NEIL CORCORAN

Neil Corcoran is Emeritus Professor of English at
the University of Liverpool and has published
widely on modern literature.

Do You, Mr Jones?

Bob Dylan with the Poets & Professors

EDITED BY
Neil Corcoran

With a new foreword by Will Self

VINTAGE

1 3 5 7 9 10 8 6 4 2

Vintage
20 Vauxhall Bridge Road,
London SW1V 2SA

Vintage is part of the Penguin Random House group of companies
whose addresses can be found at global.penguinrandomhouse.com.

First published in Great Britain by Chatto & Windus in 2002
First published in paperback by Pimlico in 2003
This edition reissued by Vintage in 2017

penguin.co.uk/vintage

A CIP catalogue record for this book is available
from the British Library

ISBN 9781784706807

Printed and bound by Clays Ltd, St Ives plc

Penguin Random House is committed to a sustainable future
for our business, our readers and our planet. This book is made
from Forest Stewardship Council® certified paper.

CONTENTS

FOREWORD

With the Nobel Committee's award to Bob Dylan of the Nobel Prize for Literature in 2016, the controversies surrounding the status of his work re-erupted. Why wouldn't they, since they were simmering all along. To my way of thinking, Dylan's status – as the most significant Western popular artist in any form or medium of the past sixty years – is always going to rub people up the wrong way, whether they be poets, professors or novelists. The signature capability of Dylan's creative being – as these essays splendidly attest – is its ever-protean character. The lazy shorthand for this is to say something like, 'He ceaselessly reinvents himself'; but we're not really interested in anything ad hominem, or psychoanalytic, when it comes to judging what qualifies as literature, and whether that literature is to be classed as canonical. These judgements were first published fifteen years ago – since then Dylan has released a further seven studio albums, collaborated on numerous others; the series of bootleg recordings have continued to be issued, there have been innovative video responses to the new work – while the never-ending tour has indeed continued. Then there's Dylan's memoir, *Chronicles: Volume One*, which – perhaps rather more than *Tarantula*, the Lennon-esque poetic grab bag that was published in samizdat dribs and drabs throughout the late 1960s – properly qualifies as a work of literature.

In his remarkable biography of Coleridge, Richard Holmes concludes its first volume, *Early Visions*, with a thought experiment: What if the poet had died – as he very much believed he would – during his trip to Malta in 1804, aged thirty-two? Holmes's view is that Coleridge's reputation might well have been higher, had he not drowsed on in his opiated reverie for another thirty years. The died-young Coleridge would have been remembered as a great poet to rank alongside those others extinguished tragically young – Shelley, Keats and Byron – while Coleridge's as-yet-unpublished *Christabel* would have had the status of a numinous urtext, known only from its author's own recitation, yet mysteriously animating the entire English-language Romantic movement. By contrast, if Dylan had died when this collection first appeared, his reputation wouldn't have stood any higher or lower than it does now. No. In my view Dylan's reputation has been effectively sealed since the 'comeback' album *Time Out of Mind* was released in 1997 – and it's this unassailable quality that critics of all kidney find so intolerable. I remember hearing a review of *Modern Times* (2006) on the BBC Radio 4 arts programme, *Front Row*. I can't recall which pundit it was who dismissed Dylan as a lyricist on the basis of this couplet: 'They say low wages are a reality / If we want to compete abroad', but I hope he or she's feeling pretty small now: after the 2007/8 financial collapse and the rise of anti-globalisation right-wing populism, the lyrics for 'Workingman's Blues #2' now seem starkly prescient.

Notwithstanding diversity of tone, differences of emphasis, methodology and the material they consider, all the poets and professors in this collection are united in this regard: while deeming Bob Dylan's writings as worthy of a scholarly response, the way in which they deliver that response remains severally qualified. All work hard to annul the popular perceptions of Dylan: the sheer fact of his cultural ubiquity, and the performative or recorded mode in which his words have, for the most part, been received. The first great wave of Dylan exegesis had long since crashed on to the muddy beach of English literary studies when this collection first appeared in 2002: many works had already been published in which Dylan's lyrics, without circumlocution, are treated as possessing prosody and poesis, if not as being 'poetry' in any narrowly defined way. The essays in this volume do the vital work of refracting a sense of Dylan's writerly sensibility – its timbre, if you like – through the sensibilities of other writers. Yet here we are, in 2017, still agonising over whether his creative output can – or even should – be conceived of as 'literature'. My argument, in what follows, will be that this has as much to do with literature's own permanent revolution as it does with anything especially antinomian in Dylan's corpus.

Anyway, there's a sense of special pleading in these essays, which makes for stimulating reading if you're a Dylan enthusiast. (And if you're not partial to his work, what the hell, Mr and Mrs Jones, are you doing here?) Why? Because no true Dylan believer is without his or her own special pleading: when it comes down to the wire – or the communion rail, for that matter – we all feel just a little uneasy about the sincerity of our devotion, which is based, let's face it, on justification by faith alone. As the 1960s graffiti so sparingly put it: 'Bob is God'. Ours may be a wildly heterodox faith – a church way broader than it is long – but we all feel ourselves to be within the same communion. Reading these essays, I encountered not just the writers' credos, but also read about their conversion experiences: for faith – at least in the Protestant understanding – remains a null category, if not contrasted with unbelief. And the time when his conversion takes place will ever after remain significant for the convert: an eternal recurrence for the baby-boomer generation of the cultural renaissance of the 1960s, which has made of us (born in 1961, I just qualify to be born again) the cynosure for all subsequent generations, trapped as they are in an ever-inflating bubble of the bi-directionally, digitally mediatised Now.*

There's special pleading in these essays, I suppose, because many of these Mr and Mrs Joneses feel themselves to be still slumming it – despite all their devotion – in Dylan's church of the poisoned mind. We plead for Dylan's genius – and literary significance is surely a Rushmore-sized facet of this – because without its being acknowledged, our own passion will appear, at best, misguided. It only takes someone to say something along the lines of 'I can't stand it when he opens his mouth' for the whole giddy edifice of Dylan's majesty to shiver, then crumble before us. At least for a moment. As a novelist myself – one completely dedicated to this form, and convinced of its importance (if not superiority) – I nonetheless cavilled not one jot at the Nobel Committee's decision. My only caveat concerned Dylan's acceptance: surely, like Jean-Paul Sartre before him, he would regard the Prize as both *de trop* and beside the point – so refuse it. My sister-in-law wanted to push the point

---

* My son and I watch Scorsese's *No Direction Home* together, and both of us start crying when we see the footage of Dylan singing with Joan Baez at the 1963 Monterey Jazz Festival. We weep because we're both overcome by the ethereal beauty of this juvenescent couple – and their bright, shining talent. My son is six years older than they were at the time. Sometimes I feel I've done very little with my life besides listening to Bob Dylan – and passing it on.

(well known to her, as a historian) that lyric poetry – if, that is, you allow Dylan's lines to be poetry at all – has always been considered a minor genre within the canon. My brother, another historian, looked up the list of previous Nobel laureates and began comparing Dylan with each in turn; observing that the prize is awarded either for short-term political reasons – Winston Churchill, Bertrand Russell – or it's Buggins's turn yet again: so many globally significant Scandinavian scribes, of whose work we've read not a jot or a tittle. This must have been the fourth or fifth such dispute I'd had since the award was announced – wrangles I found it difficult to engage in wholeheartedly, because the subject remains so dear to my heart, rather than my head.

The place Dylan's lyrics occupy in my personal canon is precisely that accorded to poetry by earlier generations: his taglines, couplets, exploded metaphors and twisted jibes have, over the decades, become my own psychic shorthand. I've only to think of lost loves to recall, yet again, that while I once held mountains in the palm of my hand – I did, indeed, throw it all away. I've only to think of one dreadful *mésalliance* or another, to feel once more the pain that stops-and-starts, as the corkscrew of resentment twists in my heart – and who can count the jingle-jangle mornings on which I've sallied forth with my ragged company?

I once had a spirited debate with the music writer Barney Hoskyns over the relative strengths of Smokey Robinson and Dylan as lyricists. Barney maintained – and probably still does – that there was really no comparison to be made between an effortlessly lucid couplet, such as 'Now if there's a smile on my face, it's only there to fool the public / But when it comes down to fooling you, now honey that's quite a different subject', and a typical piece of Bob's public-fooling: 'On the back of the fish truck that loads / While my conscience explodes'. But just looking at these lyrics laid out on the page makes me feel splenetic all over again: how could anyone prefer the simple Robinsonian prosody – elegant as it may be – to the semantic convolvulus of the Dylan lines?

To me, the juxtaposition of something that seems not only quotidian – the loading of a fish truck, presumably with fish – but also an activity merely glimpsed, with this other phenomenon – a sense of responsibility at once violent and evanescent – lies at the very core of Dylan's literary sensibility. In a fine introductory essay to his translation of Franz Kafka's *Metamorphosis*, Michael Hofmann coins the term 'Kafka Time' to describe those minutely calibrated passages in which Kafka effortlessly manages to convey the simultaneous – yet variably paced – actions of a series of agents. For Hofmann, such passages are homologous with the condition of utter intractability with which Kafka's oeuvre has been received: all those agents, labouring simultaneously, at variable rates, to extract determinate meanings from the corpus. Well, as a response to the fish-truck couplet, I'd like to propose 'Dylan Time', a mode of expression in which thought and action are rendered concurrently – not in anything like a stream of consciousness, but as a single gestalt, such that in a manner analogous to the philosophical *epochē*, whereby ontological judgement is suspended in order to achieve a sense of freedom. Yes – that's how I feel when I hear 'On the back of the fish truck that loads / While my conscience explodes': I feel free. I feel free time and again – and I've been feeling free for time out of mind; because Dylan Time radiates out from such couplets, shimmering a world of its own into being.

And what a world: there's also much discussion in these essays of the mythopoeic America that Dylan summons up with his lyrics. From this side of the Atlantic, and equipped with the gee-whiz spectacles with which the British regard that newfound land, Dylan's realm can appear commensurately carnivalesque – in Bakhtin's sense. But to me, the son of a Jewish-American mother who was a child of the Depression, and who filled my ears with tales of boxcars and Hoovervilles, Dylan's disunited states of mind march with my own land of childhood Nod. 'I wish I was a mole in the ground / Yes, I wish I was a mole in the ground / If I was a mole in the ground, I'd root that mountain down'. These lines, quoted by Greil Marcus in his superb liner notes for *The Basement Tapes*, are so evocative of that realm they might have been penned by Dylan in the 1960s, rather than having seeped, like lexical sink-water, up into the bottom of some southern draw. When I take my own children to the States, and they have a typically European – and unjustified – reaction against the brashness of American commercialism, I always tell them what they fail to understand: in America commercialism *is* authentic popular culture. Dylan Time – Dylan's mythopoeic realm, which both borrows from, and pays back to, the melting pot from which it emerges, these too are authentic responses to the problematic of American being.

Arguably the entire post-war generation of American male novelists spent the balance of their working lives hunting – like desk-bound Ahabs – for the white whale of the Great American Novel. Mailer, Bellow, Styron, Roth: each in their own way exposed the soft underbelly of his anxiety as he zeroed in for the impossible kill. The legacy of slavery – the ever-present stain of misogyny: male American novelists of this generation threshed about in the turbulent currents of collective immorality that undercut their own master narrative – meanwhile, Dylan breasted his own turbulent word-soup. 'I've seen an arrow on a doorpost / Saying this land is condemned / All the way from New Orleans / To Jerusalem'. Manifest destiny has always been the key to understanding the male American psyche: with no fresh territories to conquer, in the twentieth century the American masculinist mind began to box itself in, nailing together mea culpas with countervailing – and quixotic – imperialistic gestures. Dylan hasn't escaped this tendency: the Great Helmsman of a thousand thousand white boys moaning about their romantic angst, there's a queasy threnody that runs through his lines – the silvery spunk-trail of desiccated lust, voiced with a slave's whinny. But I'd argue that it's precisely in these areas, where Dylan's oeuvre is so wide open to retrospective political correction, that he shows himself to be the most responsive to emergent realities. Dylan, the frustrated and inadequate lover, not only anticipates but enacts the knock-kneed postures of a senescent patriarchy – Dylan, that hokey Jewish song-and-dance man; a vaudevillian hoofing it at the end of history, has more to say with his 'cultural appropriations' than many – if not all – more 'authentic' voices.

Why? Because his lyrics freewheel out of any metrical constraints, and so point the way to the emergent narrative forms of the twentieth century: not boxed-in texts which can be piled up into the battlements of a Eurocentric canon to keep out the world's ragged company, but a sort of never-ending news thread, the polymorphously perverse captioning of an equally proliferative stream of imagery. Yes, with its capacity to connect entirely and remotely – yet evanescently – and to suggest a veridical map of the territory that is the same size as the virtual territory itself, Dylan's literary oeuvre not only confirms his position as one of the most influential writers of the twentieth century, it announces him to be the representative type of the twenty-first.

Will Self
London, 2017

PREFACE

> In the 20th century, the fan had a language.
>
> Alice Fulton

I'm a fan, of course, as well as a critic and a professor. This is why.

I had an American friend at school called Hughes: at that school we were all known by the priests who taught us, and more or less knew one another, by our surnames, and in any case he didn't stay at the school long so I can't now recall his first name. His father was stationed at a US airforce base in Lincolnshire and every summer the family returned to New York. This seemed very glamorous to me, and Hughes was an adventurous and exceptionally mature person, in the way of much-travelled children, so probably he actually did what he said he'd done one summer, when we were both only twelve or thirteen: he'd been to Greenwich Village and seen someone called Bob Dylan in concert. I remember liking the spelling of the name. He brought back to school Dylan's first album, *Bob Dylan*, and played it for me in Fr Benignus O'Rourke's house room in Lincoln House, Austin Friars School, Carlisle, in 1962 – clandestinely, I remember, which would have given it a sheen of even greater glamour. But only if I'd been ready for it. I wasn't. I quite liked Cliff Richard and the Shadows at the time, and Dylan pretending to be an old blues man was completely beyond me, although I did register the attractiveness of his impudent, scruffy, knowing surliness on the album cover.

So that was the first time I listened to Dylan, but not the first time I really heard him. That was a year or two later during a school trip to Stratford where, in one still intensely memorable week, I discovered the joys of live Shakespeare (David Warner, the 'Russian' Richard II), Wimpy Bars (they were different then, and this one, the 'Judith Shakespeare', was the first time most of us had ever eaten a hamburger), illicit beer (in the Dirty Duck, where we encountered the gangling Russian Richard himself, hunched beneath the rafters), and Dylan's second album, *The Freewheelin' Bob Dylan*. I saw it in the window of a record shop and immediately liked its title, the chunkily elegant lettering of its design, and of course the perfect, James Dean-influenced icon of its snowy New York City cover image, Dylan huddled against the weather in an immensely desirable and entirely inappropriate little suede jacket, Susie Rotolo adoringly clutching his arm but looking as though she had a mind of her own too. I bought it and played it over and over again in the early pre-performance evening on the old Dansette in the hostel we were staying in. Its songs, ever since, play in the back of my head when I read *Richard II*, 'I wasted time and now doth time waste me' forever ghosted by 'A Hard Rain's A-Gonna Fall'.[1]

I saw him first in Newcastle during the 1965 tour, the one commemorated in Donn Pennebaker's movie *Dont Look Back*.[2] He was entrancing: playful, witty, the perfectly dressed epitome of cool, bringing an audience for the earlier songs along with him into the startlingly original new work ('Mr Tambourine Man', 'Gates of Eden') with elegant ease and assurance. The *Dont Look Back* book says that the scene during which the microphone breaks down happens in Sheffield, but this certainly also happened in Newcastle: perhaps microphones broke down all the time in those days? In Newcastle, after recovering briefly, the mike went dead once or twice again. Dylan seemed entirely patient and relaxed, sitting on the edge of the stage and talking to the immediate audience. His cool or *chic*, though, wasn't just a matter of address, or indeed of dress, but of the way he moved, or carried himself, on stage. 'He was a great mover in the '60s, Dylan,' Patti Smith has said, 'those great little curtsies he used to do'; and many others testify to the way this Dylan was riveting when he walked into a room.[3] What I still remember, vividly, from the Newcastle concert is a little thing he did with his shoulders; perhaps this is what Patti Smith is referring to: a kind of shrug or twitch, which seemed a register of privacy, just something people didn't do on stage, a deconstruction of the pretence of it while still also a performance. It was alluring, don't-give-a-damn, a little come-on that was also a put-off: it was 'Dylanesque', and a new style entered the world with it.

One way in which he carried his audience along with him during that concert was in knowing pretty accurately what its primary constitution was: students of the Humanities, I imagine, at school or university, whom he flattered with such changes to the recorded versions of the songs as that in 'Talkin' World War Three Blues', where 'Abraham Lincoln said that' became 'T.S. Eliot said that' If there was ingratiation in this, there was also just fun and, I suppose, a sly little acknowledgement of at least one source for some of the astonishing lyrics we were hearing for the first time; and in retrospect, of course, we know how irrecoverably far from ingratiation he'd travelled by the time he returned to England the following year. (As far as his behaviour to his audiences goes, that's more or less where he's stayed.) It was also a nod to the fact that many members of this audience were probably more accustomed to poetry readings than to whatever this thing Dylan was doing might be called; and there was, indeed, a moment during the concert which has always been for me definitive of a transitional ethos in Dylan and in 'the Sixties'. At the line in 'World War Three Blues', 'I was down in the sewer with some little lover' some girls in the audience screamed Beatles-type screams, while others (me included) made outraged shushing noises. No prizes for guessing which side the person Sam Shepard has called 'true Dylan' must have been on, laughing behind his hand.

Since these things just vanish from the world – and doesn't *Dont Look Back*, for all its virtues, always raise the deeply frustrated desire that an entire 1965 concert filmed by Pennebaker should exist for posterity? – I want to put on record two things Dylan said during this concert. He sang 'Gates of Eden', not yet available on record, without introducing it, and afterwards said, simply, 'That was called "Gates of Eden".' He followed it immediately with 'If You Gotta Go, Go Now', again without introduction, and, finishing this hilarious and still in 1965 risqué song (in Newcastle, if not New York) of sexual innuendo and invitation, said, 'That was called "Gates of Eden" too.' He did introduce 'Love Minus Zero / No Limit', by saying, 'This song is like math, you know, a fraction' – and he drew a line in the air with his hand – 'with "Love Minus Zero" on the top line, and No Limit on the bottom.' He paused and shuffled a bit – he was a great shuffler in the sixties, Dylan – and then said, 'I made the title before I made the song.' This Dylan, charmingly communicative, even flirtatious, with an audience, has long since vanished from the world too; but the word 'made' has high sanction, and makes him, in one certain sense, very much a poet before he is anything else: since, as Sir Philip Sidney tells us in his sixteenth-century *Apology for Poetry*, 'the Greeks called him a *poet*, which . . . cometh of this word *poiein*, which is, to make.'[4]

Yet the word as Dylan used it also suggested to me a childlike vulnerability about the act of creation, and has always stayed with me as a revelation of how this extraordinarily complex and metamorphic writer and singer thinks, very simply, about his own relationship with the songs he has indeed made, and goes on making. There is something poignant in this: and when I think about Dylan there is always, despite his immense wealth and fame, poignancy in my thought, for reasons I can never fully fathom, and not simply, I think, because his songs have been a major soundtrack to the various passages of my own life. Hazlitt on *Hamlet* once came to the mind of someone writing about Dylan – 'as real as our own thoughts'. Same for me. *Salut* to a voice without restraint.

But I'm a professor and a critic as well as a fan, and I like confirmation from my authorities. Since I've written a bit about modern Irish literature, I particularly like the story about another fan told by the late John Bauldie, editor of the Dylan journal *The Telegraph*. He tells us that Donn Pennebaker asked a friend of his, Shelly, if he could locate a copy of the *Dont Look Back* paperback book. '"I need one for Beckett," Pennebaker explained. "Beckett who?" asked Shelly. "Samuel Beckett," said Pennebaker. "I've just been working with him. He loves the film. He's a real big Dylan fan."'[5]

I'm grateful to Professor Tom Roche for filling me in on the activities of the Seventeen-year Cicada and organising my access to the Mudd Library during a visit to Princeton in 2001 when I read the file on Dylan's honorary degree in 1970. I'm grateful too to Professor Paul Muldoon for inviting me to lecture in

Princeton then. For good advice on my own contibutions I want to thank several of my contributors – Patrick Crotty, Aidan Day, Paul Muldoon and Nick Roe – and also Paul Driver, John Haffednden, Neil Rhodes and Sue Vice. But I'm also grateful to all this book's contributors for accepting my invitation to write with such alacrity and enthusiasm, and for subsequently making my editorial task so rewarding. Thanks too to Lino Puertas, who recently showed me around what survives of Dylan's New York with expertise and good humour, and to the Carnegie Trust for a welcome research grant. I'm especially grateful to Jeff Rosen of Bob Dylan's office for extending great courtesy to this book in the matter of copyright permissions, and also to Jenny Uglow, my editor at Chatto, who has been a great friend and advisor to this book from the beginning.

Neil Corcorn
St Andrews
May 2002

INTRODUCTION: WRITING ALOUD

'Colleges are like old-age homes; except for the fact that more people die in college than in old-age homes, there's really no difference': Bob Dylan – previously known as Robert Zimmerman – dropout from the University of Minnesota and famous folksinger and rock star, in an interview in 1966.[1] Withering observations on the academy and the business of criticism have been a constant in Dylan's otherwise extravagantly protean work and career over the intervening years, and I suppose they should give any academic and critic pause before embarking on the editing of a collection of essays like this.[2] In 'Ballad of a Thin Man' on *Highway 61 Revisited* (1965) Dylan snarls the reproach which entitles this book:

> You've been with the professors
> And they've all liked your looks.
> With great lawyers you have
> Discussed lepers and crooks.
> You've been through all of
> F. Scott Fitzgerald's books.
> You're very well read,
> It's well known –
> But something is happening here
> And you don't know what it is,
> Do you, Mister Jones?

Mr Jones is 'thin', I assume, because the knowledge he derives from the professors, and specifically from a literary education, fails to nourish. There is also a taunt here about the suspect erotics of pedagogy ('they've all liked your looks') which implies less than single-minded intellectual motivation among 'the professors'. And true knowledge, the knowledge of the something that is happening here, escapes in the process – the academic process. Mister Jones, the critic with his pencil in his hand before the professors, the lawyers and the canonic texts of modern American culture, is here and throughout this vituperative song, hopelessly out of key with his time.

This kind of anti-intellectualism, or at least anti-institutionalised intellectualism, in an intellectual goes deep in the American tradition. It is a significant feature of Emersonian Romanticism; and Mark Ford writes about self-reliance in Dylan, which is the obverse of such hostility and may even give it motive and permission. Yet Robert Zimmerman, from a middle-class Jewish Midwestern family, must also have needed personal permission to become a university dropout in 1961, and his motivation – to escape from the Midwest to New York City, to meet Woody Guthrie, and to become famous – certainly demanded self-reliance from a very young man. Dylan is arresting in that same 1966 interview about what the alternative to college should be: 'I guess you should go where your wants are bare, where you're invisible and not needed.'[3] So if there is cultural sanction for his aggression to the professors, there must also once have been personal neediness. It enabled Robert Zimmerman to dress his wants as Bob Dylan and to begin a process in which the hitherto invisible wants of an audience were given newly shining raiment too. Whatever the truth of Dylan's choice of name – and Daniel Karlin considers this at length, calling it 'a knot which can't be undone' – it at the very least coincided with that of the poet Dylan Thomas who, some years previously, had had a huge impact on American poetry, partly through his acclaimed readings on college campuses, had inhabited some of the same Greenwich Village haunts that Bob Dylan was now making his own, and had died in New York City in 1953. So, at the time he was dissociating himself from the professors, Dylan was conceivably allying himself with an alternative source of authority, one that retained academic and critical sanction.

In fact, despite his objections to the academy, Dylan is never simply consistent. There is a touch of dewy-eyed romantic pastoralism in his spoken introduction to 'Baby, Let Me Follow You Down' on his first album, during which he says he met Ric von Schmidt 'one day in the green pastures of – uh – Harvard University', where the phrase 'green pastures' is drawn from Psalm 23, 'The Lord is my shepherd'. And in 1970 he accepted an honorary doctorate from Princeton University: a doctorate of music, not of literature. Thirty years later, in 2000, he also accepted the Willard and Margaret Thorpe Medal for Excellence in American Arts and Letters from Princeton.[4] The two moments are drawn delicately together by Paul Muldoon in the poem which opens this collection: a Princeton professor (and the current Oxford Professor of Poetry) welcoming back the honorary, or 'ornery', graduate while also honouring, in an admiringly imitative blues, that graduate's perpetually creative 'disquietude'.

In a recent book Robert Crawford uncovers the tension between bardic wildness and academic respectability as a fundamental pattern in the self-conception of the modern poet; and according to this pattern Dylan's behaviour on the 1970 occasion must seem almost the norm, because the conferment of his degree impelled him in turn to bite the hand that fed him in the song 'Day of the Locusts' on *New Morning* that same year.[5] The Seventeen-year Cicada to which Paul Muldoon's poem refers – an East Coast phenomenon encountered during the conferment ceremony – provides the image for the chorus of a quasi-surreal account of the day's events, a day when 'Darkness was everywhere, it smelled like a tomb':

> And the locusts sang off in the distance,
> Yeah, the locusts sang such a sweet melody,
> Oh the locusts sang off in the distance,
> Yeah, the locusts sang and they were singing for me.

The cicadas are figured as a biblical plague of locusts, and self-reproach is the impulse of the trope. But even when in disgrace in his own eyes for accepting the academy's approval, Dylan makes a gracefully allusive literary gesture of exactly the kind that must have attracted Princeton's notice in the first place: the song is titled after Nathanael West's great Hollywood novella of 1939, *The Day of the Locust*.

Dylan's negative attitude to academics and critics also undoubtedly has to do with his unwillingness to be classified according to the usual literary categories. In an interview in 1965 he said, 'I don't call myself a poet because I don't like the word. I'm a trapeze artist'; and he has repeated such deflective refusals over the years.[6] Possibly he rejects the word 'poet' because, truly, it does fail to fit. The lyrics without the music are not, exactly, poetry, or not always so, since they cannot always stand alone – but then, as Christopher Butler reminds us, they have no desire to do so since they are written to be accompanied. A lyric poem is always also a musical score of a kind, a set of instructions for the production of sound: Elaine Scarry says that 'the page does not itself sing but exists forever on the verge of song'.[7] Even so, axiomatically, words that cannot stand alone cannot be poems; and when Dylan has collected his song lyrics he has titled them, unpresumingly, just 'writings' and 'lyrics'. Simon Armitage discusses Dylan's impact on him, as a poet, as not merely or even primarily verbal or lyrical. Although he does identify high lyrical value in the strengths of narrative and humour apparent on *Another Side of Bob Dylan*, he also discovers something poetic in Dylan's persona, manner and style, and praises his exemplary attitude of resilience and survival.

Lavinia Greenlaw writes about what we might call the poetry, or the poetics, of Dylan's vocalising which, at least on *Nashville Skyline*, she considers as a form of delay; and this need not be dependent on the lyrics at all, which are sometimes (repeatedly) misheard. Anyone interested in Dylan will understand what Greenlaw says about responding on that 'visceral level' which is entirely dependent on hearing him in recorded performance. Indeed, the officially unreleased 'I'm Not There (1956)', which Mark Ford calls 'one of the most beautiful songs' from the Basement Tapes period (1967), has partly indecipherable, perhaps only half-written, lyrics. Lavinia Greenlaw goes so far as to suggest that 'Dylan's delivery resists the two kinds of structure it's pinned to: the words and the tune', which would make him, surely, uniquely 'ornery' as a singer-songwriter, but – I agree with Greenlaw – plausibly so. Actually I have always thought that Roland Barthes is describing Dylan in *The Pleasure of the Text* when, with his characteristically dandyish gravity, he invents 'writing aloud': 'the pulsional incidents, the language lined with flesh, a text where we can hear the grain of the throat, the patina of consonants, the voluptuousness of vowels, a whole carnal stereophony'; and, he says, 'a certain art of singing can give an idea of this vocal writing'.[8]

Christopher Butler is right, then, to remind us that the lyrics are given 'point and reinforcement in the context of musical accompaniment, which has its own ways of demanding an attention to words'. In practice, however, a criticism which does full justice to both lyrics and music is hard to achieve; and Nicholas Roe reminds us, alternatively, that Dylan's work has been extensively viewed in relation to the Western literary canon. The one major musicological study of Dylan, Wilfred Mellers's dreadfully named *A Darker Shade of Pale: A Backdrop to Bob Dylan* (1984), is absorbing on some of the American musical contexts for Dylan but pretty thin in its analyses of the songs. Michael Gray in *Song and Dance Man III* does engage with both music and lyrics, and his book is variously and fascinatingly informative and illuminating; but the engagement with music, which is impressionistic rather than musicological, usually occurs independently of his discussions of the lyrics.

So, recognising the centrality of the music, these essayists understand that Dylan cannot be viewed without reserve as a poet. But although Simon Armitage, after tracing his own journey of appreciation, ends his lengthy reading of 'Tangled Up in Blue' by observing that 'literary criticism is the wrong tool when it comes to the analysis of song lyrics', several other essayists, such as Pamela Thurschwell, Patrick Crotty, Aidan Day and myself, have close readings which implicitly make the case that Dylan's lyrics often do merit and repay patient expository and interpretative attention, just as complexly organised poems do. Songs may sometimes permit licences that poems do not, and licence – unpoetic licence, we might say – is what Simon Armitage believes he has uncovered in 'Tangled Up in Blue'; but other essayists show how Dylan's songs are sometimes much less self-permissive, or may grant themselves resourceful and enabling permissions which poems may not. When Patrick Crotty defines an 'almost uncanny instinct for fusing form and feeling' in Dylan's rhyming, he is particularly sensitive to the difference between poems and song lyrics, arguing that the latter may make genuine rhymes out of what appear on the page as non-rhymes. Crotty will not have it, as I have it in my reading of 'The Lonesome Death of Hattie Carroll', that Dylan writes, on occasion, unrhyming songs; and the difference between our approaches perhaps offers one specific disagreement, at the level of technique, about what literary criticism can and cannot do with Dylan, even as we are both certain that it can do something satisfactory.

Most of the contributors to this volume are exclusively or primarily literary, not musical, people. Aspects of the music do figure: for instance when I define an ironic discrepancy between lyrics and music on *Highway 61 Revisited*; when Aidan Day notices how Dylan's singing can carry an insinuation which could not be sensed from the printed lyric; and when Nicholas Roe shows how time is an issue in song, performance and recording quite differently from the way it is at issue in poems. But most essays focus firmly on the lyrics and their contexts. For me, although Dylan may not be a conventional poet, he moves in my mind, and moves there primarily – though not only – in his language, exactly as exceptional poets of the printed page do: he has clarity, force, resonance, grace, relevance in a wide number of contexts, and utter memorability. Aidan Day coins the phrase 'song poems' and suggests that they behave 'as if there were no wall of poetic convention separating the statement from the listener'. This may underestimate the extent to which Dylan's songs work by conventions of their own (and you could see poetic convention less as a wall than as a bridge), but Day's hybrid term nevertheless suggests that if Dylan's songs are not always, exactly, poems, they almost always have poetry in them, and the varied techniques of literary criticism and interpretation may be satisfactorily and illuminatingly applied to them. That is the contention of this volume: and one of its stories is that Dylan has been an important, quasi-poetic presence in the emotional and intellectual lives, and in the imaginations, of its contributors, who are notable contemporary poets and critics.

When he surveys some of the kinds of critical activity already performed on Dylan, Christopher Butler controversially observes that academics, as 'the museum curators of the future', must make the 'implicitly canonic' judgements that really matter. His crucial criterion of value is that the complex modes of articulation in Dylan's work give it 'some kind of life beyond the contemporary'. One of his examples is 'Highway 61 Revisited', and in my own essay I propose that specific Dylan songs, including this one, transcend topicality in their dealings with contemporary American history. All of these essays, some in less overt but nevertheless substantial ways, adumbrate what a life beyond the contemporary might be like for a great many of Bob Dylan's songs.

But the question of what exactly constitutes the Dylan 'text' is one that I must address more pragmatically here too. 'The song disappears in the air, the paper stays. They have little in common,' Dylan has said himself.[9] Stephen Scobie has a good discussion of the matter in his valuable book *Alias Bob Dylan*, where he says that 'Every time a critic quotes from a Dylan song, the quotation is in some way provisional, hedged around with qualifications.'[10] Dylan's work is creatively unstable in a way that makes the text very difficult to establish. Different performances will inflect songs in ways that demand fundamental reinterpretation, so that the lyrics without the voice and music are only ever what Frank Kermode and Stephen Spender call 'reminders, hints, or shadows'.[11] In addition, some songs, even the greatest, exist in several radically different variants – 'Tangled Up In Blue' and 'Caribbean Wind' are outstanding instances – but only one version is given in the published *Writings and Drawings* (1973), in *Lyrics 1962–1985* (1987) and on the official Bob Dylan website (www.bobdylan.com). These collections are incomplete in many other respects, while some of the published lyrics bear only scant relation to what Dylan actually sings, even on the officially released recordings. And even when they do, the lineation of the version on the page often very inadequately represents what we hear on the record: Dylan breaks the line at a different point from the printed lyric, often to great expressive effect, and internal rhymes and assonances dependent on his pronunciation are not conveyed in the printed version. In addition, some printed songs have relatively full conventional punctuation, while others have none whatever.

The critic is therefore faced with difficulties which even critics of the poetry of W. H. Auden, Robert Lowell and, today, Derek Mahon – all energetic self-revisers after first publication – do not confront. In the present collection the printed version, or the version on bobdylan.com, is taken as text for purposes of quotation, but individual essayists cite alternative versions, and some comment on the whole issue of the Dylan text. I would like to think that when Dylan revises himself in performance we may regard him as his own first critic: bringing out different nuance and emphasis, interpreting and reinterpreting in ways that serve the original text while also acting to reintroduce it to the contemporary moment, and so to bring it newly alive. So, against Dylan's own assault on the professors, I take solace from the way he offers here almost a paradigm of the critical activity and a validation of it in relation to his own work.

In his earliest creative years Dylan sometimes claimed to be writing novels and plays as well as songs. I have no idea whether he actually was or not – *Tarantula*, the 'novel' eventually published in 1971, was the only fruit of this – but he clearly wanted then to be considered a 'literary' figure. Writing 'Like

A Rolling Stone', he said shortly after he had done so, 'changed it all; I didn't care any more after that about writing books or poems . . . All my writing goes into the songs now. Other forms don't interest me any more.'[12] He didn't care, I think, because the kind of literary quality he wanted had now, in the scope and amplitude of this song, been successfully translated into something so dizzyingly radical in its formal inventiveness that it exploded all the usual categories: Mark Ford notes the song's 'exhilaration at the possibilities suddenly discovered within a seemingly exhausted genre'. When Dylan hazards a further self-definition in 1969, it is, precisely, an inclusive amplitude that he is describing: 'I see myself as it all . . . poet, singer, songwriter, custodian, gatekeeper . . . all of it. I feel "confined" when I have to choose one or the other.'[13]

The idea of Dylan as custodian and gatekeeper is suggestive and ramifying, given the various traditions, both literary and oral, that he has preserved, melded and furthered. Some of these are specifically American, and several essays examine aspects of what Daniel Karlin calls Dylan's 'self-conscious and constructed' Americanness. Karlin himself considers the 'American abundance' of names and naming in the work, which has Walt Whitman, Woody Guthrie and Jack Kerouac behind it, but he also points to its connection with a species of American breakdown and apocalypticism, which Patrick Crotty discusses in other contexts. Naming in Dylan, Karlin thinks, is an attempt 'to make sense of things not making sense any more'. Richard Brown's exploration of American (and other) place names in the songs discovers in them not only geography but a figuring of subjective states of being. Referring to contemporary theories of social space, Brown's essay reads America in Bob Dylan's work as 'a primary site of semantic instability'. Mark Ford's interweaving of Emerson and Dylan traces a long

American Romantic-individualist tradition in which Emersonian 'self-reliance' is transformed latterly into Dylanesque 'dignity'.

Where Nicholas Roe's study of time in, and in relation to, Dylan considers the personae of his songs as constantly about to leave, Mark Ford inflects this with a specifically American accent, linking it to a shared tradition of the American Jeremiad. Arguing for the constructedness of Dylan's Americanness, Daniel Karlin insists that it is not regional or ethnic; but Bryan Cheyette proposes, against a teleological view of the career, an American-Jewish context for many of these matters and motifs, urging that the extensive figuring of the railroad in Dylan – the 'carnival train' of licence and the 'slow train' of Christian conversion – charts a complex process of departure, separation and reconfiguration. He adduces Al Jolson, Jewish blackface minstrel, in his contextualising of Dylan's self-departures; and others draw the minstrel analogy too, Susan Wheeler in her study of Dylan's humour – 'the riffing mind at work' – and Sean Wilentz in his examination of the loving larceny of *'Love and Theft'*. For both these writers Dylan is an American whiteface minstrel (Wilentz reminds us that he literally whited up for the Rolling Thunder tours in 1975–6). Wheeler proposes that the mimicry of his humorous characterisations catches the American idiom 'with an ear akin to Robert Frost's or James Tate's' – which is the highest praise, from a contemporary American poet, for Dylan's American ear; and in my essay on Dylan and death I attempt an account of some of the ways in which he is, in the dialogue of his 1960s songs, a strikingly capable dramatist of some intrinsically American tones and modulations. Wilentz admires Dylan's unpredictably subversive insistences on 'his own version of "America"' over the course of his career, and outstandingly when he draped the Stars and Stripes on stage behind him in Paris in 1966; and he reads *'Love and Theft'* not only as larceny but as self-plundering or self-recycling too. The loving theft, making so much Americana newly contemporary, is jocular but also troubled, a 'serious and fearful play'.

An element of Dylan's work which has caused furious debate from time to time is its attitude to women. Simon Armitage says that 'on some very basic level' Dylan's reception 'is a man thing', although he discriminates the actual from the initially apparent gender politics of 'Sweetheart Like You'. But there is some truth in what he says. Pamela Thurschwell discusses the whole issue of women's responses to Dylan, and in the light, or shadow, of charges of misogyny (and of a story by Joyce Carol Oates) she reads certain songs as a tracking of 'continuing disturbances in the interaction between the realms of the sexual and the socio-political'. Nicholas Roe reminds us of the Renaissance tradition of mutability which lies behind attitudes in some of the songs, in which women become an element in the singer's sometimes 'troubled relationship with time'. And Aidan Day, particularly in his reading of 'Highlands', also detects 'trouble' in the 'self-consciousness about masculine drive' in Dylan's more recent work, believing that its demythologising unsettles stereotypes of male sexual authority. Alert to Dylan's strength as a writer of 'older age', Day describes the moral gains as well as the physical depredations of the sense of 'impasse' in songs which 'speak authentically of having lost all sense of authenticity'. I would add something which, surprisingly enough, no contributor mentions: that the carefully constructed and very striking image Dylan made of himself in the mid-1960s was a distinctly androgynous one, and that some of the songs of that period – on *Blonde on Blonde* (1966), in particular – have an element of camp. Before that he may have been imitating Woody Guthrie in vocal manner, but for the image of 'Bob Dylan' he was leaning heavily on James Dean and, to a lesser extent, Marlon Brando, and also on the poets of the Beat generation. In all of these masculinity as chosen style, of an unconventional and ambivalent kind, rather than masculinity as essence, is very much part of the point.

In a chapter of *I'm a Man: Sex, Gods and Rock 'n' Roll* called 'Dylan: Creativity, Misogyny and Echo', Ruth Padel declares that 'Dylan is the hero of creative maleness. But to many women's ears, the whiny, insistent masculinity of his voice also carries an edge of supremacism and misogyny. He is brilliant. But it is nearly always men who go on about him.'[14] This latter may be true, and the phenomenon needs explanation, and gets some in this collection – for instance when Richard Brown refers to Dylan's 'acute vernacular articulations of masculine emotional vulnerability and sexual need'; but I would argue with Padel's readings of individual songs. For instance, she contrasts what she regards as the relatively woman-appreciative 'All I Really Want To Do' on *Another Side of Bob Dylan* (1964) with what she calls the 'utterly vicious' 'It Ain't Me, Babe', on the same album.[15] This seems to me utterly wrong. 'Babe' as an address to a woman from a man could be thought problematic, but it would not necessarily have had the same resonance in 1964. In any case, that the Dylan of this album understands all that is clear from the final, equalising lines of the luminously tender 'To Ramona': 'And some day maybe, / Who knows baby, / I'll come and be cryin' to you' – so who's the cry-baby now? And subsequently, on *John Wesley Harding* (1969), Dylan sings a song which radically undermines, while still in some ways following, the conventions of songs of seduction: 'I'll Be Your Baby Tonight' infantilises, even as it yearningly presents, the would-be male lover himself. Never has attempted seduction seemed less aggressive.

I read 'It Ain't Me, Babe' as a song that not only rejects the bourgeois ideal of a settled relationship (which would make it relatively conventional for its time) but scrutinises, with devastating honesty, the inability of the singer to measure up to the ideal proposed by the woman. This is that of the traditionally perfect male lover, and therefore a preposterous stereotype which demeans both of them. The woman is not blamed for having such an ideal, exactly. In fact, the song prominently tells us what she 'says' she wants, not what she wants: 'You say you're looking for someone / Never weak but always strong' means something quite different from 'You're looking for someone . . .' The song puts the emphasis on the discourse used, and implies that this is both constructed and exhausted, making it impossible for her to read the situation between them adequately. She sounds scripted, and is, of course: by the script of patriarchy. 'In that cruel-whine voice Dylan delivers each clause as a triumphant nail, skewering her emotional coffin,' says Padel.[16] I hear no triumphalism, and to me the voice has no cruelty or whine: it sounds wearily sad, strained and tense. And does she mean these clauses?

> Go melt back into the night, babe,
> Everything inside is made of stone.
> There's nothing in here moving
> An' anyway I'm not alone.

This may be hurtful to her, but it is also hurtful to him. 'Melt' certainly invites her to disappear, as Antigonus tells us the Hermione of his dream does in *The Winter's Tale* – 'With shrieks / She melted into air.' But the word has a residual tenderness in it too, figuring her as liquefied by tears. And if she has melted like this because of him, then he self-reproachfully represents himself, alternatively, as petrified: since, if 'everything inside is made of stone', then he is stone too, and his heart is stone. In these dehumanising transformations, which are shadowed by a virtually Ovidian metamorphosis, both he and she are destroyed by the ending of their relationship.

What may appear the most intense cruelty is delayed until the last line of the quatrain and emphasised by its rhyme: the fact that he is not alone. But actually he is alone, because he is stone, the word that rhymes with 'alone'; and if you are stone it hardly matters whether you are alone or not, because you are alone anyway in your unfeelingness: there is, precisely, 'nothing in here moving'. The lines have an almost surreal quality, and I always think, when I hear them, of Magritte's 1950s stone interiors with stone people, works like *Souvenir de voyage* and *Le chant de la violette*: paintings of solitude, stasis, the terrifying frozenness of everything for ever. 'It Ain't Me, Babe' is a great song of regret, in mourning for an irretrievable loss, the loss of what would otherwise have been 'you' and 'me' together, not alone. It is also, beyond this, a brave farewell to an audience and to a particular phase of creativity – a resonance which both Pamela Thurschwell and Patrick Crotty pick up.

I like to think of the final verse of 'I and I' on *Infidels* (1983) as offering a less hostile encounter between singer and critic, or at least singer and listener, than that offered in 'Ballad of a Thin Man'. Alluding disconsolately enough to Isaiah 59: 10 – 'we stumble at noon day as in the night; we are in desolate places as dead men' – it goes like this:

Noontime, and I'm still pushin' myself along the road,
    the darkest part,
Into the narrow lanes, I can't stumble or stay put.
Someone else is speaking with my mouth, but I'm
    listening only to my heart.

> I've made shoes for everyone, even you, while I still go
> barefoot.

The address to the listener in the final line is a kind of Baudelairean gesture, as when 'Au Lecteur', the poem which opens *Les Fleurs du mal* – to which Dylan alludes in 'Every Grain of Sand' – addresses the reader as '– Hypocrite lecteur, – mon semblable, – mon frère!' – a line which T. S. Eliot famously appropriates for *The Waste Land*. Unlike the Baudelairean line, however, Dylan's lines invoke no dark complicity between writer and reader but insist rather on the chasm opened between the two by the human cost involved for the writer. That 'everyone, even you' forces us to acknowledge that we are the comforted beneficiaries of another's suffering.

If there is challenge and affront here, there is also generosity. The metaphor of the song's final line is a rich one. Songs are shoes for their listeners: ways of proceeding, forms of protection and comfort on a journey; and it is salutary to be reminded of the comfortless bare feet of the shoemaker, of the crippling self-exposures involved in bringing into public discourse the sometimes painful hoard of privacies behind Bob Dylan's work. (In fact an autobiographical detail, of an affecting kind, must inform the metaphor here: Bob Dylan's paternal grandfather, Zigman Zimmerman, emigrated from Odessa, in the wake of an anti-Semitic pogrom, in 1905, to Duluth, Minnesota. In Odessa he had run a substantial shoe factory; in Duluth he was obliged instead to take up a pedlar's cart.)[17] I do not believe that the final line of 'I and I' is looking for gratitude, exactly: the song's sense of how impossible it would be, despite the difficulties, to 'stay put' seems to place the singer isolatedly beyond the need for reciprocity. And in any case 'barefoot' may suggest a Whitmanian or even Native American preference for keeping the skin in contact with the ground; and we could read the lines as a recasting of Yeats's request to his song to throw off its coat, since 'there's more enterprise in walking naked.' Nevertheless, gratitude is what the line compels from me, and it is in gratitude for a lifetime of pleasure from the variety, breadth and weight of Bob Dylan's work that I have edited this volume.

Sam Shepard has said that 'The point isn't to figure him out but to take him in.'[18] I am all for taking in Bob Dylan but I am perfectly certain that there is point in trying to figure him out too. Indeed, a proper act of the critical intelligence does not differentiate between the two. The essays in this book are, I believe, eloquent displays of such decorum and such acumen. Something is happening here all right, and Mr Jones may just have an inkling what it is.

1

BOB DYLAN AT PRINCETON, NOVEMBER 2000

Paul Muldoon

We cluster at one end, one end of Dillon Gym.
'You know what, honey? We call that a homonym.'

We cluster at one end, one end of Dillon Gym.
'If it's fruit you're after, you go out on a limb.'

That last time in Princeton, that ornery degree,
those seventeen-year locusts hanging off the trees.

That last time in Princeton, that ornery degree,
his absolute refusal to bend the knee.

His last time in Princeton, he wouldn't wear a hood.
Now he's dressed up as some sort of cowboy dude.

That last time in Princeton, he wouldn't wear a hood.
'You know what, honey? We call that disquietude.

It's that self-same impulse that has him rearrange
both "The Times They Are A-Changin'" and "Things
    Have Changed"

so that everything seems to fall within his range
as the locusts lock in on grain-silo and grange.'

2

BOB DYLAN'S NAMES

Daniel Karlin

Tell me, is my name in your book?

'Tell Me', 1983

Bob Dylan was given a name: Robert Allen Zimmerman. He gave himself others. In 1958 he fronted a band in Hibbing, Minnesota, called Elston Gunn and the Rock Boppers, and when he briefly joined Bobby Vee's band it was as Elston Gunn. Subsequently he guested on various records under various aliases, including 'Bob Landy', 'Tedham Porterhouse', 'Blind Boy Grunt', and 'Robert Milkwood Thomas'. But the change that matters is from Robert Zimmerman to Bob Dylan. It took place in 1958 or 1959, and was made legal in 1962, when Dylan was twenty-one. Everything starts from this re-naming, but I'm going to delay considering it. First I want to look at some of the names in Dylan's songs.[1]

Song titles carry the names or nicknames of real people: 'Song to Woody' (Woody Guthrie), 'Ballad of Donald White', 'The Death of Emmett Till', 'Who Killed Davey Moore?', 'The Lonesome Death of Hattie Carroll', 'Sara' (Sara Dylan), 'George Jackson', 'Hurricane' (Rubin Carter), 'Joey' (Joe Gallo), 'Julius and Ethel' (the Rosenbergs), 'Lenny Bruce', 'Blind Willie McTell' and 'High Water (for Charley Patton)'. Titles also carry the names of real places: 'Hard Times in New York Town', 'Kingsport

Town', 'Oxford Town', 'Spanish Harlem Incident', 'California', 'Positively 4th Street', 'Stuck Inside of Mobile with the Memphis Blues Again', 'Goin' to Acapulco', 'Mozambique', 'Romance in Durango', 'Caribbean Wind', 'Brownsville Girl', 'Mississippi'.

Place names in titles are a fraction of those found in songs from every part of Dylan's career, forming a map of America with crazy zigzagging lines of connection to Europe and Africa and the Middle East. The same is true of people: the songs play host to a vast population of named figures, real and imaginary, drawn from literature, popular song, folk-tale, history, legend, myth, the Bible, the movies: here are some of them, in more or less alphabetical but no other order: Abraham, Achilles, Aladdin (and his lamp), Captain Arab (alias Ahab), St Augustine, Brigitte Bardot (followed by Anita Ekberg and Sophia Loren), Samantha Brown, Madame Butterfly, Cain and Abel, Casanova, Fidel Castro and his beard, Cassius Clay (before he changed his name), Cinderella, Cisco and Sonny and Leadbelly too, Columbus, Walter Cronkite, Charles Darwin (trapped out on Highway 5), Bette Davis, Bo Diddley, Delilah, Cecil B. DeMille, Einstein, F. Scott Fitzgerald, Robert Ford and Jesse James, Clark Gable, Galileo, Pat Garrett and Billy the Kid, Genghis Khan, Barry Goldwater, the Good Samaritan, Homer, Henry Hudson, the Hunchback of Notre Dame, Isis, Little Jack Horner, Jack the Ripper, Thomas Jefferson, Jesus Christ, John the Baptist, Erica Jong, Judas Iscariot, Jupiter and Apollo, John F. Kennedy, Martin Luther King, the Lone Ranger and Tonto, Lucifer (the name of a new pony), Bertha Mason, Willie Mays, Michelangelo, Napoleon (three times), Nietzsche coupled with Wilhelm Reich, Ophelia, Othello and Desdemona, Don Pasquale, Tom Paine, Gregory Peck, St Peter, Peter O'Toole, Prince Philip, Ezra Pound and T. S. Eliot (fighting in the captain's tower), Ma Rainey and Beethoven (unwrapping a bed roll), Rasputin, the reincarnation of Paul Revere's horse, John D. Rockefeller, King Saud and his four hundred wives, Romeo (rebuffed in 'Desolation Row' and brushed off again in 'Floater'), his maker Shakespeare (in the alley with his pointed shoes and his bells), Belle Starr (twice, once paired with Annie Oakley), Big Joe Turner, Tweedle Dum and Tweedle Dee (pronounced with an extra 'ee' as three-syllables 'Tweedle-ee-dum and Tweedle-ee-dee'), and Link Wray.

And then, of course, there are the made-up names, some of them ordinary, such as the names of women to whom love songs are addressed (Corinna, Ramona, Angelina, Johanna, Magdalena), or the names of characters from ballads and other stories: Old Reilly who is hanged for stealing the stallion in 'Seven Curses', John Brown who goes to war, John Thomas, the un-Lawrentian miner who marries the narrator of 'North Country Blues', Will O'Conley (Rambling, Gambling Willie), Frankie and Albert and Blackjack Davey, Jim Jones (who declares his intention of joining a gang of 'brave bushrangers' led by the historical Jack Donohoe), Arthur McBride and Diamond Joe, Silvio and Stack-a-Lee, the mysterious Henry Porter about whom the only thing we know for sure is that his name isn't Henry Porter, Aunt Sally who isn't really his aunt, and Mr Goldsmith (a nasty dirty double-crossing back-stabbing phoney). And last but not least, either in number or significance, the names of freaks and quirks of fancy, crazies and masked or disguised creatures, of whom these are only a handful: Gypsy Lou and Baby Blue, Dr Filth and his nurse, Frankie Lee and Judas Priest, Lucky and Mighty Mockingbird, Queen Jane and Quinn the Eskimo, the king of the Philistines and Gypsy Davey, the kings of Tyrus with their convict list, Mr Tambourine Man and Miss Lonely, the *other* Jones (not the one who doesn't know what's happening, but the one who came along and emptied the trash), Silly Nelly and Fat Nancy, Tiny Montgomery (along with Skinny Moo and Half-Track Frank), Henry and Mrs Henry, the Jack of Hearts, Tweeter and the Monkeyman, Mr Jinx and Miss Lucy who jumped in the lake, a retired businessman named Red (cast down from heaven and out of his head), the Sad-Eyed Lady of the Lowlands and the Man in the Long Black Coat.

It seems right to begin with catalogues, with their primitive order and abundance. It is an American abundance: Woody Guthrie, Jack Kerouac, and Walt Whitman, among many others, offer the enchanted recital, the incantation of names of states and towns, rivers and roads and streets; but the simple form of this is quite rare in Dylan and tends to be early, as in 'Gypsy Lou' or the very Guthrie-like 'Dusty Old Fairgrounds' (1962):

> From the Michigan mud past the Wisconsin sun
> Cross the Minnesota border, keep 'em scrambling
> Through the clear country lakes and the lumberjack
>   lands,
> We're following them dusty old fairgrounds a-calling.
>
> Hit Fargo on the jump and down to Aberdeen
> Cross them old Black Hills, keep 'em rolling
> Through the cow country towns and the sands of old
>   Montana . . .

What matters more are the gestures of grasping and embracing, arcs of naming that take you from coast to coast or from north to south, that bridge or traverse or circle or encompass the distances of the continent. Like Whitman, Dylan rolls up the map with his tongue, claiming to own everything and belong everywhere:

> Go out in your country where the land meets the sun
> See the craters and the canyons where the waterfalls run
> Nevada, New Mexico, Arizona, Idaho
> Let every state in this union seep down deep in your souls,

And you'll die in your footsteps
Before you go down under the ground.

('Let Me Die in My Footsteps', 1962)

Yes I'm a walkin' down your highway
Just as far as my eyes can see
From the Golden Gate Bridge
All the way to the Statue of Liberty.

('Down the Highway', 1963)

Idiot wind, blowing like a circle around my skull
From the Grand Coulee Dam to the Capitol

('Idiot Wind', 1974)[2]

Whether solemn or jaunty or despairing, these gestures assume that the nation, the union, has meaning and can be encompassed, that it can be 'sung' and sung to. In 'Blind Willie McTell' (a song from the same year as 'Union Sundown') Dylan gives the sweeping, encompassing gesture a metaphysical dimension:

I see the arrow on the doorpost
Saying this land is condemned
All the way from New Orleans
To Jerusalem.

What gives Dylan the authority to make such visionary statements? He comes from a particular place: he was born in Duluth and raised in Hibbing, Minnesota, and he has songs which remind you of that, which are founded on a personal locality and speak of desire or rejection. Yet his Americanness is not regional or ethnic, but self-conscious and constructed. Art liberated him

31

from a single place, as it liberated him from a single name. '*Love and Theft*' (2001) is a recent reminder of the way his accent can shift from country boy to bluesman, from New York synagogue cantor to jazz crooner. He is promiscuously at home in America, as though every state in the union had indeed sunk down deep in his soul; he adopts Americanness as though he were not American to begin with.[3]

Turning from places to people, you notice a sharp divide between the songs about real people and the others. The songs about real people don't play games, or at least not with the identities of their subjects.[4] Not that Dylan's songs about real people are always accurate – very much the reverse in the case of 'Joey', which romanticises a New York gangster to death and beyond – but the focus is on action or emotion, and the name is a sign of an integral self: substantial, essential, given:

This boy's dreadful tragedy I can still remember well,
The color of his skin was black and his name was Emmett Till.

('The Ballad of Emmett Till', 1962)

Hattie Carroll was a maid of the kitchen.
She was fifty-one years old and gave birth to ten children

('The Lonesome Death of Hattie Carroll', 1964)

Lenny Bruce is dead
But he didn't commit any crime

('Lenny Bruce', 1981)

The name denotes an identity which is stable, partly because, in most cases, it belongs to the public world and circulates in other media and other discourses: in politics, in newspapers, in the courts. In 'Hurricane' (1974) we hear of the boxer Rubin Carter 'fighting for his name' in South America, but his real fight is back home, where the police justify their framing of him by sneering 'he ain't no Gentleman Jim' and where the story 'won't be over till they clear his name'.[5] The most direct and powerful statement of the song therefore appropriately leads with the name: 'Rubin Carter was falsely tried.' In another such song, 'Who Killed Davey Moore?' (1963), the dead boxer's name appears only in the refrain, 'Who killed Davey Moore, / Why an' what's the reason for?' Each of the main verses is devoted to an anonymous figure or group, all of whom disclaim responsibility: '"Not I," says the referee . . . "Not us," says the angry crowd . . . "Not me," says his manager . . . "Not me," says the gambling man', and each verse finishes 'It wasn't me that made him fall. / No, you can't blame me at all', whereupon the refrain, and the name, comes back: 'Who killed Davey Moore?' The last verse of all is devoted to Davey Moore's opponent, whose name was Sugar Ramos but who is un-named in the song, denoted only by periphrasis: 'the man whose fists / Laid him low in a cloud of mist'. He at least can't claim not to have made him fall, but he has if anything a worse excuse: 'Don't say murder, don't say kill. / It was destiny, it was God's will.' But the song does say kill: Davey Moore's name, and the question of who killed him, begin the song, and punctuate it, and end it, and all around the name, like a rock, swirls the language of hypocrisy, evasion, and cliché – especially, of course, from the 'boxing writer', whose hands are 'pounding print on his old typewriter' and who thinks that the pounding of flesh is 'just the old American way'.

Another song which opposes a named figure to an anonymous group is 'Only a Pawn in Their Game' (1963), which commemorates the assassinated civil rights leader Medgar Evers by contrast with the 'pawn' of the title, the poor white who 'Like a dog on a chain ... ain't got no name', his identity indifferent to those who use him.[6] Medgar Evers, therefore, is accorded the dignity of a name: indeed his killing is represented as an attack on his name: 'A finger fired the trigger to his name'. And this dignity is then enhanced by a pun which Dylan allows himself in the final verse: 'Today Medgar Evers was buried from the bullet he caught. / They lowered him down as a king'. The honour due to Evers isn't lessened by his making this appearance on the chess board, where he is revealed as the most important piece, if also the most vulnerable. The pun plays like lightning around his head, but doesn't strike and deform him.

There is a radical difference between this treatment of real people, and the use which is made of names from the grab-bag of culture. Disrespect is the order of the day here, identity is unstable and subject to transformation and degradation, characters from 'real life' rub shoulders with invented or mythical figures, as though freedom of association were not only a right but a duty under Dylan's artistic constitution. All this is clear, but how should it be interpreted? 'Desolation Row' (1965), the most famous example of this technique, is 'a deliberate cultural jumble', according to Frank Kermode and Stephen Spender:

> history seen flat, without depth, culture heroes of all kinds known only by their names, their attributes lost by intergenerational erosion – all of them so much unreality against the background of Desolation Row ... the general deviance, the lack of stereoscopy in the cultural reference, gives the poem its whole force.[7]

Yet the song doesn't work unless the names are known to be deformed – that is, unless they are known to name something which once had integrity, but which has now lost it. The song is about loss, about desolation, but Desolation Row is also a place, an order, an American way. Kermode and Spender's term *deviance* is more useful than *unreality*: it speaks of a swerve away from the 'natural' or given attributes of names, but deviance implies a *from* and a *to*, a process of unmaking. It is this which the singer describes in the final verse:

> Yes, I received your letter yesterday
> (About the time the door knob broke)
> When you asked how I was doing
> Was that some kind of joke?
> All these people that you mention
> Yes, I know them, they're quite lame
> I had to rearrange their faces
> And give them all another name
> Right now I can't read too good
> Don't send me no more letters no
> Not unless you mail them from
> Desolation Row

This isn't a denial of reality but a cry which echoes through Dylan's writing: it's the same cry as in 'Visions of Johanna' (1966), 'Name me someone that's not a parasite and I'll go out and say a prayer for him', and in the last verse of 'Señor' (1978):

> Señor, señor, let's overturn these tables,
> Disconnect these cables,
> This place don't make sense to me no more.

A place that don't make sense no more *made sense once*; 'Everything Is Broken' (1989) is a song title and refrain, but something that is broken was once whole; when Dylan sings 'Broke Down Engine' (a blues associated with Blind Willie McTell) and does so on an album called *World Gone Wrong* (1993) the same applies. The engine *once* ran, the world was *once* right. The broken doorknob in 'Desolation Row' is a figure of lack, but not of emptiness. The narrator's response to the 'lame' people he is offered is to rearrange and re-name them. I don't see Bob Dylan's names as empty, floating, post-modern signifiers, I don't think they are flat and without depth, or that they are playful in a way which discounts notions of substantial identity and value. They're notations of despair at the spectacle of disorder, recorded in the concluding lines from 'I Dreamed I Saw St Augustine':

> I dreamed I saw St Augustine
> Alive with fiery breath
> And I dreamed I was amongst the ones
> That put him out to death
> Oh, I awoke in anger
> So alone and terrified,
> I put my fingers against the glass
> And bowed my head and cried.

St Augustine may be appearing here out of his time – or the legendary radical Joe Hill may be appearing in the costume of a saint – but you couldn't argue that the name lacked meaning.[8] It's a long drop from St Augustine to Prince Philip, but even here the satire doesn't consist in hollowing out the subject or accusing it of unreality:

> I met Prince Philip at the home of the blues
> Said he'd give me information if his name wasn't used
> He wanted money up front, said he was abused
> By dignity

> ('Dignity', 1991 [first released 1994])

His Royal Highness is plunged into incongruity here, and into indignity, playing the low-life informant to Dylan's noir detective (and not getting his wish, either, since his name *is* used), but what comes out of this exchange isn't the feeling that Prince Philip has no identity and might as well have been King Kong, but that his real identity has been travestied, that his appearance here is a twisted truth, and that this fits the pattern of the song as a whole, amidst the chaos of whose terms and names is a persistent beat, the beat of the word *dignity* at the end of each verse, the rhythm of an unending search for what has been irretrievably lost.

In the late 1970s and early 1980s, the period of his conversion to Christianity, Dylan found a way of describing this loss by reflecting on its origin. In 'Man Gave Names to All the Animals' (1979), he goes back to a primal myth of naming:

> Man gave names to all the animals
> In the beginning, in the beginning.
> Man gave names to all the animals
> In the beginning, long time ago.
>
> He saw an animal that liked to growl,
> Big furry paws and he liked to howl,
> Great big furry back and furry hair.
> 'Ah, think I'll call it a bear.'
>
> He saw an animal upon a hill
> Chewing up so much grass until she was filled.
> He saw milk comin' out but he didn't know how.
> 'Ah, think I'll call it a cow.'

Of course these childlike perceptions, and the sensuous clumsiness with which each animal is denoted, are a product of art; the names cannot be other than arbitrary, and have no right to represent themselves as 'natural': indeed they seem generated as much by rhyme as by reason. But suppose we allow this naming to stand for the blissful innocence with which the world is first perceived. Leapfrogging over the bull, the pig, and the sheep, we get to the last verse:

> He saw an animal as smooth as glass
> Slithering his way through the grass.
> Saw him disappear by a tree near a lake . . .

We are left to supply the rhyme for 'lake', and to guess which tree the snake is headed for. What does this ending imply? Not that original sin breaks an innocent connection between the name of something and its essential identity, because that connection never existed; what is broken (after which *everything is broken*) is the innocence of naming itself.

'Desolation Row' represents an American way of viewing this world of lost or broken names in its humour, its taste for the outlandish and its refusal of deference, but above all in its appropriation and naturalisation of names, symbolised by Cinderella putting her hands in her back pockets 'Bette Davis style'. The song is aggressively hospitable to these figures, compelling them to come in, indelibly marking them with American idioms and accents: the Good Samaritan getting ready for the show, Ophelia peeking in to Desolation Row, Einstein bumming a cigarette, Casanova being spoonfed to get him to feel more *assured* (listen to the dragging accent on that word), the Phantom of the Opera shouting 'Get outa here', Neptune presiding over the sailing of the *Titanic* to the tune of 'Which Side Are You On?' (Florence Reece's classic of the Depression era which Pete Seeger had been singing with the Almanacs twenty years before). You have to listen to this American accent in the song to understand its yeasty ferment, its sour energy and craft: the carnival of names, in this

song and in Dylan's work generally, is an American attempt –
an attempt of American language and music – to make sense of
things not making sense any more. A version of pastoral, perhaps,
which returns us to 'the hills of old Duluth':

> Thought I'd shaken the wonder and the phantoms of
>   my youth
> Rainy days on the Great Lakes, walkin' the hills of old
>   Duluth.
> There was me and Danny Lopez, cold eyes, black night
>   and there was Ruth
> Something there is about you that brings back a long-
>   forgotten truth.

The rhyming names, 'Duluth' and 'Ruth', a place and a lover, are
clasped by the enclosing rhyme of 'youth' and 'truth', long gone
and long forgotten. It is beside the point whether the names are
biographically authentic (they're not, as far as I can tell) or the
memory real. It doesn't have to be real to be true: the imprint of
a personal memory is rhetorically powerful and self-justifying.

Yet Dylan can't rest here, can't find creative authority in
Romantic memory; in order for him to do this, he would have
to be self-possessed, that is, he would have to know who he
was and where he was bound. In 'Brownsville Girl' (1986),
what substitutes for the wonders and phantoms of youth is a
movie starring Gregory Peck, whose memory haunts the singer
and which becomes, in the end, a point of origin which cannot
be reached or understood, but only mourned. Here is how the
song begins and ends:

> Well there was this movie I seen one time
> About a man riding cross the desert and it starred
>   Gregory Peck

He was shot down by a hungry kid trying to make a
   name for himself
The townspeople wanted to crush that kid down and
   string him up by the neck.

. . .

There was a movie I seen one time,
I think I sat through it twice,
I don't remember who I was or where I was bound.
All I remember about it was it starred Gregory Peck,
He wore a gun and he was shot in the back,
Seems like a long time ago, long before the stars were
   torn down.

The movie is *The Gunfighter*, directed by Henry King in 1950, and the character played by Peck is shot down by, as Dylan tells us in the first verse of the song, 'a hungry kid trying to make a name for himself'. He's terrifically like Dylan, this hungry kid, the Dylan who thought that the hobo's worst fate was not just 'to lie in the gutter' but to 'die with no name' ('Only a Hobo', 1963).[9] The kid wants so much to be like Gregory Peck, utterly authentic and self-possessed – except that Gregory Peck is a famous actor of authenticity and self-possession. The name of the character he plays in *The Gunfighter* is Jimmy Ringo,[10] but Ringo is not named in the song and the grammar of the opening lines can make it seem as though Gregory Peck himself is shot down. To have your own identity erased by a fiction: that's the meaning of being an actor and being spellbound by acting: *I don't remember who I was . . . All I remember about it was it starred Gregory Peck*. You can't *make a name for yourself* under these conditions, not when the stars themselves have been torn down.[11]

By the time he wrote this song Dylan had made a name for himself; even in 1963 the opening line of 'With God on Our

Side', 'Oh my name it is nothin'', was already incongruous. 'Bob Dylan' is a made-up name, and according to one theory represents the son's assassination of his father and the Jew's rejection of his Jewishness; an originating murder *to make a name for himself*.[12] Yet it's such an American thing to do, to change your name: 'a common thing', Dylan said in 1968: 'It isn't that incredible. Many people do it. People change their town, change their country. New appearance, new mannerisms'.[13] The immigrant, the gangster, the social climber – all these American types do it; so do movie stars, though not, as it happens, Gregory Peck, who somewhat surprisingly turns out to have been Gregory Peck all along. Corporations and sports teams do it; the country itself did it. Re-naming oneself is a way of rejecting the past and claiming the future; the name-changer acquires magical powers over the world of names, is able to see through them (in both senses), is a trickster who can't be caught, and rejoices above all, as we have seen, in his power to change the names of others.[14] This magical transforming power is the source of some of Dylan's greatest songs – his funniest, his most savage, his most exultant and inventive – but it is shadowed by a corresponding terror.

Changing your name is a Jewish as well as an American thing. Zimmerman is too long, too ethnic. The Broadway musical star Ethel Merman was Ethel Zimmerman: she had the inspired idea of dropping the 'Zim', saying 'Can you imagine the name Zimmerman in bright lights? It would burn you to death!'[15] Dylan also joked about this; the prose piece 'Advice to Geraldine on Her Miscellaneous Birthday' (1964) ends 'when asked t' give your real name ... never give it', advice which he takes himself at a press conference in 1965:

> *Bob, is it true that you've changed your name? If so, what was your real name?*

My real name was Knezelwitz and I changed it to avoid obvious relatives that come up to you in different parts of the country and want tickets to concerts and stuff like that.

It was Knevevitch?

Knevovitch yes.

That was the first or last name?

That was the first name. I don't really want to tell you what the last name was.[16]

At one stage Dylan considered abbreviating it to an initial: Bobby Zee, like Bobby Vee. He would be a dead letter by now. The whole of Zimmerman, the Jewish patronymic, had to go. That sons should feel threatened by fathers is nothing new: Dylan reminds us of it in the opening line of 'Highway 61 Revisited' (1965), 'Oh God said to Abraham, "Kill me a son"'. As it happens Abraham is also a changed name. He was originally Abram: God awards him the extra syllable in chapter 17 of Genesis as a sign of the covenant between them. The new name means 'father of a great multitude'. Dylan's father was called by the earlier, primitive form: he was Abram Zimmerman, or 'Abe', as God also calls him in the song (though not in the Bible). So you might say that the son re-names the father, and not with the intention of honouring him.

Dylan's change of name is the subject of controversy. One of his earliest Hibbing girlfriends, Echo Helstrom, tells a story which seems to have been refined over the years until it reached its final form, appropriately enough, in the biography I always think of as 'Bob Spitz on Bob Dylan'. According to this version:

One afternoon in 1958, Bobby pulled up in front of Echo's house and hopped out of the car. He had a small book in his hand and waved it wildly at her as he walked up the front steps. 'I've finally found a name. I'm gonna call myself Bob Dylan,' he said, pronouncing it *Dial*-in. 'Whaddya think?' Echo agreed it was a splendid name, although Bobby never specifically acknowledged it corresponded to his discovery of Dylan Thomas.[17]

'Call me any name you like, I will never deny it . . .' ('Farewell Angelina', 1965). But not only did Dylan never *specifically acknowledge* that the name Dylan came from Dylan Thomas, he did specifically deny it, to Robert Shelton among numerous other friends and reporters.[18] Spitz makes play with 'Bobby's' hick inability to pronounce the European name correctly,[19] and has Echo appropriately echoing the false note, but the whole thing is made up, if we are to believe Dylan himself, who states that the name came to him while he was standing in a coffee-house in Minneapolis in his first weeks at college. In any case there's a lively other version of the origin of the name, in the TV Western lawman Matt Dillon; certainly there are plenty of people who remember Dylan touting his new name in that form before he settled on Dylan.[20] We're never going to know the truth of this: Echo Helstrom's story has a kernel of truth, I think, in that Dylan did tell her of a change of name, but the name then was probably Dillon and it got changed later by association with Dylan Thomas, who would thus be responsible for the spelling but not the sound. But the spelling matters, and so does the dissociation between Western hero and European poet and wild man. The name is a knot which can't be undone, an American chemical compound.

Or half of one. Because the other half often gets left out – the displacement of 'Robert' by 'Bob'. One of Dylan's aliases, 'Robert Milkwood Thomas', expresses his exasperation, or amusement, at being thought to have emerged from *Under Milk Wood*, but it also points at the impossibility of Robert. Can we imagine Robert Dylan? As difficult for me as to imagine that great Victorian poet, Bob Browning – though Ezra Pound tried it.[21] And Bob is not Rob, not Bobby, not Robbie. 'You can call me Bobby, you can call me Zimmy,' Dylan invites us in 'Gotta Serve Somebody' (1979); but no one does.[22] What is it about *Bob*? The movie which is partly a parody of Dylan, *Bob Roberts* (1992), cleverly uses both names in a way which suggests how impossible it would have been to have them the other way around.[23] In the presidential campaign of 1996, Bob Dole went around America telling people to vote for him because there had never been a president named Bob. *The Bob Book: A Celebration of the Ultimate OK Guy*, by David Rensin and Bill Zehme, appeared in 1991, the same year as Elmore Leonard's *Maximum Bob* (a less OK guy by any measure). According to *The Bob Book*,

> Bobs are never overwhelmed by circumstances; they face the music one note at a time. They do not dance; they hum. There is nothing flashy about Bobs. They put forth only what they are capable of expending; they can afford to promise little more. It's not as though they can hide behind their name. There isn't room.[24]

There is a literary precedent for this humdrum image in *Tristram Shandy*, a book fascinated by names and aliases; in book I, chapter 19, Mr Walter Shandy, Tristram's father, expounds his theory 'That there was a strange kind of magick bias, which good or bad names, as he called them, irresistibly impressed upon our characters and conduct.' But, Tristram goes on,

> there were still numbers of names which hung so equally in

the balance before him, that they were absolutely indifferent to him. *Jack*, *Dick*, and *Tom* were of this class: These my father called neutral names; – affirming of them, without a satire, That there had been as many knaves and fools, at least, as wise and good men, since the world began, who had indifferently borne them; – so that, like equal forces acting against each other in contrary directions, he thought they mutually destroyed each other's effects ... *Bob*, which was my brother's name, was another of these neutral kind of christian names, which operated very little either way; and as my father happen'd to be at *Epsom*, when it was given him, – he would oft-times thank Heaven it was no worse.

Does Bob Dylan fit this 'neutral' pattern? Rensin and Zehme sent a 'Bob Survey' to 'celebrated Bobs'; led by Bob Hope they all responded dutifully to the twenty-odd comedy prompts ('Why I'm Bob', 'What being Bob means', 'Boyhood dream', 'Favorite sandwich') – all except Dylan, who responded only to the request for 'Free advice': 'Don't do to someone something you wouldn't want them to do to you'.[25] According to Rensin and Zehme, Dylan is 'unlike many Bobs in that he is enigmatic', but 'in the truest spirit of Bob, he is at least *dependably* enigmatic. As George Harrison succinctly put it: "Bob is still out there, and whether you like him or not, he's still Bob."'[26]

But it isn't just the first name, or the last, but the way they fit together. It's to do with the stress pattern – Bób Dýlan – which is why it's so disorientating to talk to French fans who say Bób Deelán. The first name is easygoing, simple, transparent, reversible – you can say it any which way, it's impossible to misspell and almost impossible to mispronounce. It invites familiarity: Dylan fans refer to him amongst themselves as Bob, and the group which follows him on tour is known as the Bobcats. Using someone's first name without knowing them is a liberty, even in the land of the free; then there's the fake ingratiation of those who have power over you, like the dentist in Robert Lowell's monologue who has Lowell in the dentist's chair and calls him 'Bob', which no one ever did;[27] politicians specialise in this, as Dylan knew early on:

> Well, my telephone rang it would not stop,
> It's President Kennedy callin' me up.
> He said, 'My friend Bob, what do we need to make the
>   country grow?'
> I said, 'My friend John, Brigitte Bardot.'

('I Shall Be Free', 1963)

You know from this exchange how far they are from being friends; you sense Dylan's wariness and scorn, but also his realisation that the name 'Bob' lays him open to this treatment, and he has chosen it partly for that reason.

'Bob' goes with 'Dylan' like milk in coffee: from light to dark, simple to complex, transparent to opaque.[28] The name is balanced and divided against itself. It is phoney because it is made-up, but its fictiveness is also protean and fertile, in a way that the singular and limited 'self' is not. It serves a purpose:

> I'm only Bob Dylan when I have to be.
> *Who are you the rest of the time?*
> Myself.[29]

When does Bob Dylan *have to be* Bob Dylan? When he performs, presumably, as 'Bob Dylan': this assumed character is the horn of plenty (the father of multitudes) from which the songs pour. A real 'self' can put off this disguise, disclaim its truth. On the other hand that very self, essential and irreducible, inheres in the name:

> I didn't create Bob Dylan, Bob Dylan has always been here ... always was. When I was a child, there was Bob Dylan ... sometimes your parents don't even know who you are.[30]

As with the origin of the name, the truth of either of these statements is less important than the fact that they can both be made with conviction. They are linked, also, by the assumption that there is such a thing as a self which can be either truly or falsely denoted by a name. Dylan has held to this assumption: he doesn't worry that signs might be arbitrary and empty, but he worries that they are, like the sign of his own name, duplicitous. The duplicity has something to do with fame, the condition for which *making a name for yourself* is a periphrasis; fame is the unspoken rhyme-word which lurks between *flame* and *name* in these lines from 'Every Grain of Sand':

> I gaze into the doorway of temptation's angry flame
> And every time I pass that way I always hear my name.

Dylan's interest in famous outlaws is, in part, a response to this problem, and accounts for his name as the sidekick of the most famous outlaw of all, Billy the Kid, in the film *Pat Garrett & Billy the Kid*: 'Alias'. Better be that than Einstein, the figure and near-synonym of 'genius', so painfully down and out in Desolation Row, 'disguised as Robin Hood'; certainly a more home-grown hero doesn't need the disguise:

> John Wesley Harding
> Was a friend to the poor,
> He travelled with a gun in every hand.
> All along this countryside,
> He opened many a door,
> But he was never known
> To hurt an honest man.

('John Wesley Harding', 1968)

Yet Harding's unequivocal self-possession carries a price, something like the price of fame or endless travelling for the singer. The outlaw opens doors into every house except his own. Whether he is being welcomed into these houses or robbing them is hard to tell, but the one thing he is not doing is living in them. 'Down in Chaynee County,' we are told, 'He took a stand', but has no roots there. And it also becomes clear that fame, like crime, makes you a *wanted man*: Harding's name resounds 'all across the telegraph' with sinister intent.

The song 'Wanted Man' (1969) playfully expounds this double meaning: to be wanted is both to be desired, and to be liable to capture and punishment.

> Wanted man in California, wanted man in Ohio,
> Wanted man in Kansas City, wanted man in Buffalo,
> Wanted man in Oklahoma, wanted man in old Cheyenne,
> Wherever you might look tonight, you might see this
>   wanted man.
>
>   . . .
>
> Wanted man in Albuquerque, wanted man in Baton
>   Rouge,
> Wanted man in Tallahassee, wanted man in Syracuse,
> There's somebody set to grab me anywhere that I
>   might be

> And wherever you might look tonight, you might get a
>   glimpse of me.

'There's somebody set to grab me': this may be an erotic or a judicial ambush, but in either case you want out. The wanted man is always on the lam, always on the move, from town to town and state to state, naming and eluding the places and the women in which and by whom he is wanted. Nobody can track or chain him down, not even in Chaynee County. He is boastful, but he is also disorientated and lost. 'I've had all that I've wanted of a lot of things I had', the wanted man sings, but to have had *all you wanted* is also to have *had enough*, to be fed up. It's great to be wanted, and we, too, are teased by the desire to glimpse the singer, to grab a piece of him ourselves, for we, like him, may be anywhere on the map. But though we may recognise him, the singer withholds his name.

3

DYLAN AND THE ACADEMICS

Christopher Butler

The textual materials offered by Dylan for study are impressively extensive – 500 pages of lyrics from 1962 to 1985, and more waiting to be printed in book form – and there are plenty of variant texts, particularly if we take into account the transcriptions of the words Dylan actually uses in performance. There is scope for all sorts of scholarly activity here. Other factors make Dylan (by now) like many other established poets. One is the interpretative tradition. The many published interpretations of Dylan's songs are not all 'academic' ones. Controversies on the local fanzine level are very different from professorial deconstructions, or exercises in political correctness which purport, with one of the typical hypocrisies of academic convention, to be addressed to the intellectual world at large. There are already plenty of impressive book-length studies of his work, which relate and compare it to earlier literary and musical traditions, most notably those by Michael Gray, on music and text, and Wilfrid Mellers, for musical analysis.

Many critics have shown how the different kinds of songs which Dylan sings have a complex relationship to cultural traditions in popular literature and in music – from themes derived from Woody Guthrie and others to parodic tributes to Elvis Presley.

Beyond attention to an evolving historical tradition within popular music, some critics also wish to make connections to a broader and 'higher' literary tradition (which is, e.g., more difficult, more acceptable to educated elites): for example to Elizabethan troubadours and even to the Metaphysicals. Michael Gray thinks that 'Go 'way from my window, / Leave at your own chosen speed' ('It Ain't Me, Babe') has a certain Donnean immediacy as the opening of a song.[1] It is easy to go too far along this road. Beginning a love lyric with an imperative may not be enough. The window from 'The Sunne Rising' may simply be a distraction here. And this looks suspiciously like what Philip Larkin called dipping in to the myth kitty. What we may need more are more plausible influences from within the zeitgeist – for example from William Blake, who also influenced Michael Horovitz's Children of Albion and many others in the Sixties. If the drug culture really can produce any original visionary insights they ought to be here, without too much need for Blake, and there is no doubt that Dylan's 'surrealism' (often euphemistically so described) may fit in here. *Tarantula* aside, Dylan's lyrics are generally far more intelligible than William Burroughs, and songs like 'Gates of Eden' may indeed fit into this context. It is less easy to agree that (as Gray suggests) an economy of language, a concentration, and a tone of disinterestedness about deep emotion can make Dylan's 'Love Minus Zero / No Limit' comparable to Blake's 'O rose thou art sick', because the thematic links here are weak.[2]

Plenty of poets have had these characteristics, including lots of Americans nearer in time and culture to Dylan. But the point of the comparison for the critic is as much to suggest something about the status of Dylan's work as a contribution to the tradition of high literature – as visionary, as dissenting, and prone to express abnormally elevated states of mind. We need to distinguish between high to low comparison which is mere cultural compliment, and the use of allusion which brings two contexts together in a metaphorical interaction. There is a large cast of characters in 'Desolation Row' – Cinderella, Ophelia, Cain and Abel, Noah, Einstein, Bette Davis and Dr Filth, along with Ezra Pound and T. S. Eliot. But this lyric is more of a hilo carnival night out than an attempt to succeed Pound and Eliot (or even Ed Dorn) as an allusive monologuist for the Sixties. The imagery is brilliant, the comedy exact – 'spoonfeeding Casanova / To get him to feel more assured' – but Dylan's imagery creates a fairly shallow post-modernist world of popular culture, which we need to accept on its own terms, rather than to give it a specious mythical depth. You can't turn Paul Auster into Tolstoy either.

When Robert Shelton asked Dylan for his reaction to the idea that he is a 'poet', he made it clear that his poems obey the conventions of the song lyric first of all. 'Allen Ginsberg is the only writer I know. The rest of the writers I don't have that much respect for. If they really want to do it, they're going to have to sing it . . .' Otherwise 'all that' would put him 'in a category with people who would just bother me'. And he cites a nice middlebrow lot – 'Sandburg, Eliot, Spender, Rupert Brooke, Edna St Vincent Millay and Robert Louis Stevenson and Edgar Allan Poe and Robert Lowell'.[3] This certainly shows Dylan's sense of humour: he knows too that Frost is popular for his 'poetry about trees and branches'. But as a writer he's more likely to be influenced by Ginsberg, William Burroughs and Jean Genet, whom he read. And *Tarantula* shows, unreadable as it is, that Rimbaud and Surrealism and City Lights in general can be added to this list. It's not Dylan's pseudo-Modernism that counts here, but something much more important, which is the way, at a particular historical period, and under the social and political pressures of that period, a songwriter of genius comes to terms with the ideas within *his* culture, in a way that is unique and no longer a matter of the dutiful allusion and disguised quotation which still lends authority to the Modernist tradition. The nearest Dylan gets to authority of this kind is in his many allusions to the Bible. Robert Christgau may think he is attacking Dylan, but I think he reveals very well how some of Dylan's ideas actually work, when he says that he wrote 'like a word-drunk undergraduate who had berserked himself into genius, his only tradition the jumbled culture of the war baby – from Da Vinci to comic strips, from T. S. Eliot to Charlie Rich'. So that his surrealism owes 'as much to Chuck Berry as to Breton or even Corso'.[4]

Dylan's use of this kind of material can be obscurely personal and autobiographical – it is often this voyeuristic play with 'real life experience' that is exploited by the great rock stars, who know that they can rely upon the obsessional biographical tracking of their fans. In *Renaldo and Clara*, Dylan puts himself (and his friends) firmly within this self-indulgently persona-ridden, self-revelatory tradition.[5] This paradoxical conflict between 'persona' and genuinely self-revealing work is typical of the pop world, in which 'revelatory' publicity is so often also fiction.

Christgau also points out that Dylan's imagery may have 'broadened the stream of songwriting' but it is only really useful as 'a background' for Dylan's 'endless stream of epigrams – which songwriters call good lines – flowing in our language, some already clichés such as "The times they are a changin'", "Something is happening here / But you don't know what it is"'.[6] Dylan may not be as good a read as Corso or Ferlinghetti or O'Hara or Ginsberg or whoever, but as a song lyricist, in the great American tradition of revivified cliché, wit, rhyme and everyday speech (just like Cole Porter and Rogers and Hart), he is far better than most of his contemporaries to listen to, because his epigrams, judgements, and bizarre narratives are given point and reinforcement in the context of musical accompaniment, which has its own ways of demanding an attention to words. Here as elsewhere Dylan makes the miserably cliché-ridden self-pity and aggression, churned out to mechanically repetitive rhythms, which is the norm for so much popular music, far more interesting.

What the parallels of Dylan to literary tradition can show is that he is of that irrationalist family of poets and prose writers for whom the process of writing derives, as Aidan Day puts it, from a conflict between the 'socialised self that has its being in language' and 'those drives of personality that exceed rational formation and social definition'.[7] Or to put it another way, between the 'bourgeois conformity' of, say, Hibbing, Minnesota, and the various hobo, outsider and criminal myths of Woody Guthrie, John Wesley Harding, Hurricane Carter, and the sexual intrigues of Lily, Rosemary and the Jack of Hearts, in their various *ménage à trois* manifestations. Not surprisingly, middle-class academic critics mimic this development when they praise what they hear as 'carnivalesque', and as an 'experimental' irrationalism, which 'contests' ideologically tired, i.e. 'bourgeois', attitudes. But Dylan already knows this – that's what the folksingers in the leftist tradition in America did anyway; it is the irrationalist turn against the 'very well read' Mr Jones, who has 'been with the professors' and who is a representative of the 'dominant rationalist culture', which is distinctive. According to Day, what Jones can't see is 'the interdependence of the rational and the irrational', and of 'meaning and the absurd':

> Now you see this one-eyed midget
> Shouting the word 'NOW'
> And you say 'For what reason?'
> And he says, 'How?'
> And you say, 'What does this mean?'

> And he screams back, 'You're a cow
> Gimme some milk
> Or else go home.'

('Ballad of a Thin Man')

The things that are 'happening' and which Jones doesn't understand are 'deeper than the reach of the merely rational self'. Dylan seems to appeal here for an understanding which not only evokes the solidarity of (his) group, for whom Mr Jones, like most of the contributors to this book, is entirely square, but also asks us to allow that 'the energies of the unconscious graphically break through the strict, constraining orders of reason', as Day puts it, though it is difficult to know why he believes that the work of Kristeva is a good route for coming to a conclusion like this.[8] It may well be that it is post-Derridan theory that allows the academic critic to see such metaphoric excess as liberating a polymorphously perverse identity. I think it just makes Dylan, like so many in the Sixties, into a not quite Maileresque absurdist-existentialist-hipster.

We go further towards what I am calling an 'academic' judgement when we ask how far work like this deserves to be part of a literary tradition and so part of whatever more general literate consciousness the academy imagines to be valuable. There is no significant difference so far between Dylan and Tennyson or Dylan and Dylan Thomas, given the difference between Dylan and those singers preceding him who simply purveyed what Tin Pan Alley provided. It's the singularity of his vision which intrigues those who care for him.

There are then traditionally oriented methods for comparison between his work and that of others. But these bring with them implicit standards of judgement for Dylan's canonic status within the larger contexts of the 'high' culture, but perhaps more particularly within a post-modernist culture, which, as so many have argued, doesn't mind mixing, within works of art, and within the minds of those of its creators and users who were born after, say, 1940, the originally 'high', the formerly 'low', and the currently popular. The question then is, how sophisticated and enduring a contribution is made by artists like Warhol, Lichtenstein, Dylan, Schnabel, Adams, Glass, Laurie Anderson, Stephin Merritt, Baz Luhrmann, Judy Chicago (to offer some surreal juxtapositions of my own), to those who defend a high cultural canon, or do they really appeal to those who accept this post-modernist mixed culture?

I mean by 'academic' here, with some irony, those who accept procedures which involve an appeal to universalisable standards of judgement, at least in the sense that the values involved are supposed to apply to the whole field (of song in this case). And so if you write about Dylan as a poet, then the whole of the accepted canon from the ballads on is indeed implicitly acceptable for purposes of comparison – and the same goes for the musical accompaniment. The corollary of this is that the values involved are not just relative ones, as they are if the exercise is just a kind of special pleading for the values expressed within an historical period (like the post-modernist), or a particular subculture. This special pleading is indeed typical of much recent work in Cultural Studies, often on the grounds that through this kind of popular work it can interpret the politics of a supposedly valuable 'difference' or discern the expression of a (supposedly not enough appreciated) social, ethnic or gender 'identity'. Bruce Springsteen and Michael Jackson would indeed be very different in these respects.[9] By earlier 'academic' standards, this kind of particularism used to be ruled out: the anger or compassion which Dylan expresses towards other people was to be assessed by the same moral standards as would be applied elsewhere, and not in a purely anthropological sense. It's not much of an excuse to say, for example, that it's just a particular artistic convention within a particular social group, that in rock music from Dylan to punk, to rap and onwards, you just do get a lot of male chauvinist violence, and expressions of contempt for various kinds of person. Dylan's lyrics are frequently misogynistic. This is more of an issue for academic criticism in my sense than it is for cultural studies.

This is not to say that such special pleading, of what I am going to call an 'anthropological' kind, cannot be justified, when it is indeed the study of effects on particular audiences which is at issue. That is why you can argue that Dylan's songs are indeed significant (even if not *ipso facto* particularly valuable), because they are better memorised by the many than are the texts of many 'canonical' poets by the minority. Hence the pardonable exaggeration of the claim that Dylan 'has done more than anyone else – and far, far more than formal mass education systems – to develop in a mass audience the kind of receptiveness to things imaginative and non-trivial that was, before, the sole prerogative of elite minorities'.[10]

But the history and society here won't bear much examination either, because if the 'imaginative and non-trivial' had really been the sole prerogative of the elite up to about 1960, we wouldn't have any jazz, any Cole Porter, or anything like the 'elitist' art which arises out of popular culture, such as *Porgy and Bess*. These are sociological rather than cultural claims. What is often more seriously implied by such observations is the claim that plenty of mass art (along with newspapers like the *Sun* or the *Daily Mail*) can be seen as providing powerful legitimating myths. As Dylan puts it, with a typical bit of sentimental over-simplification, 'Popular songs are the only form that describes the temper of the times ... It's where the people hang out'.[11] Of course this applies just as much to Bing Crosby's 'White Christmas' and to the awful songs for peace and the relief of famine evolved by the popular music community, as it does to such songs as 'With God on Our Side', 'Masters of War' or 'Like a Rolling Stone'. But Dylan's claims to importance on these grounds depend less on relationships to 'the people' who like these sorts of things, than on his very complex relationship to the student and protest culture of the 1960s. For Dylan was lucky enough to begin his career within the relatively sophisticated, politically dissentient audience for folk music, which was to that extent already willing to think for itself against some of the dominant social attitudes of the late Fifties and early Sixties.

It is these political criteria which govern the interest of some critics in the 'oppositional' character of popular work in general. John Fiske, for example, asserts that popular cultural commodities 'bear the interests of the people', and that 'all popular culture is a process of struggle, of struggle over the meanings of social experience, of one's personhood and its relation to the social order'. That is why, for him, 'there can be no popular dominant culture, for popular culture is formed always in reaction to, and never as part of, the forces of domination'.[12] Even if this were empirically correct, which it isn't since it is just political wishful thinking by prescriptive definition, we would still have to make some distinctions between Frank Sinatra, Bette Midler, Dylan and Springsteen. Joan Baez saw this pretty well: 'He criticises society, and I criticise it, but he ends up saying there isn't a goddam thing you can do about it, so screw it. And I say just the opposite.'[13] Much of the interest of what Dylan has said arises from his position within a distinctively leftist oppositional culture. He has never had to rely on the sloppy impression that the popular culture of rock is somehow 'inherently' oppositional, when in fact it is far more obviously open to conservative economic pressures and inducements than his own. And in any case the political implications of Dylan's born-again Christianity are far from obviously radical in the American context.

But this sociological analysis only approaches (a bourgeois, universalising, rationalistic) academic criticism in my sense when the values involved, however oppositional, are seriously brought into comparison with such canonic standards for works of art, as well as those for political correctness, as the academy and the generally well-educated listener might be expected to support in the longer run. (In the longer run, stick with the *Antigone* rather than a novel by Andrea Dworkin.) This formulation runs counter to the post-modernist defence of multicultural relativism, by which popular music can be justified on the grounds of the study of identity politics.[14] It also conflicts with the current distrust of consensual or ethical criticism. But it seems to me that Dylan's major work can be examined apart from any such appeals to social and cultural history, or to the way in which he articulates the values of any particular political grouping. Many great works of art arise out of or contest the values of some group or another, from the Greek gods to the later masters of war. It is the way in which serious artists articulate such problems and oppositions so that they have some kind of life beyond the contemporary, that counts – and for that you need Dylan. His work is quite different from the sort of cheery protest previously to be found in pop songs, such as 'Sixteen Tons', as sung by Tennessee Ernie Ford, where some sort of point about workers' exploitation through debt is indeed there, but the way that it is sung is jolly rather than critical. Dylan brings real anger into political songs (and into love songs too). You can see how 'Sixteen Tons' simply points to an abuse as mythically well known, and is ultimately as condescending in effect as references to happy 'darkies' singing their 'hymns' of Christian reconciliation to their lot would be.

The whole thing is neutralised by becoming almost comic. 'Sixteen tons, and what do you get, another day older and deeper in debt.' It's almost the successor to the Seven Dwarves singing 'Heigh ho'.[15] My comparison here is fairly ludicrous, but reminds us that the cultural context that soon after produced 'Oxford Town', or even 'The Death of Emmett Till', was articulated by Dylan in a quite different way. These songs transcend newspaper reactions, to involve the whole community in a disgrace of which it pretends to be unaware.[16] It's this combination of historical and communal embeddedness in so many of Dylan's songs, along with their protesting vision, that gives them their continuing moral relevance, so long as nations still claim to fight 'With God on Our Side'.

And so, if we look at a popular and quite obvious song like 'Highway 61 Revisited' we find a successfully continuous mythopoeia, combined with the immensely powerful implied historical context – of the Vietnam war (perhaps the first war to have been watched by millions on TV from the 'bleachers'). 'In the Spring of 1965, following the start of a sustained U.S. bombing campaign against North Vietnam, "teach-ins" on the war were held on college campuses across the country.'[17] But the context of the song's appeal to a then young audience, and also its continuing power, depends on its also being a great song about conflict between the generations, and one which dares to see its perpetuation by complicity with a religious culture which takes a very explicit form within American political rhetoric. Fathers demand obedience and sacrifice their own sons. Dylan, like Joseph Heller or Stanley Elkin, makes Abraham and Isaac, and the Judaeo-Christian theology of sacrifice, into an American tragicomedy. For him, the wickedness of war and the wickedness of this theology are the same thing. The scene of sacrifice of the first stanza turns into a surreal sequence of American myths, all of which can be directed to Highway 61, which is not so much the site of a private sacrifice as of the kind of war which naturally follows from the theology. Here come the poor men like Georgia Sam, the flag and telephone dumpers, and the second mother and her seventh son, so that by the last stanza the bored 'rovin' gambler' easily finds a 'promoter' to stage the 'next world war' in front of 'bleachers out in the sun' . . . on Highway 61. The song rises to a level of generality and universality characteristic of major art.

The Vietnam war is now nearly thirty years in the past, but Dylan's song, in articulating part of this conflict, both recalls and shows the underlying basis for a revolt by many young people against war and their elders in that period. And it's far from being a nostalgic evocation. Shelton found 'a disturbing undercurrent of probability' in this song.[18] I find much more, in retrospect, about the business of America, about spectacle, and about fathers consenting to the killing of sons.

Dylan's greatest songs are also serious art in other more conventional ways. Gray's judgement on 'One Too Many Mornings' (1964) is for me entirely representative of what Dylan can do as other great songwriters can. For him it expresses

A wonderfully clear sighted, calm-centred, complex compassion that conjured up in a few attentive, human strokes the particularities and atmosphere of real people in real moments and real places: living individuals glimpsed in the living, breathing night, evoked without recourse to formula or filler-lines, sung out on a melody of infinite space with a consummate syllable-by-syllable accuracy, with grace – heart and head in balance . . .[19]

A central question that remains to be asked once all these background explanations and justifications have been given, is this –

What sorts of persons are projected in Dylan's songs? To ask Wayne Booth's question, 'What kind of company do we keep?'[20] This is a question that particularly arises for mass culture, where audiences are so acutely aware of the artist as role model. Dylan's angle on this involves an interesting conservative reliance on the heroic. In 1991 he told an *LA Times* reporter: 'There used to be a time when the idea of heroes was important. People grew up sharing myths and legends and ideals. Now they grow up sharing McDonald's and Disneyland'.[21] Dylan often enough casts himself as the larger-than-life and often martyred hero of his own songs, which ties his fans to the idiosyncratic development of his own mythicised life story – which is full of an American dream of self-fashioning and self-transformation.

His successive albums present changed 'identities', and along with that, different types of narrative: hence the shock to many of *John Wesley Harding*, where Dylan explores his cowboy hero and others like him in portraits which offer little indication of the narrator's attitude. What emerge are the traditional American cultural values more associated with country and western music, which is interestingly counterpointed to warnings against categorising people. Or *Street-Legal*, which brings together 'the moralist, the writer who draws heavily on the Bible, Dylan caught in the struggle between the flesh and the spirit, Dylan ending his relationship with Sara, Dylan the betrayed victim', in Gray's words.[22] This is the album as confessional poetry, with its insatiable demands for a sympathetic, interpreted understanding of the song, though Dylan is never as sentimentally demanding as, say, Joni Mitchell or Leonard Cohen and many others. And Dylan's becoming a Christian in *Slow Train Coming* was an identity change which many of his admirers found it very hard to take, although Christopher Ricks managed some 'gratitude' for a 'heartfelt expression of faith' and says that even he would become a Christian not for any poem by Gerard Manley Hopkins, but for George Herbert, and Dylan's 'What Can I Do for You'.[23] But then these songs are matters of dogma, and fairly explicitly exclude the unsaved.

Dylan's further self-identification with Christ here and elsewhere can be hard to take. If it was a hard life being Judy Garland, it has clearly become even harder for the rock stars of the Seventies and Eighties. And it doesn't help when academic critics wrap all this up in the jargonised assertion that 'This obsessive identification with Christ can be seen as a product of Dylan's intense awareness of the negative end of the public axis.'[24] From the post-modernist perspective – one which doesn't particularly look for depth or autonomous control – this instability of identity within the texts of his songs, and the different pressures on it of social construction, are endlessly interesting.

A good deal of mass art expresses sloppily adolescent self-centred emotions and so depends upon sentimental beliefs which, compared to those of the elitist culture, are narcissistically self-promoting, let alone sexist, vulgar, and violent. Such characteristics are not really well defended by claims like Simon Frith's that such music can have a unique – if 'haphazard' – effect upon our feelings:

The experience of pop music is an experience of placing: in responding to a song, we are drawn, haphazardly, into affective emotional alliances with the performers and the performer's other fans.

He adds that sport can have the same effect. In such cases popular music is seen as offering a uniquely immediate experience of a collective identity. (Just the sort of thing of which writers like Jung and Canetti and Adorno and Marcuse strongly disapproved.) And for Frith, whereas 'Other cultural forms – painting, literature, design – can articulate and show off shared values and pride . . . only music can make you feel them'.[25] (So much for the emotional impact of Shakespeare's *Henry V* and the paintings in the Tate Modern in general.) This emotional immediacy is often to be bought at the cost of attention to vulgar, base, coarse, disgusting, crass, raw and primitive, sentimental, maudlin, mushy, pathetic and kitsch types of art. All in their ways immensely enjoyable. Dylan is rare, in avoiding most of these traps. It's his quality of feeling, arising from complex beliefs and a complex musical context, that brings his work to the level of what John Pasmore calls 'serious art'.[26] Not always, however. You don't have to be merely politically correct to feel that there is no way that Dylan can sing

> . . . she aches just like a woman
> But she breaks just like a little girl

without being deeply embarrassing.

All these judgements of course carry with them a number of potentially offensive social values, but I don't see how they can be avoided in claiming serious aesthetic status for Dylan's work.[27] Rock indeed leads us to look at the contrast between crowd, mass or group emotion, and the responses of the (sophisticated) individual in isolation, in appreciating great art. For such as Robert Pattison, (vulgar) rock in live performance is 'the glorification of untranscendent instinct, in which taste and discrimination disappear into the celebration of infinite possibility'.[28] This happy illusion, whether generated by the Doors, the Stones or Dylan, or their successors, is extremely powerful. But that will not be the case made for Dylan by most of the contributors to this volume, who know that their settled response to him is as far from this as it is from the parody offered by such as Allan Bloom, who evokes 'the thirteen year old with his Walkman' who is no more than 'a pubescent child whose body throbs with orgasmic rhythms; whose feelings are made articulate in hymns to the joys of onanism or the killing of parents; whose ambition is to win fame and wealth in imitating the drag-queen who makes the music.'[29] 'Maggie's Farm' is not like this.

The short reply to all this disapproval is 'So what, I enjoy it.' And that also goes for those who enjoy rock as well as high art, and therefore have avoided the fate predicted for them by Bloom, who says that rock 'ruins the imagination of young people and makes it very difficult for them to have a passionate relationship to the art and thought that are the substance of a liberal education.'[30]

There is a problem here all the same, and one which is rarely faced up to by academics, concerning the nature of the pleasure to be got from sophisticated rock, and *a fortiori* from listening to Dylan, within the general context of popular music. It is not enough just to read Dylan, and to conclude (correctly) that he can be an extraordinarily complex, witty, self-aware and dramatic user of language. As the books written by Paul Williams show, a response to actual musical performance can be at some distance from academic appraisal. If for example we track some of the 1974–1986 performances of 'Lay, Lady, Lay', the *Before the Flood* version excites Williams to respond 'What a great guitar player Robbie Robertson can be! So much is said between the words in this performance, it's like Dylan's singing (the way he stretches the word "brass" for example) in percussive accompaniment for the lead guitar'. And in 1975, says Williams, the song 'moves from being a sweet sexy song of courtship to a purposely crude (and joyous) assertion of male sexuality'. But by 1976's *Hard Rain* album it 'expresses the expansive and awkward sexuality of the newly or not-quite-single 35-year-old male'.[31] This can be way over the top, wilfully subjective, and more like a fan than a critic, but these judgements on the differing aspects of the song are far from unintelligible, and that is my point.

The academic barriers to our treating Dylan seriously seem then to be of two complementary kinds. The first stems from the (now fast-diminishing) belief that the popular culture is too low to be worth serious critical as opposed to sociological attention. This is the 'bottom up' view. The second depends on a more loftily well-informed 'top down' comparative value judgement: 'Dylan may think he is like Rimbaud and take his name from Dylan Thomas, but he isn't nearly as "good" a poet as they are.' (Good for what?) I am arguing that in the long run this second, implicitly canonic judgement is the one that counts, and that it is the task of academics, as the museum curators of the imaginary of the future, to try to decide where it applies.

In making it we must not yield to the temptation of thinking that the text can be 'saved' by an interpretation made independent of music, even if the practice of some academic critics tends to suggest that it can, when they listen to the songs for the amazing subtleties of their poetry and message, at the cost of leaving out any consideration of the interactions between the text and the genre of the accompaniment. For example, as Mellers put it, Dylan's 'main sources' in his early career are 'North American (Yankee) transformations of British ballads, Southern Poor White (Appalachian) metamorphoses of them, cowboy or hillbilly songs, Negro hollers and blues, and gospel music both black and white.'[32] It is only by seeing how Mellers' musical analyses arise out of Dylan's songs that we can appreciate, paradoxically, the uniqueness of his art, based as it is on an extremely sophisticated synthesis of musical materials, *along with the emotional commitments that they traditionally imply*. And these styles change from album to album. Dylan's relationship to the musical traditions of folk song and the blues, much of which seems to get into his songs by a kind of subconscious assimilation and transformation of past traditions and conventions, is just as important as the question of literary allusion.[33]

And this musical allusion is not exactly 'literary' either, because it depends entirely upon auditory and oral transmission if, like Dylan, you don't read music. This relationship of a song to its musical performance raises a number of very interesting considerations. Dylan's lyrics carry rhythms and rhymes and emphases which are designed for musical performance, and play off against all sorts of musical accompaniments. His texts are not poetry, designed to be read autonomously, because they do not need to aim at the poem's autonomy – at an internal music, or metrical organisation, or syntax that will carry and articulate exactly the emphases that go with the thought. Song lyrics can be quite sloppy in this respect, and leave a good deal of their significant implications up to the varying emphasis that the singer and the band can make in different types of performance. (The Budokan song style is very different indeed from that of the albums on which the songs first appeared.) Conversely, when we read a song lyric, knowing something of its performances, these inevitably echo round and supplement our reading. But there are no hymns hovering around in the background of Larkin's 'Church Going', or real organ music to accompany Milton, or Browning's 'Ben Ezra', and no real melodies to be slipped alongside even the poetry or prose that Pater and others may have thought aspired to the condition of music.[34] There are no tunes in Mallarmé or even in the *Four Quartets*, though there are plenty of vital articulating rhythms.

The importance of this performance style is intuitively obvious when we listen to some of the truly awful cover versions of Dylan songs, such as Sam Cooke's 'Blowin' in the Wind', with its jaunty, unthreatening up tempo, which boogies along in a way which transforms Dylan's song into an old swing band tune. Many of these cover versions unsurprisingly move Dylan's tempo up, to a much more obviously danceable beat – and so smooth out the amazingly well articulated, jagged conceptual emphases of Dylan's own versions. (On the other hand, the similarly easy way in which Bobby Bare can sing 'Don't think twice' reveals how close Dylan sometimes comes to the lyric of a standard pop song. And it is none the worse for that.) With few exceptions, and perhaps the most enjoyable on '*Love and Theft*', you don't expect to dance to Dylan.

Betsy Bowden's pioneering book-length study looks closely at Dylan in performance, but her method is all the same very text-based. She looks for the sound patterns of rhyme, assonance, alliteration and so on in the text, for example in pointing out the alliteration of 'doll, deal, dime, how does it feel?' or 'prime, proud, princess, pretty', in 'Like a Rolling Stone'.[35] It's difficult to see much point to this part of her analysis even when she goes on to give an impression of the varyingly expressive ways in which Dylan pronounces such words in performance: for example her remarks on 'din yoo' for 'didn't you' in the same song.[36]

This may also sell short the experience of a Dylan song, by stressing the immediacy and contingency which many see as typical of popular art (and something we would never attribute to German lieder or opera), particularly when Bowden suggests that:

A listener to a song doesn't need the rational, narrative, or even imagistic links that a reader would. A listener experiencing each emotion while the phrase evokes it understands what these third stanza lines have to do with the rest of the song ['Sad Eyed Lady of the Lowlands']; they share its vowel/consonant patterns, its syntax, its rhymes; they are delivered in the same velvety voice and the same instrumentation.[37]

This is perhaps more true of the averagely banal and repetitive forms of much popular music, but Dylan's work is exceptionally good at provoking us into paying attention to complex narrative. (He once claimed that he 'could sing *Porgy and Bess* with two chords, G and D, and still get the narrative across'.)[38] That is basically what he does – narrative much of the time. Real melodic invention accounts for a relatively small part of his output, and that is why the 'imagistic links' within and between his lyrics are indeed the staple of so much academic interpretation of his work.

Even if a transition from the complexities of classical music to the sometimes crude and repetitive procedures of rock may seem to be difficult to negotiate, and vice versa, for the generation that grew up with Dylan these are two differently effective musical styles, and not much more than that. This is partly because 'elitist' preferences for coherence and complexity in art have become critically less popular, and partly because of the contemporary taste for surface, for contradiction, and for the affirmation of socially constructed identities rather than of a deeper humanist portraiture. It is style that counts, and within Dylan's combination of folk, country and rock music there is an extraordinary range of them available.[39] Ultimately, the pleasure of Dylan as music is intimately related to our awareness of the implications of musical accompaniment, and to the unique kinds of emotional stance that, *ipso facto*, this music alone can express. He refuses to work on Maggie's Farm, gets tangled up in blue, drinks one more cup of coffee, and frequently regrets the passing of a love affair, in forms of expression which only differ from the great arias of the past (or the songs sung by Sinatra or Fitzgerald) in that they are almost impossible to reproduce, except in his way, in his own recordings. Such uniquely individualist pleasures are well worth preserving, and always rewarding to revisit.

4

BIG BRASS BED: BOB DYLAN AND DELAY

Lavinia Greenlaw

When I was eight, I thought of Bob Dylan as a music box or wind-up toy. I already had a blue satin jewellery case in which a plastic ballerina rotated to *Für Elise* plucked out on a tiny metal harp. This dancer was invested with my dreams of a future self – all glamour, grace and shine. Dylan's 1969 album *Nashville Skyline* became a different kind of soundtrack: the sad rough noise of my present self.

Nashville Skyline was one of a handful of 'pop' records my parents acquired at what my mother later referred to as 'the time when your father tried to be swinging'. I can't remember them actually playing it, and it never occurred to me that they might do so after the four of us had gone to bed. With a child's egotism, I assumed that Dylan was my discovery and my secret.

There was a box gramophone in the corner of the living room and I would crouch over it and close my eyes. If I could, I would have dug a foxhole in the parquet or put up a tent. Here was someone whose feelings, like mine, were too big for comfort. He had difficulty finding words and then couldn't get them out straight. I imagined them swelling on his tongue and pushing each other out of shape. I recognised the rhymes and repetitions of the ballad form from nursery rhymes and camp-fire sing-songs, but here the structure had gone badly wrong. Except for two jittery numbers, these songs were too slow; they were falling apart, leaning so far back that they were bound to crash. The voices of Dylan and Johnny Cash were falling apart too. They sounded like men who were being made to sing for centuries, not for pleasure but as a punishment from the gods.

In 1970, the American voices I knew best were those of cartoon characters, pop stars, cowboys and the plosive slang of my other favourite record, *West Side Story*. Dylan's shambling manner did not fit with these polished performances. Nor was his vocal roughness the smoke and grit of country and western. It was something just as stony but altogether more urban and neurasthenic. It sounded like the voice of someone who had lived a little and I, of course, thought that I had too.

The Elliot Landy cover picture didn't add up either. It has the country attributes of hat and guitar, even a hint of Southern manners in the tipping of the hat. But this is a Jewish guy from Minnesota, the air is full of northern chill (it was taken in Woodstock) and he looks warmly dressed. London was full of young men sporting beards and guitars but they were hippies, colourful and sloppy; and I'd never seen a cowboy with a neatly trimmed beard, let alone one wearing a (tweed?) jacket.

I can't remember what other such records my parents had, except for *Yellow Submarine* and the Moody Blues' *In Search of the Lost Chord*, which comes back to me as moments of tinkling serenity interspersed with electronic efflorescences. I relished an absurd spoken interlude, something like 'Face piles of trials with smiles, it riles them to believe that you perceive the web they weave, so keep on thinking . . . free.' The best part was that caesura, which built up a sense of finale and then sprang its surprise: the big word, 'free' was thrown away, almost whispered. I had this album – lumbering, high-concept, over-egged – in mind as antithesis but now see that that pause, coming as it did after a verbal pile-up and just when one expects a crash, is the kind of thing that intrigued me about Dylan. Later, when I got onto meaning, I threw out the Moody Blues, appalled by what might be called their air rhetoric, as in air guitar.

I knew all the words to *Nashville Skyline* long before I knew what they meant: LAY LAY DEE LAY, LAYER PONYA BIG BRA SPED ... UNTILLA BRAKE ODAYEE ... LEMMY CEEYER MAIKIM SERMIYUL. Singing along was much harder than it should have been and the timing of certain phrases continued to elude me. The words 'big brass bed' in 'Lay Lady Lay' are equally stressed but, to my ear, do not fit as a triplet within the existing tempo.

This difficulty with 'big brass bed' got me thinking about how Dylan's delivery resists the two kinds of structure it's pinned to: the words and the tune. He injects tension by holding a song back from its natural tempo and adds more by tearing the lyric away from its expected cadence. On top of all this, he holds back the words, releasing them in bursts that skew emphasis and pull meaning adrift.

Being able to push a song out of shape, to stretch it to breaking point but keep it intact, is a technique one associates most with jazz: Ella Fitzgerald forgetting the words to 'Mack the Knife', Billie Holiday measuring out 'I Get a Kick Out Of You' against a bossa nova, John Coltrane ripping into 'My Favourite Things' or Chet Baker sucking the air out of 'My Funny Valentine'. It's not the same thing as a folk or rock singer's tonal roughness and vocal ad libs, and is one of the non-country elements that make *Nashville Skyline* so interesting.

The ballerina in the jewellery case was more intriguing than she might have been because of the effort it cost her to make it through each pirouette. She wasn't slick and I liked that. It made her glamour all the more possible. Now, I think of her timing as being like Dylan's, one of delay. It is this quality, delay, that charges *Nashville Skyline* with deferred feeling and deflected meaning. The album is so gradual and refractive in its revelations that I was astonished to discover it is just twenty-nine minutes long. What takes three minutes to play seems to take ten minutes to listen to. My experience of this record as slowed down is so ingrained that I was taken aback to realise that there are not only a couple of upbeat numbers but two more that ought to be described as fast.

For me, the dominant mood remains one of delay, the more so now that I have got to know and think about the words. Delay breaks up narrative and isolates images. To my ear, the phrase 'big brass bed' bears no musical relation to what is going on around it, which might be why, once I realised what the words were, the image came to stand out so. I wasn't interested in the drama of the man asking a woman to spend the night with him. I was captivated by the emblematic vision of that huge, golden, shining, empty bed.

Nashville Skyline was recorded in eight sessions in February 1969 in Columbia Studios, Nashville. The album was released in April, the same month in which Simon & Garfunkel released *The Boxer*, Sirhan Sirhan was convicted of killing Robert Kennedy, Paul McCartney was quashing rumours that he was dead and Concorde 002 made its maiden flight. '68 was over and Woodstock was four months ahead. Although the festival took place on his doorstep (*because* it was his doorstep), Dylan did not play there. *Nashville Skyline* is the early fruit of the sidestep he took at this point.

The opening duet with Johnny Cash, 'Girl of the North Country', is an anti-'Scarborough Fair' set in a landscape devoid of parsley, sage, rosemary or thyme. It is a desperate plod in which each laden strum drags along so painfully that even if, like me, you have sung along for thirty years, you find yourself leaping ahead and coming in too soon. The physical effort required to hold back the next phrase, let alone the next syllable, demonstrates the power of Dylan's delay. I used to think of these men as struggling through the snow, barely able to gather the strength to hit the note. The high notes, though strong, sound painful. Cash has a granite lump in his throat, and Dylan hangs on to his words until they start to unravel and the syllables come out bigger or smaller than they should. When he lets go towards the end, this skews the emphasis as if to protect his true meaning: 'Well, if you're travelin' in the NORTH country fair'.

When they duet, Dylan tends to trail behind Cash, who either couldn't figure out how Bob was going to take it or didn't much care. Their fraying harmonies are the most moving thing on the record, especially when they lift at the end, becoming freer and higher as they repeat the barely recognisable phrase, 'True love of mine', approaching it each time from a different angle as if trying to circle or grasp this elusive woman. Meanwhile, the solid backing remains under tight rein, with even the brief instrumental break just going round in a small circle. Like most of the other tracks, this arrangement has a discrete ending, in this case the tiredest drum roll I've ever heard.

Although this song is not new to *Nashville Skyline*, its words have the austerity and lack of narrative progression that characterise the lyrics on the album and stand apart from the epic litanies of 'A Hard Rain's A-Gonna Fall' or 'Sad-Eyed Lady of the Lowlands' or the knowingness of the slapstick surrealism of 'Bob Dylan's 115th Dream'. The singers are stuck where they are and their plea is couched in uncertainty, 'Well, if . . .' Among all this wind, ice and snow, two sources of shelter beckon: the hair that 'rolls and flows all down her breast' and the 'coat so warm'. Until I saw a lyric sheet, I thought Dylan was singing the far more obvious 'curls and falls' only rounding out his vowels. (Now I tend to hear both versions at once and can't decide what exactly is being sung, but will go by the published lyrics here.) This repeated 'o' echoes that of 'coat' and 'so', and puckers the mouth, which is then released into the sensual pout of 'warm'. This might be stretching it, but I can't help noticing how what Dylan does with vowels relates to what's being expressed.

In 1968 Dylan had released *John Wesley Harding*, an album of trademark ballad narratives about a holy fool, a femme fatale, the drifter, the joker, the judge and the thief. These are conventionally populated songs, heavy on dialogue and plot, which continue the hobo theme that began with 'Freight Train Blues' and 'Song for Woody' with allusions to steamboats, landlords, immigrants and outlaws. Before this, he had turned out seven albums in five years, the last of which was a punctuation mark of sorts, the 1967 *Greatest Hits*. *John Wesley Harding* was the first step in the direction of *Nashville Skyline* but, to my mind, is a far more formulaic work. The vocal and musical delay and the enlarged present tense which intrigue me so much are only evident in the earlier album's last track, 'I'll Be Your Baby Tonight'. This is, again, a relatively simple lyric dramatically broken up and delayed. It points back to 'It Ain't Me, Babe' and 'It's All Over Now, Baby Blue', songs to which the phrasing and timing of *Nashville Skyline* owe a great deal. (The commas in these titles might just be good punctuation, but they also insert delay into emphatic statements.)

The album's second tune, 'Nashville Skyline Rag', is an instrumental ditty that bowls along with only a slightly discordant harmonica putting on the brakes. I have never got used to the abruptness of this ordering. One minute we are on our knees in the snow, the next trotting through the Southern countryside on a sunny day. J.J. Cale does a similar thing on *Naturally*, where the soporific 'Magnolia' has us just about rolling off the porch only to be shaken awake by 'Clyde'. Perhaps this tune acts as a decent pause between ruing the loss of one woman and courting another. It is also very orderly and polite, giving each of the boys a turn to do their stuff.

When I learnt to play the piano, I discovered more about the pleasures of delay and how hard it is to accomplish. I loved Scott Joplin's rags, although the word 'rag' confused me at first because, thanks to *Nashville Skyline*, I thought that it meant something to be played fast. I was quickly bored by the best-known Joplin, 'The Entertainer', made famous by *The Sting*, and preferred those like 'Bethena', to which Joplin had attached the dictum: 'Do not play this piece fast. It is never right to play ragtime fast.' He was another king of delay, resisting a melody, pulling back from its momentum. Because of him, I understood why Chopin's *Prelude in E Minor* was so difficult to play and got the joke when Jack Nicholson hammered it out in *Five Easy Pieces*. Since then, I have noticed that the music I love best is driven by delay: Glenn Gould's 1981 recording of *The Goldberg Variations*, to which he found he'd added 12 minutes and 48 seconds over the timing of his first in 1955; Diana Ross and The Supremes holding off in 'Some Day We'll Be Together'; the mid-air suspensions in Satie's waltz, *Je te veux*.

'To Be Alone With You' takes its time getting going, beginning in fact before itself with the procrastinating out-take, 'Is it rolling, Bob?' The feeling Dylan defers here is, like the best lyrical romancing, speculative. That may sound contradictory but push-and-pull is what Dylan's delay is all about. The phrase that stands out is 'Night time is the right time', in which each slamming monosyllable (except for 'the') is evenly stressed. It is, again, more measured than it appears and hard to sing along to. Dylan concentrates on restraining the vocal while the band rocks away behind him, the piano turning up the temperature as it vamps behind the second verse. When Dylan does let go, he picks his emphases more extremely than ever: 'You'reall WAys whatI'm THIN kingof!'

The slog returns in 'I Threw It All Away.' These anodyne lyrics ('Love is all there is,/It makes the world go round') are saved by Dylan's stately and melancholic delivery. Here, he is feeling out the big words in particular and letting them go only when the edges have been worn down. For years, I didn't realise that these spasmodic moans were in fact 'cruel', 'fool', etc. This is a song about faltering belief, the moment at which a long-held assumption crumbles and so the words falter too, their connections fail in an awkward pause like 'she said she'd always ... stay' or an odd moment in which the word gets stuck and there is, if you like, a syllable of silence: 'de ni – ed', 'tri – ed'.

'Peggy Day' is another deflected narrative moving more slowly than seems good for it. Weirdly upbeat and slyly throwaway ('By golly, what more can I say'), it melts into liquid phrases such as 'she'smylittlelady' and 'wellyouknowthatevenbeforeIlearned her name'. In the end, the song switches tempo and style to nail down the line Dylan has let go as an aside throughout his foot-shuffling, lowered-eyes performance. It swings into pure raunch: 'Love to ... spend the night ... with Peggy ... DAAAAAY'. This line has been repeated throughout the song with a very light stress on the word 'love' but when Dylan finally lets rip, his emphasis is not on the woman or the feeling but on the pun. I think he's attracted to what that rounded 'a' does in his mouth and the raw noise it produces as he cracks the word open, a noise that has all the urgency and avidity he has put off exposing. The fluidity of the vocal reminds me of the sure-footed and featherlight delivery of Louis Jordan, the kind of patter that gives the impression of barely being sung at all but that is as difficult to mimic as 'big brass bed'.

'Lay Lady Lay' has a complicated percussive backing which flutters away behind Dylan's unusually regulated delivery. The out-of-joint phrasing of 'big brass bed' is repeated in the triplet of '(Stay with your) man a while'. Although Dylan's voice is notably constant here and his timing is absolute even when offbeat, there is still evidence of delay. He breaks a line at a point that dislocates an image or pauses a scene so, in keeping with the theme of the song, everything is caught, step by step, on the verge of consummation: 'I long to see you in the/morning/light', 'when he's standing/in front of you', 'the night is/still ahead'.

The urgency of 'One More Night' is most apparent in its brisk tempo and staccato, nervy guitar. This is the most upbeat number on *Nashville Skyline* and has the album's most overt lyric about delay in the form of the world moving on and trying to take someone with it, who is either stuck fast or trying to resist. This is the same atmosphere as that of Robert Lowell's poem 'Window'[1], which begins and ends with the same image: 'The tops of the midnight trees move helter skelter'. For Dylan, 'The wind blows HIGH above the tree'. Even the arrangement resists progression as it repeats and returns until the piano winds things up. Dylan gives the song a relatively upbeat delivery, only really dragging out the wailing 'i' sounds – 'high', 'night', 'bright', 'light', 'sight'. He hasn't quite managed to put off moving on yet.

'Tell Me That It Isn't True' has the stately rhythm of 'Lay Lady Lay' but a quietly desperate lyric. Delay bolsters hopes: 'come . . . through', 'isn't . . . true'. There is an interesting moment in which Dylan produces a run of rapid triplets in 'all of these/awful things/that I have', isolating the crucial word – 'heard'. The parts of the arrangement – voice, guitars, drums and keyboards –

remain discrete, more so here than in the other tracks, underlying how things are straining to cohere.

'Country Pie' is another turn round the local landscape, electrified but laid back, its lyric more colourful than that of any other track. Brought up on apple pie and rhubarb crumble, the litany of flavours, including some I had never tasted, pumpkin and blueberry, made it all the more vivid. The 'hogshead' and 'fiddler' were confusingly English-sounding to me then and the whole now seems frothily picturesque when compared with what is going on around it.

With the final track, 'Tonight I'll Be Staying Here With You', Dylan's delay comes to a (very gradual) end. There is no sign of urgency but the man is giving way, holding on to his pauses even when up to his neck: 'I went . . . under'. The crescendo on 'I find it so difficult to . . . LEAVE' is underpinned by a descending guitar line and Dylan, who 'should have left this town this morning', pushes back: 'It was MORETHANI could do.' The resolution, the admission that he is sticking around, is expressed all on one note: 'staying here with you'. All the drama was in the delay and now that that is almost over, he can be both straightforward and quiet.

Back in the days when I didn't understand the words, *Nashville Skyline* would leave me exhausted. It provoked feelings of pressure, difficulty and suspense at a visceral level, one on which I felt through sound and rhythm. The words only confirmed that this was all about tension and the different ways it can pull: being trapped by regret or riveted by desire; trying to be offhand about passion or grown up about loss; moving on or giving in. Dylan's technique of delay, conscious or not, is the centrifugal force with which the tension is sustained, keeping everything apart but, like that north country girl, tantalisingly just about in sight.

5

PLAYING TIME

Nicholas Roe

Time held me green and dying
Though I sang in my chains like the sea.

Dylan Thomas, 'Fern Hill'

all the time out of my mind

Bob Dylan, in *Rolling Stone* (22 November 2001)

29 July 1966, Woodstock, New York. Bob Dylan crashes his motorbike and survives the accident, escaping the Romantic myth of genius dead in its prime. Instead of joining Thomas Chatterton, Robert Burns, John Keats, T. E. Lawrence (motorcycle crash) and James Dean (car accident) in the pantheon of doomed youth, Dylan recovers and becomes an eternal survivor – a sentinel of time, not unlike his own Tambourine Man or Samuel Taylor Coleridge's Ancient Mariner.

Since the 1960s each decade has been marked by headlines such as '50 Fascinating Facts for Bob Dylan's 50th Birthday', or 'Eccentric '60s hero Bob Dylan turns 60'. An article in the *Boston Herald*, May 2001, noted ruefully that '[w]hen the voice of the '60s generation turns 60, it only serves as a reminder to baby boomers of their approaching senior citizen status'.[1] Not a reminder about Bob Dylan, notice, but of 'the voice of the 60's generation' and '[t]hose great Sixties albums [which] somehow helped define . . . perception of self'.[2] Dylan's listeners have always collaborated in creating the meanings of the songs; equally, and from the first, 'Bob Dylan' has been the servant of other selves, others' memories – personal, communal, generational. He 'hears the ticking of the clocks', and in some recent photographs has appeared, obligingly, in the sombre attire of 'the eternal Footman': a pall-bearer in a black frock coat, black top hat, and black leather gloves.

I would argue that Bob Dylan's achievement as a poet, musician and singer, a 'Song and Dance Man', is the resourcefulness with which he confronts, responds and plays to the passing of time. In this he is like all poets, no doubt, even though his lyrics – recorded and performed – are not straightforwardly literary or poetic compositions. A search of the on-line concordance to Dylan's songs reveals some 156 instances of the word 'time', while other key areas of his vocabulary – which one might have expected to be more extensively present – receive less emphasis: love is cited 132 times, home 65, life 60, and death 28 times.[3]

As a musician Dylan is brilliantly responsive to the demands and permissions of tempo and rhythm. His work as a recording artist brings contractual demands and deadlines; the constraints of hours in the studio, and, equally pressing, the 'playing time' of the recorded songs and albums. The sleeve notes to the original LP issue of *Bringing it all Back Home* described the record as 'a picture of what goes on around here some-times. tho I don't understand too well myself what's really happening', and proclaimed, in upper case letters, 'THE SELECTIONS ARE FOLLOWED BY THEIR TIMINGS.'[4] Listing track durations on LP and CD packaging was and is routine. To draw attention to 'TIMINGS' gave unusual emphasis to the recording, marketing and consumption of time – to the songs as some time happening. In these ways, and more, I shall be arguing, Dylan's art is intricately and rewardingly tangled-up with time.

I

Rejecting the suggestion that 'Not Dark Yet' is about his own mortality, Dylan observes: '[i]t's one thing that we all have in common, isn't it?'[5] Many of his songs are meeting points, passages from common life, and in these senses Dylan preserves the 'folk-like integrity'[6] of his earliest songs in the different lyrical idioms of his later work. In seeking to account for Dylan's appeal, Frank Kermode and Stephen Spender identified a 'suggestiveness', or 'organised ambiguity' in the songs which invites listeners 'to do the work of interpretation' and 'fill in' meaning. So the surreal world of 'Desolation Row' deliberately presents a 'cultural jumble', providing material from which each of Dylan's listeners constructs his or her interpretation (to take just one example, Robert Shelton's claim: 'Unless we renounce materialism, this will be our future').[7] In this case comparisons have been made with T. S. Eliot's *The Waste Land*, and in a more general sense Dylan's achievement could be described as the negatively-capable lyric; that is, poetry which deflects and simultaneously invites 'meaning' or 'message'.

Dylan adopts various techniques to achieve this manner of evasive or elliptical significance, the most obvious of which are perhaps questions: 'Who killed Davey Moore, / Why an' what's the reason for?'; 'How does it feel . . . ?'; 'Because something is happening here / But you don't know what it is / Do you, Mister Jones?'; 'Won't you come see me, Queen Jane?'[8] Some of his lyrics don't conclude so much as deliquesce into strange, evocative images – 'And we gazed upon the chimes of freedom flashing'; 'My love she's like some raven / At my window with a broken wing'.[9] Others wind up portentously, or enigmatically: 'The answer is blowing in the wind'; 'It's a hard rain's a-gonna fall'; 'And there are no truths outside the Gates of Eden'; 'Two riders were approaching, the wind began to howl'.[10] Several of Dylan's songs abandon themselves with a shrug: 'I just said "Good luck"'; 'I do believe I've had enough'; 'And then I shut all the doors'.[11] Questions, quasi-symbols, an oracular mistiness – all are strategies for evading definitive statement, self-dismissals which create a sense of elusive significance. Philip Larkin said he had 'poached' a copy of *Highway 61 Revisited* and discovered that although '"Desolation Row" has an enchanting tune' this was overlaid by 'mysterious, possibly half-baked words'. Larkin sounds dismissive: underlying 'poached' and 'half-baked' may be an insinuation that the songs are faked or 'cooked' poetry. But, following up the other sense of 'poached', it was Dylan who turned out to be gamekeeper: 'mysterious, possibly half-baked words' describes very accurately the fertile lack of precision of some of Dylan's lyrics, reminiscent of Larkin's own *symboliste* sketch 'Absences': 'Such attics cleared of me! Such absences!'[12]

Dylan thrives by creating a sense of enthralling absence, 'thoughts unexpressed but compelling', in lyrics which are 'open, empty, [and] inviting collusion'.[13] 'Collusion' here echoes Larkin's sense that 'Bob Dylan' had been fabricated by Robert Zimmerman and a welcoming public, much as Robert Burns had introduced himself as 'an obscure, nameless Bard' to eager readers who then collaborated in filling out his identity.[14] Both 'nameless Bards', Bob Dylan and Robert Burns, are eerily alike in being common property, the creations of their admirers and detractors: peek behind the masks, and you discover – us, the colluders, playing along.

Some of Dylan's commentators have sought to place him in relation to the English Romantic poets. On a BBC radio programme to celebrate Dylan's sixtieth birthday, for example, Christopher Ricks explored Dylan's treatment of mortality through a close reading of 'Not Dark Yet', teasing out echoes of and parallels with the darkling scene of John Keats's 'Ode to a Nightingale'.[15] That Dylan's songs are remarkably susceptible to intertextual collusion is demonstrated by the numerous writers and literary traditions with which they have been linked. Here are just a few of them: W. H. Auden, James Baldwin, William Blake, the Bible, Bertolt Brecht, André Breton, Robert Browning, William Burroughs, Lord Byron, Albert Camus, Joseph Conrad, Gregory Corso, Hart Crane, Leonardo Da Vinci, Charles Dickens, John Donne, T. S. Eliot, William Faulkner, F. Scott Fitzgerald, the French symbolists, Allen Ginsberg, the Gothic novel, Robert Graves, Greek tragedy, Arthur Hallam, Hamlet, Ernest Hemingway, Hermann Hesse, Geoffrey Hill, Homer, James Joyce, Carl Jung, Franz Kafka, Jack Kerouac, Arthur Koestler, F. R. Leavis, Louis MacNeice, Norman Mailer, Andrew Marvell, John Milton, Friedrich Nietzsche, Thomas Pynchon, John Crowe Ransom, Arthur Rimbaud, Christina Rossetti, Carl Sandburg, Scandinavian epics, Scottish ballads, William Shakespeare, John Skelton, John Steinbeck, Dylan Thomas, Henry David Thoreau, twelfth-century troubadours, François Villon, Walt Whitman, W. B. Yeats, and Yevgeny Yevtushenko.[16]

The list is extraordinary. Unlike nearly every other writer, for whom 'finding a voice' or unique verbal identity may be an imperative, Bob Dylan is apparently most himself as a sublimely capable alias, merged into a babel of others' voices. As a performer, too, Dylan's voice is utterly unmistakable yet endlessly modulated, by turns harsh, gravelly, bawling, sneering and honey-pleading. The peculiar vocal inflections of Dylan's singing voice lend further diversity to the songs, sometimes slurring pronunciation so that listeners may hear their own versions of some lines. I long thought that lines in the second stanza of the *Blonde on Blonde* version of 'Visions of Johanna' ran, 'She's delicate and seems like Vermeer', when the lyric is actually: 'She's delicate and seems like the mirror'. Which isn't to dismiss Vermeer entirely.

This might be thought a Shakespearean virtuosity, except that where Shakespeare's was an extravagant realisation of multiple identities Dylan's hunger is for another's world and others' words.[17] A cultural ragman, he draws a circle around the entire Western literary tradition – and the Devil has all the best tunes. He complements the elusiveness of his songs (a greed for meaning) by existing most fully only at the moment of performance, and in so far as his listeners locate his work in relation to other cultural forms. So if Dylan does resemble Keats, this may be through verbal similarities and also in his having no stable identity, like Keats's 'chameleon Poet' who, like the 'nameless Bard', has no self.[18] A wardrobe of identities is stock-in-trade for many popular musicians – think of David Bowie as Ziggy Stardust and then Aladdin Sane in the 1970s; of Madonna's various incarnations; of Michael Jackson's grotesque metamorphoses. This is show-business, stimulating or adjusting to a fickle market by attempting to set, stay ahead of, or maybe just keep up to date with musical trends (a creative irrelevance which Jim Miller has neatly described as 'cultural static').[19] In Dylan's case, by contrast, multiple aliases are conditions of being.

Over the years Dylan has responded to changing times by recasting his image and music. In the 1960s he moved from Guthriesque folk-protester to electric rocker to ballad-preacher, all the while restlessly inventing his songs afresh in concert performances where his extraordinary voice mutates them into new shapes and inflections. Continuously evolving and changing shape and form, Dylan's songs also amount to a protracted clearance:

Hibbing's a good ol' town
I ran away from it when I was 10, 12, 13, 15, 15½, 17 an' 18
I been caught an' brought back all but once[20]

As these lines from 'My Life in a Stolen Moment' suggest, running away may have a biographical context in that, here, Bob Dylan is articulating something apparently felt (and maybe actually experienced) by 'Robert Zimmerman'. In speaking of his family home Dylan remarked, 'Hibbing was a vacuum . . . I just wanted to get away'.[21]

In 'getting away' Dylan resembles a poet with whom, so far as I know, he hasn't yet been linked: John Betjeman. There are parallels in their backgrounds, in that both came from immigrant families, Dylan's from Eastern European Jewish stock (Lithuania, Latvia, the Ukraine) and John Betjeman's from Dutch or (more likely) German forebears.[22] For John Betjeman, who was born John Betjemann, it was the surname 'that first made [him] aware of insecurity' when the First World War broke out:

'Your name is German, John' –
But I had always thought that it was Dutch . . .[23]

And so began the self-creation of John Betjeman, who in his autobiographical poem *Summoned by Bells* embraces, and creates out of, that formative experience of insecurity – at a remove from the traditional family business of cabinet-making. For Robert

Zimmerman, whose father was 'in a furniture and appliance business', it may have been that '"Bob Dylan" was a self-conscious attempt to reinvent himself as anything but a Zimmerman', although at the same time carrying the feelings of 'separateness, persecution, and . . . insecurity' that the family had brought with them as immigrants and as part of their Jewish heritage.[24]

That has to be speculation. However, it's evident that an urge to 'get away' finds expression in many of Dylan's lyrics, for example in 'Don't Think Twice':

Look out your window and I'll be gone

– in 'Ballad in Plain D':

All is gone, all is gone, admit it, take flight

– in the refrain of 'Farewell Angelina', 'I must go . . . / I must leave . . . / I'll see you in a while . . . / I must leave fast . . . / I must be gone', and, most starkly, from 'Going, Going, Gone': 'So I'm going / I'm just going / I'm gone'. In all his various guises, 'Bob Dylan' amounts to an affirming absence, 'I'm going . . . I'm gone', keeping in play what seems to have been a formative impulse 'to get away'. If the idea of Dylan as 'alias' focuses the way in which he has assiduously moved through identities to exist otherwise, 'alias' also places those other selves in a temporal perspective through the original Latin sense of the word, which means 'at another time'.

At all times Dylan has fought to escape the fixity of his recorded work – ironically, therefore, to extricate himself from the medium through which his work reaches his audience, and is familiar to his listeners. In the commercial world of show-business this might appear to be a kind of death-wish; in Dylan's case it's a matter of artistic survival. Recorded material, which might well be a 'live' performance, can be endlessly repeated and duplicated, so encouraging audiences to expect – if not angrily demand – songs performed in concert exactly as they have already been recorded. This was especially apparent in the mid-1960s, when Dylan moved from acoustic folk-protest to electric rock. At Manchester, 17 May 1966, for example, he responded to uproar and jeering from the audience. 'This is called "I don't believe you"', he announced; 'it used to be like that, and now it goes like this'. Playing upon what he knew the audience expected, 'it used to be like that' referred to the familiar acoustic version on *Another Side of Bob Dylan*, whereas 'now' the song is electric. Recording music is a special kind of entanglement, a circle of the damned, in that it makes Dylan a prisoner of his past, forestalling future creativity.

Dylan's genius is to sing in these chains, to place time out of mind for a time: 'With all memory and fate driven deep beneath the waves, / Let me forget about today until tomorrow'. A prayer to forget, his song is an expiation or atonement releasing the past – and here once again Dylan is in company with Coleridge's Ancient Mariner and his biblical forebear Cain (living, still, in the land of Nod). Dylan interprets his songs in performance so that they are not inevitably recognised by the audience. Over the years these performances have often proved to be not so much 'Bob Dylan in concert' as Dylan decomposing and forgetting songs he has already recorded, disconcerting his listeners by exploring new possibilities in his own work and so keeping tomorrow open and his art in touch with life.

The point is made in one of Dylan's responses to an interview in the Italian newspaper, *La Repubblica*:

Q: Mister Dylan, in your concerts it seems that the songs,

even the older ones, are changing every time. Why are you
changing them so often?
A: Time lets me find new meanings to every song, even in
the older ones, and it's important to be always looking for
new meanings. Yes, the body of the song remains the same
but it wears new clothes.

And, later in the interview:

Q: Which of your albums is your favourite one?
A: The one I still have to do![25]

Braced between possibility ('still to do') and compulsion ('still
have to do!'), Dylan is a writer for whom the clearance of self,
being 'gone', is also to be 'always looking'.

Bob Dylan's interview with *Rolling Stone* magazine, 22 November
2001, reveals a writer possessed by time. In describing the
recording of *Time Out of Mind*, he recalls 'we set aside a certain
amount of time and place. But I had a schedule – I only had so
much time . . . At that point in time, I didn't have the same band
as I have now'. This might be thought no more than an easygoing
conversational idiom, opening up in response to the interviewer's
questions. But I don't think it is just that, for the interview reveals
a complex interweaving of references: 'I don't remember the time
and place'; 'at that time'; 'All those things happened at the same
time'; 'More than a few times I probably felt I had retired'; 'I felt
like I had retired from the cultural scene at the time'; 'I follow
the dictates of my conscience to write a song, and I don't really
have a time or place I set aside'; 'It just happens at odd times, here
and there'.[26] A couple of Dylan's remarks place this interview in
a metaphysical frame: for example, 'if we know anything about
God, God is *arbitrary*' – that is, both despotic and capricious in

presiding over the temporal mesh from and against which Dylan creates. 'I don't walk around all the time out of my mind with inspiration', he says, suggesting that although this doesn't happen 'all the time' it may be possible, 'with inspiration', to be 'out of [his] mind'. And at such ecstatic moments time is 'out of mind' – and, too, the sense of repetition captured in the phrases 'walking around'/'walking a round'.

In contrast to the circularity implied by 'walking around', when recalling his life in the 1960s Dylan says '[w]e were sort of living from this place to that – a kind of transient existence'. This sense of 'transient existence' as a passage through time and place is apparent in a number of the quotations above (not least so in one of the senses of 'arbitrary') and also in Dylan's idea of 'career' as a desultory 'something that takes you from one place to the other' – a form of time-travelling. The transient has some appeal for Dylan: he remarked in 1969 to Jan Wenner, '[w]e don't choose anything ... we just go with the wind'. But this seemingly carefree acceptance of circumstance (and, by implication, the chanciness of 'inspiration') can produce disorientation, 'I was just being swept by the wind, this way or that way', eventually becoming insidiously random: 'at times I felt like, "I don't want to do this anymore." Then something would always lead me to something else, which would keep me at it'.[27] On the other hand, the more overtly controlled and directed trajectory of a 'career' carries with it the risk of reiteration, in the requirement 'just to make another record at this point'.[28]

When seen in this way, creating 'at this point' freezes into a predictable commitment – merely the latest in a long sequence of other such moments. Viewed in a slightly different aspect, it becomes a torment in which the 'end' of being is to be condemned endlessly to do over again:

> deep inside my heart
> I know I can't escape.
> Oh, mama, can this really be the end,
> To be stuck inside of Mobile
> With the Memphis blues again.

And again and again. The refrain to Dylan's song is repeated nine times, every time the song from *Blonde on Blonde* is played (ten times, if one includes the title of the song, 'Stuck Inside of Mobile with the Memphis Blues Again'). And every one of those times the refrain is inseparable from the lyric's burden, 'I can't escape', which the final stanza shifts onto the listener:

> An' here I sit so patiently
> Waiting to find out what price
> You have to pay to get out of
> Going through all these things twice . . .

'Going through things twice' is a reprise, and in terms of lyrical form it constitutes a refrain or chorus,

> To be stuck inside of Mobile
> With the Memphis blues again.

In another, older sense of the word a 'reprise' was a cost or burden imposed in retaliation, a reprisal that

> You have to pay to get out of
> Going through all these things twice . . .

– and, by paying, permit Dylan, here a figure of 'patience' before his listeners, to escape and make an end.

Dylan is scathing, humorously so, about critics who persist in comparing his albums:

> You know, comparing me to myself [laughs] is really like . . . I mean, you're talking to a person that feels like he's walking around in the ruins of Pompeii all the time.[29]

Pompeii isn't just any old ruin, but a town in which time stopped, its citizens fixed forever in the act of trying to free themselves from entombment in volcanic lava and dust. To compare 'me to myself' is a laughable pastime, seeming to be 'walking around all the time' in a scene of life that was long ago arrested, a scene which brings startlingly into focus the dilemma against which Dylan is constantly struggling. The reason for this struggle is not far to seek; revealingly, he describes 'comparing my new work to my old work' as 'a kind of Achilles heel'. This is of course a point of vulnerability, but also and more urgent, I think, is Dylan's sense that such comparisons have about them the touch of death. This is why Dylan wants 'done with' songs he's 'turned in' at the recording studio: 'I don't want to hear them anymore. I know the songs. I'll play them, but I don't want to hear them on a record'.[30]

II

While recuperating from the effects of his 1966 motorcycle crash, Dylan disappeared for a while – encouraging rumours that he was disabled or, maybe, dead. From now on he no longer heard the expansive lyrics and 'wild mercury sound' of *Highway 61 Revisited* and *Blonde on Blonde*, forsaking these for the compact stanzas and acoustic idiom of *John Wesley*

Harding. Quicksilver electric cadences were now succeeded by more restrained ballad rhythms, although the songs on *John Wesley Harding* were no less compelling than Dylan's earlier, surreal narratives in which Paul Revere, Napoleon, Cecil B. DeMille, Beethoven, Ezra Pound and T. S. Eliot had mingled with Cinderella, Jack the Ripper, John the Baptist, 'Mr Jones' and 'the mystery tramp'. In *John Wesley Harding* Dylan moved from the exotic and outlandish to an arbitrary, insecure world inhabited by outlaws, drifters, hobos, tenants, thieves, gamblers and immigrants – a world in which there is '"no place to hide"' and where excuses, cover stories and alibis are stripped away. This is Dylan's version of the third act of *King Lear*, in which the mighty men are brought to confront 'the thing itself; unaccommodated man' (III. iv. 104–5).

Many of the songs on *John Wesley Harding* are concise parables concerning unforeseen turning points and moments of 'fatal doom', preoccupied with honesty and flattery, choice, questing, remorse, judgement, ideas of home and belonging, burdens and dreams. These are themes which open unsettling questions of 'the way you feel that you live' ('Dear Landlord'), and over the songs broods a sense of expectation and foreboding, most explicitly so in the thief's words from 'All Along the Watchtower': '"let us not talk falsely now, the hour is getting late"':

All along the watchtower, princes kept the view
While all the women came and went, barefoot servants, too.

Outside in the distance a wildcat did growl,
Two riders were approaching, the wind began to howl.

The elements of this scene are simple, yet enigmatically so – 'women came and went', 'Outside in the distance', 'Two riders were approaching' – and they gather an ominous power by echoing the Revelation of St John in which appear the watcher, the princes, the horseman, and Christ as a thief. The effect of this is to make Dylan's songs attentive to eternity from within the world of time, aware of and dealing with the arbitrary spirit that governs the universe:

> Just then a bolt of lightning
> Struck the courthouse out of shape,
> And while ev'rybody knelt to pray
> The drifter did escape.

In this passage from 'The Drifter's Escape' is an aspect of time which exerts a continuous hold on Dylan's songs: the relationship between time and the exigencies of justice. Just as Shakespeare's Bolingbroke in *Richard II* marvels at the sovereign's power to pronounce or revoke a sentence of banishment –

> How long a time lies in one little word!
> Four lagging winters and four wanton springs
> End in a word: such is the breath of Kings.

> (I. iii. 213–15)[31]

– so the figure of the judge stalks through Dylan's imaginative world, dispensing arbitrary justice and determining 'in one little word' the duration of (in this case) exile. The questionable authority of the law in relation to time is the subject of some of Dylan's finest songs. In 'The Lonesome Death of Hattie Carroll', for example, the judge

> spoke through his cloak, most deep and distinguished,
> And handed out strongly, for penalty and repentance,
> William Zanzinger with a six-month sentence.

The infinitesimal pause in the final line above, before 'a six-month sentence', is calculated to maximise the audience's outrage at the leniency of the prison term given to Zanzinger. The song weighs the brevity of this sentence against other temporal markers such as Hattie Carroll's age ('fifty-one years old') and all the things that she and her ten children 'never' did (including 'never done nothing to William Zanzinger'). 'Never' underlines the finality with which she was banished in life to 'a whole other level', and, after her death, the thoroughness of the cover-up ('spoke through his cloak') which excludes her from justice. Throughout three of the song's verses, Dylan sets the narrative of Hattie's life and death against the song's chorus –

And you who philosophize disgrace and criticize all fears,
Take the rag away from your face.
Now ain't the time for your tears.

– in a way that presses home an urgent temporal awareness. The song repeatedly cautions 'Now ain't the time for your tears', until we hear 'a six-month sentence' and the refrain resolves itself, and the song, into 'Now's the time for your tears'. 'Now's the time', of course, when such cruelty and injustice are 'philosophized' into acceptability.

In the same genre of protest 'Percy's Song' questions why another judge, who also 'spoke / Out of the side of his mouth', sentenced a young man to 'Joliet prison / And ninety-nine years' for a road accident. The song juxtaposes the mishap in which 'he was at the wheel' with a Shakespearean refrain (recalling Feste's last song in *Twelfth Night*) about the constant mutability of the elements:

Turn, turn to the rain
And the wind.

In the uncaring business of the rain and the wind, the song tells us, we hear the music of a universe in which tragedy and injustice are inevitable and inescapable:

> And I played my guitar
> Through the night to the day,
> Turn, turn, turn again.
> And the only tune
> My guitar could play
> Was, 'Oh the Cruel Rain
> And the Wind.'

Both Hattie Carroll and Percy are presented as victims 'who never done nothing':

> What happened to [them]
> Could happen to anyone

– and the songs bind around their hapless lives and deaths a legal authority which cruelly emulates that of the vengeful, arbitrary God of the Old Testament. The expanse of 'ninety-nine years' is set against the peremptoriness of 'leave / My office now', the single 'door slam' and the insistent rounding of the song's refrain. In a world where all walks round, turns, and turns again, Percy's doom is cased in stone: 'His sentence is passed / And it cannot be repealed' ('Percy's Song').

Away from overt forms of protest, the judge figure and his close associate, the hangman, have significant walk-on parts in some of Dylan's more narrative songs in which they function like 'the ticking of the clocks'. The lines 'he went to fetch the hanging judge / But the hanging judge was drunk' in 'Lily, Rosemary and the Jack of Hearts', for example, articulate the tension between

control and chaos – a tension wrought up by the headlong tempo
of the musical accompaniment and the gambling-hall setting
where all depends upon the turn of a card. Throughout, this
complex ballad steers a disturbing course, playing across and
between different histories, time zones and measures of time.
As well as the mysterious past and presence of the Jack of
Hearts –

> 'I know I've seen that face before,' Big Jim was thinkin'
>   to himself,
> 'Maybe down in Mexico or a picture up on somebody's
>   shelf.'

– there is Lily's damaged odyssey –

> She'd come away from a broken home, had lots of
>   strange affairs
> With men in every walk of life which took her
>   everywhere

– the ongoing activity of the boys 'drillin' in the wall', and
Rosemary's troubled 'tiredness' and doomed sense of her own
future in which a little vowel separates 'deed' from 'died':

> She was tired of the attention, tired of playing the role of
>   Big Jim's wife.
> She had done a lot of bad things, even once tried suicide,
> Was lookin' to do just one good deed before she died.

The song presents a scene '"set . . . up for everyone"' in which
each character has a role, and stanza by stanza it cuts between the
lives of Big Jim, Lily and Rosemary. These scenes heighten the

drama of 'Lily . . . took her dress off', 'a cold revolver clicked' (did you hear it as 'Colt revolver'?), 'the boys finally made it through the wall', and the even more immediate and suggestive present: '"Be careful not to touch the wall, there's a brand-new coat of paint"'. The upbeat tempo has relentless momentum, hurrying the song onwards so that when we reach the line, 'they say that it happened pretty quick', hearsay has the force of inevitable doom. In this way the song plays between the different senses of 'arbitrary' Dylan has more recently associated with God:

> . . . nothing would ever come between Lily and the king,
> No, nothin' ever would except maybe the Jack of Hearts.

'[N]othing would ever come between' opens a prospect in which 'the king' has eternal sway, until, that is, the rearrangement of a word in the succeeding line returns him to the world of time and chance: 'nothin' ever would except maybe the Jack of Hearts'.

Appropriately, the denouement of the song, following the murder of Big Jim, has a fatalistic aspect, recapitulating an earlier scene but incorporating significant variation. The encounters with the characters come around again, for example the introduction of Lily in stanza three –

> Backstage the girls were playin' five-card stud by
> the stairs.
> Lily had two queens, she was hopin' for a third to match
> her pair.
> Outside the streets were fillin' up, the window was
> open wide,
> A gentle breeze was blowin', you could feel it from
> inside . . .

– later contributes to the rising tension in the middle of the song:

> The backstage manager was pacing all around by
>   his chair.
> 'There's something funny going on,' he said, 'I can just
>   feel it in the air'

The dramatic setting refreshes the Romantic cliché 'you could feel it from inside', firstly by literalising it – 'the window was open wide' and so 'you could feel [the breeze] from inside' – and then by making the 'breeze blowin'' correspond to and externalise the manager's feeling of unease.[32] The rhyme sequence also links the two passages, so that 'stairs' and 'pair' and 'chair' rhyme with, and internalise, 'air'.

When Rosemary entered the song, 'slipped in through the side door' in the fifth stanza, she had 'fluttered her false eyelashes'. In the penultimate stanza she leaves the song on the gallows, where, suspended over a different kind of door, 'she didn't even blink'. This time, too, 'the hangin' judge was sober, he hadn't had a drink', and Lily, who 'had already taken all of the dye out of her hair', is left

> . . . thinkin' 'bout her father, who she very rarely saw,
> Thinkin' 'bout Rosemary and thinkin' about the law.
> But, most of all she was thinkin' 'bout the Jack of Hearts.

The last harmonica flourish rounds off the song, in which the rondo or refrain has proved to be its enigmatic, unpredictable focus. 'The only person on the scene missin' was the Jack of Hearts', another alias for Bob Dylan.

Lily and Rosemary are two figures from the gallery of Bob Dylan's femmes fatales. Throughout his work women, and women leaving, provide markers of time which are at once sharply particular and cruelly archetypal. Since the Elizabethan sonnet female mutability has produced some of the most piercing songs in the English language. Bob Dylan knowingly borrows from this tradition, which had roots in the European Renaissance, when in 'Tangled Up in Blue' he is handed a book of poems 'Written by an Italian poet / From the thirteenth century'. The women in his lyrics are, like the songs themselves, constantly inconstant and it is often capricious changes of mood which create turns in the narrative: 'Dupree came in pimpin' tonight to the Thunderbird Cafe, / Crystal wanted to talk to him, I had to look the other way'.

Like the hanging judge, then, women in Dylan's songs present dramatic instances of the ways in which 'time is an enemy' ('Up to me'). 'Lily had already taken all of the dye out of her hair' is one such moment, in which the dye suggests duplicity and, by punning on 'die', mortality. Likewise, 'already' is disconcertingly pre-emptive, suggesting an ability to put the past (and the song) behind her with remarkable, even ruthless, speed. Throughout his lyrics, women fracture the possible continuity of relationships and narratives by abandoning their partners (often the singer) to a kind of limbo:

If you see her, say hello, she might be in Tangier
She left here last early spring, is livin' there, I hear
Say for me that I'm all right though things get kind of slow
She might think that I've forgotten her, don't tell her it isn't so.

In this instance resolution – 'passing back this way ... if she's got the time' – proves to be out of reach (presumably she still hasn't the time). Elsewhere in the songs, however, ex-partners can turn up again with uncanny readiness, to disconcert the singer all over again:

> She was standing there in back of my chair
> Said to me, 'Don't I know your name?'
> I muttered somethin' underneath my breath,
> She studied the lines on my face.
> I must admit I felt a little uneasy
> When she bent down to tie the laces of my shoe . . .

In all of these ways women in Dylan's songs are reminders of the singer's own troubled relationship with time:

> When we meet again
> Introduced as friends
> Please don't let on that you knew me when
> I was hungry and it was your world.

Dylan's treacherous women preside over the imaginative dynamics of his art traced in this essay. Their disguises and props – 'fog', 'amphetamine', 'pearls', a 'leopard-skin pill-box hat' – are gaudy reminders of the aliases of the singer himself and of the chameleon-like nature of some of his songs. So it is that the woman's failure to acknowledge Dylan in 'I don't believe you' may, with a slight alteration to the personae of the second verse, seem eerily like Dylan's own lyrical disentangling from time:

> It's all new to me,
> Like some mystery,
> It could even be like a myth.

Yet it's hard to think on,
That [he's] the same one
That last night I was with.
From darkness, dreams're deserted,
Am I still dreamin' yet?
I wish [he'd] unlock
[His] voice once an' talk,
'Stead of acting like we never have met.

Is he 'the same one'? The 'Special Limited Edition' of *Love and Theft* included a 'bonus disc with two previously unreleased tracks'. One of them is Dylan's 1961 version of a traditional ballad, 'I was Young when I Left Home'. Here the twenty-year-old Bob Dylan sings with the voice of the ages, echoing from the 'dark backward and abysm of time':

I was young when I left home
And I've been out a-ramblin' round
And I never wrote a letter to my home . . .

The song tells of a meeting with 'an old friend I used to know', a messenger bidding him return home – a 'passing back' which the song insistently defers. The other 'previously unreleased' track accompanying *Love and Theft* is an 'Alternate Version' of his early protest song, 'The Times They Are A-Changin'':

The line it is drawn
And the curse it is cast
The slow one now
Will later be fast
As the present now
Will later be past

The order is rapidly fadin'.
And the first one now
Will later be last.
For the times they are a-changin'.

In this 'alternate version' the tempo is hesitant, 'kind of slow', although the concluding line still rings out. Listening to the song now, long after it was recorded in October 1963, is to hear its prophetic assurance in ironic retrospect – aware, now, that the times have changed far less than Bob Dylan, who in keeping 'the wheel still in spin' goes on playing time's own game. He could even be like a myth.

6

ROCK OF AGES

Simon Armitage

As a poet, I'm supposed to be attracted to Bob Dylan as a lyricist. Even as a fellow poet. That's the received wisdom, and it's certainly true that I've come to Dylan through a series of recommendations and tips, nearly always from other writers. It was the poet Matthew Sweeney who first explained to me that *Highway 61 Revisited* and *Bringing It All Back Home* were the two albums I shouldn't be able to exist without, and as an example of Dylan's song-writing genius, went on to recite the whole of 'Gates of Eden'. He was word-perfect, give or take. And it was Glyn Maxwell who explained to me that the best of Dylan didn't stop with *Blood on the Tracks*. Arriving early at his house in Welwyn Garden City one morning, I sat on the front step listening to 'Don't Fall Apart On Me Tonight' from a steamy bathroom window, with Maxwell himself on backing vocals, his voice bouncing off the tiles, drowning out the doorbell. He also let me in on a fact that all Dylan fans have committed to memory. Namely, a man hasn't found true love until he finds the woman who will hang onto his arm the way Suze Rotolo hangs on to Dylan on the front cover of *Freewheelin'*. No one else will do.

To have grown up when Dylan was emerging as a musical icon must have been a compelling experience, and the spell that

Dylan still casts over his most diehard fans goes back some forty years. The image which persists is not Dylan as he is now, a chewed-up and grisly old granddad, but the Dylan of the Sixties. It's amazing how many people who are old enough to know better are still wearing that look. But because I arrived late, I neither feel possessed by him nor possessive of him. I wouldn't want to be Bob Dylan, I don't fancy him. If he came to the house one day looking for Dave Stewart and I was out, it wouldn't kill me. I have never asked what I can do for Dylan, only what he can do for me. He has to earn his place in my house, typically alongside some obscure collective of skinny, northern, white, drug-addled noiseniks whose first and only album was made for two hundred quid in an outside toilet in Hebden Bridge (what *did* become of Bogshed?). So there he is, sitting on the shelves not between Bo Diddley and Duane Eddy, and certainly not betwixt Dryden and Eliot, but sandwiched by Dexy's Midnight Runners and Echo and the Bunnymen, within The Divine Comedy (the band, not the book) and The Fall (ditto). It's in that field I position Dylan, in that company I rate him, and in that context I prefer to speak about him.

When asked, I always say the first single I ever bought was by The Sweet, after witnessing the platinum-haired Brian Connelly (now deceased) and three other interchangeable glam-rockers pouting their way through 'Blockbuster' on *Top of the Pops*. Dylan would have been thirty-two at the time and about to release the now-deleted *Dylan*. To an impressionable youngster looking for pin-ups and heroes, the choice between four glittery men in cat-suits and stacker platforms, and some clapped-out folkie singing 'Mr Bojangles' wasn't even a toss-up. Besides, 'Blockbuster' even had a siren wailing in the background. It had all the tension of a state of emergency, all the energy of a riot, all the oomph of a car chase and a blue flashing light. I didn't know what the song was about, even though I knew it by heart; I didn't even realise that 'Block' was a verb and 'buster' was a bloke. But I say it was my first single, just as I claim my first ever gig was the Sex Pistols at Ivanhoe's nightclub in Huddersfield – their last ever UK appearance. In actual fact, my first gig was the Skids at Huddersfield Poly – no shame in that – whereas my first single was somewhat less impressive.

In Bridlington High Street in 1972, at the height of the power-cut season, my Uncle Eric left the engine of his Humber Hawk running as he popped into a hardware shop for a dozen candles, two hot-water bottles, a battery-operated torch and gallon of paraffin. Returning to the car, he handed me a seven-inch circle of floppy, blue plastic, a free gift with every purchase over two shillings. It was a record. A flexidisc, in fact, almost transparently thin, with grooves on one side only and the sponsor's logo in the middle. It was a song, sung to the original Fabulous Platters' tune, and it went like this:

> They asked me how I knew,
> it was Esso Blue.

> I of course replied,
> with lower grades one finds,
> the smoke gets in your eyes.

It left a deep and lasting impression. As adverts are supposed to, I guess. It's not by accident that the other song I remember word-for-word from the same era is the Hoseason's Boating Bro-chure commercial, performed against a backdrop of deck-shoes and blazers on the Norfolk Broads. 'Sail boats, canal boats, and cruisers too, all Britain's waterways waiting for you . . .' More importantly, though, possession of the flexidisc allowed me access to that strange and rarely used contrivance, the record player. In our house, this took the form of a dusty old box containing what seemed to be a potter's wheel and windscreen-wiper arm with a needle at the end like a beggar's toenail. It was brought out at parties, but its main purpose was as a novelty piece. A suitcase that made music – what could have been more amusing than that? My father owned about a dozen records, including the double A-side single, 'The Great Pretender/Only You' by the aforementioned Fabulous Platters. The rest were long-players, some classical stuff (*Golden Guinea Family Classics*), easy listening (*Strolling with George Shearing*), songs from the shows (*Oklahoma, High Society*) and the odd cracked or chipped '78. Plus a few things less easily categorised: Victor Borge, Paddy Roberts, a Tom Lehrer album, and Bob Newhart's *The Button-down Mind Strikes Back*.

I played all the albums over and over again, especially those last two. I loved the exactness of the language, and the timing, and the delivery. Trying unsuccessfully to remember the songs and the jokes proved to me that in telling a story, diction is everything, and that actions do not, in fact, speak louder than words. And of late, I've come to think that aspirant poets could do a whole lot worse than listen to smart-mouthed entertainers and dead-pan comics like Lehrer and Newhart. A lot worse. For example, my father also had some jazz records – Dave Brubeck, Duke Ellington, Ella Fitzgerald. I didn't get it at the time, and even though I've given it every chance, it's still the only form of music I actively dislike. Either it's splodgy and haphazard, or it's that finger-clicking, foot-tapping sort of jazz which idles and revs but never actually sets off. To me, jazz is the very opposite of poetry, especially Larkin's poetry, and his enthusiasm for it has always been a puzzle and an irritation. My least favourite night out in the whole world would be an evening of improvised poetry/jazz fusion in the smoky, stone-flagged cellar of a chain-owned wine bar. All saxophones should be rounded up and disabled.

There's no reason why my father shouldn't have been into Dylan, or at least owned one of his records. He could argue, I suppose, that he was too old, being in his late twenties when Dylan released his first album. Or too concerned with conveying his baby son back from the maternity ward a year later to worry about whether or not a hard rain was going to fall. Or too busy earning a crust by the early Seventies to be shelling out good money on nonsense (or 'shit' as *Rolling Stone* magazine preferred) like *Self Portrait*. Also, photographic evidence from an earlier period shows my father to have been something of a Teddy Boy, and in all likelihood, not readily disposed to such wispy-beardy acoustic musings. Add to this a history of working-class conservatism within the family, and the odds of a new world protest singer getting on the playlist in the family home were pretty slim. Tom Lehrer's line, 'The trouble with folk music is that it's written by the folk,' made my father laugh out loud, every time he quoted it.

So there was to be no Dylan for some time yet. Not even via my cousin, who was a few years older than me and listening to a lot of music. When I was thirteen, he played me *Animals* – the new Pink Floyd album. It had a pig floating above Battersea Power Station on the front cover, and obscenities on the lyric sheet, including the word 'fuck'. I was impressed. I took a paper-round and saved up, and from an ugly shopping precinct in Ashton-under-Lyne, bought what I still reckon to be one of the greatest rock albums of all time. I'd seen David Bowie on the telly singing 'The Laughing Gnome', and didn't know if he was a pop star or Tommy Steele. I'm not sure *he* knew at the time. Next time around, he was Major Tom, a spaced-out astronaut spiralling out of orbit, and a few years later, he splashed down as Ziggy Stardust, a bisexual alien with a buzz-saw guitar, come to save the Earth. The album had been out five years by the time I bought it, but that didn't matter, because thirty years later, it still sounds like tomorrow. Bowie's transmutations, from androgynous alien to Thin White Duke to the synthesiser overlord of *Low* and *Heroes* have always had the look and feel of something new, the 'next thing'. Dylan, by contrast, has always been retro, picking up on past models of song-writing and style. He wasn't the first folksinger, just as he wasn't the first man to pick up an electric guitar, or the first bluesman, pot-head, speed-freak, or born again God-botherer. At a time when Bowie was beaming in from another planet, on all sorts of levels, the earthbound Dylan was back-tracking through images of Americana. Once again, it was a question of choice, between an exotic extraterrestrial on the one hand, and on the other, some dusty cowpoke in Stetson, corduroys and chaps.

My father, as it happened, was less keen on David Bowie than Bob Dylan. As I walked through the living room with *Ziggy Stardust and the Spiders From Mars* under my arm, he pointed at it with the mouth-end of his pipe. 'What's that then?' And he'd obviously heard of the man and his music, because when I told him, he said, 'David Bowie? He's a homosexual.' Ten minutes later I flounced back through the living room and shouted, 'So what? Beethoven was deaf.' I wasn't allowed to play David Bowie on the record player, which of course made the music more thrilling, and this injunction led me further in the direction of subterfuge and deceit. The same year, I lied about my age and joined the Britannia Music Club of Great Britain, a mail-order organisation which offered an introductory package of four free albums on the condition of purchasing at least one full-priced album per month for the next six months from their limited catalogue. With the right kind of guidance, I could have been listening to *Blood on the Tracks* or *Desire*.

But I wasn't, I was listening to Black Sabbath, Deep Purple, Yes, Tangerine Dream and the like. All well and good in itself, but somehow ... irrelevant. It was all wizards and warlocks, goat-skulls, air-brushed dreamscapes and ruched purple blouses. There was something missing, and that something came my way about a year later, in the shape of punk. In the spirit the new era demanded (two purchases short of my contractual obligation and looking down the barrel of yet another gatefold-sleeved, double concept-album with a dungeons-and-dragons cover and mind-altered lyrics) I ripped up my membership card and told the Britannia Music Club to stick it where the sun don't shine.

I was fourteen in 1977, not really old enough or brave enough to be stumbling through the northern mill-towns in a pair of bondage trousers like a bolassed ostrich, or cropping my hair in the style of a Pawnee tribesman. I could hear the exhilaration of the songs and see the energy of the bands, but I needed punk to stay around for a while, to wait for me. If it had tailed off or petered out completely, it would have left me with nowhere to go, except back to Rick Wakeman or even away from music altogether. And obligingly, punk defied most of its critics, and also some of its own revolutionary statements, if not by continuing in its pure form, then at least by evolving in several different directions and producing music and bands that outlived the era and its ambitions. The first Undertones album, in 1979, was the one that eventually encouraged me to take all those Jethro Tull and Uriah Heep and various other troll-rock albums to the local tip and Frisbee them into the path of an oncoming bulldozer. One Black Sabbath album, melted into a cone, actually made a very good vase, and some accompanying singles were morphed into ashtrays.

John Peel was the root cause of this behaviour. Hour by hour, his graveyard slot on Radio 1 was edging out the satin-trousered leviathans of old with their fifteen-minute power-ballads, in favour of demo-tapes by so-called 'shambling' bands and other three-minute wonders, whose hearts were in the right place, even if their plectrums weren't. I recorded the show almost every night for two years. On one occasion, he played a whole side from the Clash's *Sandinista*, not because he'd left the studio for a comfort break or a veggie kebab, but because *this was the stuff*. Pop and rock music would never be the same again – this time the cliché was true. Out of punk came the Ska revival (blue-beat sung by punks), the mod revival (mod and soul sung by punks), post-punk (punks in overcoats) and the whole Indie scene. Without punk, U2, REM, Oasis, and a great number of other bands who are, or were, or will be the biggest band in the world, would never have happened. The rave and dance cultures of the past dozen years also descended from the punk movement and its attitude to music and society.

Once again, if I try to slot Dylan into that environment and that atmosphere, he stands out like a dad at a disco. I can think of a particular gig, at Tiffany's, in Leeds's Merrion Centre, to illustrate the point. I'd gone to see Gang of Four, who were musical communists, or sociologists, or intellectuals at the very least. The line-up that night also included Pere Ubu, whose live album *390 Degrees of Simulated Stereo* was to song-writing what industrial noise-pollution is to opera, and the Au Pairs, a feminist foursome, whose mantric refrain, 'We're equal, but different', was the chant of the evening. It was the early Eighties by now, and this is what I wanted music to be. Antagonistic, apt, and original. To have heard Dylan, at that time, singing: 'You know, a woman like you should be at home. / That's where you belong, / Watch out for someone who loves you true / Who would never do you wrong' would have made my blood boil and my toes curl. 'Sweetheart Like You' is a beautiful, beautiful song. I can hear that now. And I can see the gender politics of it more clearly, and hear the irony of some of the lines, and the playfulness, and the triangular tension between the song's paternalism, its protective instincts, and its sexual courtship. But at the time, it would have jarred. Dylan's nationality would also have been a sticking point. It didn't matter that he'd spoken up for blacks, Jews, civil rights, the working man, the abused woman. According to the prevailing ideology, he came from a place whose name was a byword for bad taste. A country that was home to some of the most loathsome monsters of rock the planet had ever produced. A land that had seduced the likes of Lennon and Jagger and Bowie and sucked them dry of their credibility and talent. And somewhere that had broken free of the empires and commonwealths of old, only to impose its own economic and corporate imperialism on the world. 'I'm so bored with the USA,' barked Joe Strummer. 'They wouldn't let us into the USA, we didn't want to go there anyway,' sneered Sham 69's Jimmy Pursey, with adolescent glee.

That era also initiated the idea that any group or singer who grew in popularity could only be crap. For me, a band like Felt, who during one decade produced enough music to fill all my Desert Island Disc slots as well as my luxury item, had everything: shimmering music, regular output, coolness beyond language, and a cult status bordering on universal obscurity. It didn't matter to me that all musicians from the beginning of time have wanted cosmic acclaim and record sales to go with it. As far as I was concerned, success implied treachery, and fame was betrayal.

All that, then, is history, one which accounted for a long and deep reluctance on my part, and a lingering hesitation that occasionally resurfaces as doubt. Should I really be listening to this guy? In the end, though, there is something inevitable about Bob Dylan.

For me, 1984 was the turning point. Morrissey was going stale, Paddy McAloon was going soft, Ian McCulloch had gone over the top, Mark E. Smith was going through one of his phases, and my Giro had just arrived. I'd heard *Slow Train Coming* at someone's house, and even though it banged on about Jesus and trundled forwards like the locomotive of its title, I thought there was something in it. I was also coming round to realising that the days of turning up at a disco or club with a bunch of gladioli in my back pocket were numbered, and that not everyone wanted to hear 'Hexen Definitive/Strife Knot' on return from the pub. But it was more with a sense of exasperation and failure that I laid down four-and-a-half-quid's-worth of taxpayers' money on *Another Side of Bob Dylan*. I don't know why I chose that record. I suppose from a credibility point of view, the fact that it was twenty years old made it more of a historical document/research project and therefore less problematic as a purchase. It even had a black and white cover to advertise its provenance. I couldn't rightly travel on public transport with the comic-strip cover of *Shot of Love* about my person.

What I found amazing about the record was the narrative content, and also the humour. Did people actually do that? Punk had been all about slogans, and in the years that followed, lyrics had become a form of shorthand or subtitle to the experiences they described. I hadn't heard a record that told a story or made me laugh since 'Poisoning Pigeons in the Park'. But the music had an edge to it as well, an integrity that went beyond the Klaxon harmonica and the knockabout words. Here was a storyteller pulling out all the stops – metaphor, allegory, repetition, precise detail. The songs themselves were written and performed to give the suggestion of spontaneity, improvisation even, but they were too memorable to be anything less than crafted and composed. I could quote them, and sing them, though without the original voice and the ditzy guitar work they lost a great deal in the translation. In all, I had the impression of someone totally aware of his talent and totally in control of his work. I've often argued that the only skill any writer needs is the ability to see his or her work from the other side. That is, to put him or herself in the position of the reader. Musicians must be able to do something similar, and I got the instant impression with Dylan that he knew exactly how he sounded in my ears. 1984 was also the year I started writing poetry. I wouldn't claim that there's any connection, that listening to Dylan made me want to write, or that his songs influenced my writing style. But I do think his lyrics, even at that early stage, alerted me to the potential of storytelling and black humour as devices for communicating more serious information. And to the idea that without an audience, there is no message, no art. His language also said to me that an individual's personal vocabulary, or idiolect, is their most precious possession – and a free gift at that. Maybe in Dylan I recognised an attitude as well, not more than a sideways glance, really, or a turn of phrase, that gave me the confidence to begin and has given me the conviction to keep going. Oh, yes, and there were poem-looking things on the back of that album, Beat-style Skeltonic-type-things, but they were rubbish.

My collection grew very slowly. I was still more interested in new music than the old stuff, and Dylan had associations. For example, at University, the only people I knew who listened to him were the two gooks on the eighth floor of Bateson Tower who grew weed on their windowsill and conducted business through their letterbox. Five years later, Dylan was still prohibitively unfashionable, and by now I was a decent person with a proper job. So even when I rescued *Desire* from down the back of a settee in the Probation Service waiting room in Oldham, it was a couple of months before I gave it a spin. It was a great album, great tunes, but what was he wearing around his neck – a beaver? A bear? I didn't approve of the skin trade, at the time, and the barmy sleeve notes should have warned me against buying Ginsberg's Journals so many years later.

The trail could have gone cold at this stage. Very slowly I was getting the drift, and yet the sheer choice of material (twenty-four albums by now, not including live stuff, compilations and rarities) was both overpowering and off-putting. Left to my own devices I might have ended up with *Empire Burlesque*, and that would have been it. Finally, a friend had to intervene. A Dylan anorak of the first order, I don't think he could stand it any longer. Like there was something very obvious I needed to know, a sort of Bob Dylan birds-and-the-bees conversation that needed to be had. He taped me *Blood On The Tracks* and *Blonde On Blonde*, and handed them over in a plain brown envelope. I played one in the car on the way to work, then knocked off early to listen to the other on the way home. And suddenly it all made sense. A few years later he taped me the *Bootleg Series, I–III*, on three cassettes, which I gave away to some big-eyed down-at-heel student in Lodz, Poland. It wasn't intended as the patronising East–West gesture it probably looked like, neither was it a pure, altruistic act of Dylan-Aid. In truth, I'd bought the boxed CD set a few months earlier. I was, by this time, something of a fan, ranging forward and back through Dylan's output, having bought the necessary periodicals and biographies to map out the route. In fact there's an odd inversion within the strata of my record collection (as I still call it) whereby the oldest stuff is in the latest format, and the more recent stuff, up to a certain high-water mark, is on crackly vinyl. Which means Dylan actually sounds more alive than David Byrne, or Paul Weller, or Momus. It makes judging between them distinctly unfair.

I still haven't got everything he's done. I'm taking it slowly, because I think my appetite for his work is still growing, whereas his ability to make great records is narrowing to a point. Also, to find myself in possession of the entire works of Bob Dylan, like owning every copy of the *National Geographic* or a complete set of Pokemon cards, suggests to me a kind of autism that, for most of my adult life, I've been attempting to avoid. So I'm taking my time. Looking forward to it.

Of all Dylan's studio albums, *Blood On The Tracks* seems to me to be the most talked about, the most revered, a 'masterpiece' according to Q magazine's special Dylan edition (*Maximum Bob!* – 2001), and the record that announced him as a serial escapologist, if not Lazarus himself. Over the next twenty-five years, by my count, Dylan has risen on three further occasions from the musical coffin, even from six foot under with the lid nailed on. The only track I don't like on the album is the interminable 'Lily, Rosemary and the Jack of Hearts'. Everything else is spot-on. But the crowning moment has to be the opening number, the strange and wonderful 'Tangled Up In Blue', the kind of song that Wallace Stevens's guitarist might have sung, they reckon, the kind Picasso might have tried to paint. From a musical perspective, 'Tangled Up In Blue' is easy pickings, actually. Pitched in a very singable key, it invites vocal accompaniment. It's also extremely strummable ('Moderately, in 2'), and with the exception of the one bar-chord (Bm – 'the *side* of the road'), a sufficiently awake three-toed sloth could manage the finger-work on the left hand. For those reasons, amongst others, it's become something of a favourite amongst party-stragglers and within a ten-yard radius of any camp-fire, and I'd known the words for a good few years before I sat down one day to read them. In *Behind the Shades: Take Two*, and with reference to the song that supposedly took

Dylan a couple of years to write and a decade to live, Clinton Heylin talks about its author 'utilizing images in different ways' and 'playing with identities'. And Dylan himself is quoted on the subject, in terms of 'trying to do something that I didn't think had ever been done before', and how he had 'wanted to defy time, so the story took place in the present and the past at the same time'. There's more talk, from Dylan and Heylin, about the subconscious, about art, colour, symbolism and all the rest. Here's my reading of 'Tangled Up In Blue', verse by verse.

1   A man (we presume), our narrator (Bob himself, possibly), wakes up one morning (or is still dreaming), contemplating an ex-girlfriend. A sweetheart! They were an ill match, of different social standing, and he cries the poor tale. Then suddenly, subsequently, or simultaneously, or previously, he's outside on the road in the rain, cursing and moving east. It could be a flashback, a premonition, or part of the dream – it's not made clear. Now, a jump-cut like that, without particularly establishing the present or the foreground, is a high-risk strategy, and from a musical point of view, the shift is even more dramatic, being reinforced with rising chord changes – into A, through that Bm then to D. That said, there's something innocent and instinctive about its delivery, a seamlessness that disguises the compositional programming and the verbal trickery. It's the first tangle, I suppose. If Dylan is indeed 'playing with identity', it's also possible, grammatically at least, that he is suddenly switching to the woman's voice, as I once argued after a few drinks. However, the structure of the rest of the song doesn't support that theory, and there is little evidence from his other work to suggest that Dylan might abruptly start articulating things from the female point of view.

Whatever. It's an exciting moment.

The storyteller then implies that the woman experimented with her hair colour. At one point in the past it was red – presumably not her natural shade, since red hair is famously difficult to dye. In the Sixties, a lot of women with blonde or black hair used henna, I'm told. It could even be a reference to Dylan's estranged wife, Sara Lowndes, who is said to be the muse behind much of the album. But I don't know her natural shade.

2   The woman was married when our narrator met her. By means of 'force' (violence?) and a fast car, driving west, they escaped some problem, a 'jam' (her marriage? Not a traffic queue, surely?). Then we hear how they split up, with the woman calling over the man's shoulder as he walked away, 'We'll meet again/on the avenue.' It's the *avenue of life*. But is it a prophecy, a promise, or a curse? It's also this verse, in my view, that seals the fortune of the song, in terms of it being read, or heard, as a regular story. I suppose it could be argued that 'Tangled Up In Blue' is in fact a series of snapshots, like photographs in an album, and that each subsequent stanza describes a completely different set of circumstances. A series of relationships, a string of affairs, rather than one entanglement. And yet the themes of the song – reunion, coincidence, longing – compel us as listeners to think of one coupling, not many. 'We'll meet again some day', 'But she never escaped my mind', in verse 3, and later, in verse 7, 'So now I'm going back again, I've got to get to her somehow'. If Dylan is chopping and changing, and romantic involvement in general, rather than any particular woman, is the true subject of his song, then he misfires. There isn't enough detail to distinguish one woman from the next, and we know from Dylan's other writing (and some of the other writing in this song) that he is capable of finely drawn pen-pictures and character descriptions. So we are left with the story of a man and a woman – one man

and one woman – and we must continue in that vein. But even on that level, the song is problematic.

3   The low point of the song, qualitatively speaking. At some later stage, our hero found employment in the woods. But for all Dylan's proletarian kudos and working class wardrobe, a lumberjack he ain't, nor does he sail the high seas or catch fish for a living, and this alerts us to the idea that the song is a form of dramatic monologue, or that the confessional element is being voiced through a fictional character. In such circumstances, a sympathetic critic might allow for the canny joke ('one day the ax just fell') and the two makeweight syllables ('One day the ax *just* fell' and '*Right* outside of Delacroix'), claiming them to be the authentic voice of the working man. As a listener, I don't notice them, but as a reader, I think they suck. The narrator has also 'seen a lot of women'. An autobiographical intrusion, surely, given what I imagine to be the limited opportunities for courtship in the great, northern forests or aboard a gut-splattered trawler.

4   This is more like it. The man meets the woman again quite by chance, in a bar. It's a topless bar, although our man recognises the woman by her face, in silhouette, and the woman returns his look, noticing the lines and wrinkles. There's also an element of revenge in this scenario: the woman's mother sneered at the narrator's mother for wearing a home-made dress. The fact that her own daughter now serves alcohol naked from the waist up must be considered a form of poetic justice.

Words are exchanged, ordinary and exact words, nothing sentimental or hackneyed. It's a beautifully evocative description of recognition and the passage of time. The sexual bathos of the last line in which the woman bends to 'tie the laces/of my shoe' is expertly planned and wonderfully executed. And with the mundane and everyday 'shoe' paired off with the abstract and transcendent 'blue', the verse is pulled together and closed with a neat, rhyming bow. That's the way to do it.

5   There's a smoking-pipe in the house where the woman lives. A bong, I'd suggest. Or a peace pipe. But this verse is interesting because it mentions poetry, or rather 'an Italian poet/From the thirteenth century'. There are a number of candidates for this role, including St Francis of Assisi. But I take it to be Dante, which makes me think that the female character could be Beatrice, and that the whole song might be profitably interpreted through the paradigm of the *Divine Comedy*. 'And every one of them words rang true,' Dylan tells us, like a clue. Mind you, most words ring true after a few puffs on the magic pipe. This verse is also notable for its shift from third to second-person description, the introduction of a 'you' character. It's the redhead, presumably, but in the context of the song, the word suddenly pokes out, like a finger pointing at someone else, jabbing them in the chest.

6   This is the most metaphysical of the stanzas. It's a surprise to find our narrator now in a threesome, though less of a surprise to hear that the basement they live in is 'down the stairs'. The atmosphere is a twilight zone of coffee and communism, and also music, and if Dylan isn't the storyteller himself, you can almost imagine him at the back of the cafe, scratching out a tune, a minor character in one his own songs. The 'he' of this triangular relationship could be the husband – we could be back at the beginning again – or he could be the pipe-owner of verse five, who could be the lover or lodger of the topless barmaid of verse four. Surely it's not Dante? The second half of the

stanza is more enigmatic and tantalising than any other part of the song. The 'he' character suffers some kind of moral death, through 'dealing with slaves'. The woman holds a lawn-sale or house clearance, metaphorical or otherwise, and divested of her wordly goods, or her pride, is likewise overcome by inertia. 'And froze up inside,' is how Dylan puts it. An image of what? Spiritual emptiness? Sexual frigidity? Or simply the lack of a decent coat, having sold 'everything she owned'. In response, our narrator skedaddles. He tells us that this was his only option, 'The only thing I knew how to do', which is both an admission of cowardice and an honest statement of fact made by a restless traveller. It's also a reflexive comment on the nature of the song itself; the singer must now move on to the next scene, the next picture, the next verse. It's interesting that Dylan uses the image of a flying bird to describe the action of leave-taking. Typically, the bird is a timid and vulnerable creature, and pitiful when caged, but one that represents soaring freedom of the kind unavailable to mortals. Many are migratory, and sing.

7　The final verse is inconclusive, and, I'd suggest, somewhat contradictory. We are now back in the narrative present. Our hero wants to find the woman again, and yet is still preaching a code of life on the road and endless journeying. He reflects on past acquaintances, people now engaged in good, honest work (mathematicians) and domestic chores (carpenters' wives), and at the same time wonders what they are doing with their lives. Since he knows full well what they are doing with their lives (at least one is a mathematician, another a carpenter's wife), this can only be a value judgement, yet one made by someone whose own life is notably lacking in substance. Is the narrator praising himself for avoiding the trappings of family life and regular work, or is this a moment of self-deprecation – the snide comment made by someone who is no position to judge? The final lines don't resolve the issue. Referring again to his relationship with the woman, her of the once-red hair, presumably, he concludes:

> We always did feel the same,
> We just saw it from a different point of view,
> Tangled up in blue.

Elliptical, or what?

'Tangled Up In Blue' is a great song. But peering in to it like this tells us that it's something of a mess, or that literary criticism is the wrong tool when it comes to the analysis of song lyrics. There are moments in the textual life of 'Tangled Up In Blue' that are pure poetry and that any poet would have been glad to have written. I'm thinking again of the observed detail of verse four, the 'thinned out' crowd, the woman's profile in the spotlight, the trick with the shoelace, and the delicious use of conversational English: 'I's just about to do the same.' But for every highlight there is a contrived rhyme, a cornball cliché, an embarrassing tautology, a redundant syllable, a tired simile, a lame comment and a cheesy pun. Towards the end the song slews unnecessarily between pronouns. Dylan's sabotaging of the linear progression of the story is intriguing, even exciting in performance, but on paper it doesn't look so clever. Narrative disruption, not a new idea in poetry or song-writing in the Seventies, is a powerful device. Even Homer knew that. But its effectiveness relies on clarity. We can only endure the artist's emotional turmoil if we can enjoy his control over the material at the same time. And it is an early lesson of most writing classes that ambiguity is the achieved goal of precise writing, a nailed-on result, not an excuse for sloppiness or a byword for chaos.

But lest we forget, writing about music is like dancing about architecture, and Bob Dylan doesn't need the literary establishment to accredit his writing. He doesn't need to be seen in that light or spoken of in those terms. His virtue is in his style, his attitude, his disposition to the world and his delivery of his words. Even the way he pronounces 'illusion' on that track is enough to make something happen. Broadly speaking, his lyrics are beyond the ordinary: he has wide vocabulary, a storyteller's ear, and the eye of someone who paints wonderful pictures. Those things alone are enough to separate him from the vast majority of his colleagues and competitors.

In the spring semester of 2000 I was teaching at the University of Iowa's Writers' Workshop, and heard that Dylan was playing at Cedar Rapids, an airport town a few miles up the road. Iowa City being something of an intellectual enclave within a landscape of corn, spuds and sows, I thought that a ticket might be hard to come by, but at the last minute, one turned up in my pigeon-hole.

I'd never seen Dylan live. It's the baby-boom generation that seem most loyal to his cause, turning up to concerts year after year, agreeing in the rain afterwards that, yes, this was probably the worst ever, worse even than the one before, or the one before that. Then arranging to meet at the next gig. But the fanaticism isn't exclusive to that age-band. Over the years, Dylanism has caught on amongst following generations, and academia has been one of its breeding grounds. Bob Dylan appears to be the musician of choice among the teaching staff of many an institute of further education. It's quite possible to hear his lyrics being bandied around in the senior common room, amidst discussions of prosody and symbolism. Mention of his name signifies a dignified and recherché understanding of popular culture, but nothing as crass as an interest in pop music or rock 'n' roll. On some very basic level, it's a man thing. I don't listen to much Joni Mitchell myself, but from the times I have, I know she's a talented guitarist, that her compositions and orchestrations are extremely complex, that her lyrics are of a consistently high standard, and that she can sing a bit too. Sound like anyone else we know? She came out of the same folk-rock background not long after Dylan, but I don't see Joni on the syllabus.

Looking at the crowd from the middle-back of The Five Seasons Center that night, I was amazed at the demographic spread. From pony-tailed pensioners at the top end, to a baby in a papoose at the other. In between were locals, home-boys, farmers, bikers, crusties, rastas (white and black), groupies, roadies, slackers, civvies – the most diverse group of human beings I'd ever seen under one roof. Although the one thing that did unite them was dope. Even the farmers looked stoned.

Dylan was quite something. In his Zorro outfit, he played for almost two hours, with an appetite and enthusiasm for the songs that defied logic, given the thousands of times he must have sung and played them. In a move that typifies my approach to research, I wrote the set list on the bottom of a wax-coated drink-holder, the surface of which rubbed off in my pocket on the way home, and with it the ink. But there are internet sites dedicated to such things, so I can confidently report that he played 'Desolation Row', he played 'Mama, You Been On My Mind', he played 'Gotta Serve Somebody', he played 'Tombstone Blues', he played 'I'll Be Your Baby Tonight', and he played 'Leopard-Skin Pill-Box Hat'. And they were just the highlights of the first half. Oh, and he played 'Tangled Up In Blue' (acoustic). The encore included 'Like A Rolling Stone', 'Knocking On Heaven's Door', 'Don't Think Twice, It's All Right', and finished with 'Rainy Day Women #12 & 35'. I didn't need the web-site to remember the sight and sound of a thousand or so stoners, dancing to their anthem, singing along with the man himself, under a swirling cloud of exhaled dope. It was the stuff of writing. Dylan was poetic – not the words themselves, I could hardly hear them – but the whole thing, the spectacle as it happened, and the image that remains.

The man in the next seat kept looking at me and shaking his head, like, 'I can't believe this guy has written all these songs.' I kept looking at Dylan's feet. He was hopping from one to another, like someone with shin-splints or suffering from a circulatory problem. It was only towards the end of the evening I realised he was dancing.

7

TRUST YOURSELF: EMERSON AND DYLAN

Mark Ford

'I was simmering, simmering, simmering; Emerson brought me to a boil,'[1] Walt Whitman once remarked when trying to account for his sudden transformation, in his early thirties, from hack journalist and jobbing printer to the poet of *Leaves of Grass*. He reverently dispatched one of the 795 copies, whose printing he had paid for and overseen, to the Sage of Concord, and was delighted to receive back a letter acclaiming his book as 'the most extraordinary piece of wit and wisdom that America has yet contributed'. 'I rubbed my eyes a little,' Emerson wrote, 'to see if this sunbeam were no illusion; but the solid sense of the book is a sober certainty ... I wish to see my benefactor, and have felt much like striking my tasks, and visiting New York to pay you my respects.'[2]

And yet although Whitman, and – at least initially – Emerson were convinced that at last America had produced the transcendent poet it deserved ('He is seer ... he is individual ... he is complete in himself ...'[3] the never-bashful Whitman enthused in his own preface), Whitman did not in his own lifetime achieve anything like the status of national bard his poems so assertively claimed was his due. It was not until some time after F. O. Matthiessen's pioneering *The American Renaissance* of 1941 that Whitman's poetry began to figure regularly on school curricula, such as that followed at Hibbing High School in the mid-Fifties.

The possible influence on Dylan of Whitman (in particular as mediated through Allen Ginsberg and the Beats), and of nineteenth-century American poets such as Edgar Allan Poe, Emily Dickinson and even Longfellow and Edward Arlington Robinson has been interestingly discussed by Michael Gray in the various editions of *Song and Dance Man: The Art of Bob Dylan*.[4] Whitman and Dylan might each be said to have created an artistic persona that seems to promise an intimate relationship with the reader, listener, or spectator, but at the same time each continually insists on his ultimate unknowability. On the one hand they urge us to open up and accept not just their art, but their presence, both spiritually and physically:

> yes, it is I
> who is poundin' at your door
> if it is you inside
> who hears the noise[5]

Dylan declares in one of the poems used as liner notes to *The Times They Are A-Changin'* (1963). 'I wait on the doorslab,' Whitman proclaims in 'Song of Myself' (1855):

> You will hardly know who I am or what I mean,
> But I shall be good health to you nevertheless,
> And filter and fibre your blood.[6]

Yet almost in the same breath we are warned never to think we can control or measure or even understand this potentially redemptive visitor who so insistently demands our attention: 'Encompass worlds but never try to encompass me,'[7] admonishes Whitman; 'And there was no man around / Who could track or chain him down,'[8] Dylan asserts of his outlaw alter ego, John Wesley Harding. With both we are in the situation of the disciples to whom Christ appeared on the road to Emmaus: 'And their eyes were opened, and they knew him; and he vanished out of their sight.'[9] 'I depart as air . . .' Whitman writes as the end of 'Song of Myself' approaches, 'I effuse my flesh in eddies and drift it in lacy jags.'[10] Dylan, likewise, is almost always on the point of moving on, of bidding farewell, and of course the only answers he offers are those that are blowing in the wind.

But if it was Whitman who first embodied in poetry the ideal of the archetypal American self journeying down the open road into a future where anything might happen, it was, as he acknowledged, Emerson's writings of the 1830s and 1840s that brought his conception of the democratic hero 'to a boil'. Emerson, during this period, frequently figures himself in the role of a kind of John the Baptist: in essays such as 'The American Scholar' (1837) and 'The Poet' (1844), he both condemns the current state of American culture and boldly predicts the imminent arrival of a genius whose vision will consummate the new reality of the new republic. His rhapsodic descriptions of the true poet, who 'stands among partial men for the complete man, and apprises us not of his wealth, but of the commonwealth',[11] are attempts to conjure into existence this 'sovereign' being, rather than an appraisal of the works of poetic contemporaries such as Bronson Alcott or William Cullen Bryant. 'I look in vain for the poet whom I describe,'[12] he laments, and even his enthusiasm for Whitman (whose overt homosexuality in the Calamus poems Emerson found deeply shocking) eventually waned. Emerson's ideal poet is an impossible fusion of prophet and hero ('words are also actions, and actions are a kind of words'[13]), of national spokesman and interpreter of nature, of Christic redeemer and Adamic namer. Like Dylan's Wanted Man or Jack of Hearts, he is everywhere and nowhere, absolutely necessary to his disciples but reviled by the institutions of society, a loner who can trust only his own vision. 'Doubt not, o poet, but persist,' Emerson exhorts:

> Say, 'It is in me, and shall out.' Stand there, baulked and dumb, stuttering and stammering, hissed and hooted, stand and strive, until, at last, rage draw out of thee that *dream*-power which every night shows thee is thine own; a power transcending all limit and privacy, and by virtue of which a man is the conductor of the whole river of electricity.[14]

Has there ever been a finer description of Dylan's 1966 tour with The Band (known then as the Hawks), whose glorious climax was the performance at the Free Trade Hall in Manchester on May 17, when Dylan, wired in every way, the 'conductor of the whole river of electricity', responded to the aggrieved Folkies' heckles and boos, and an applauded catcall of 'Judas!', by fiercely drawling 'I don't believe you, you're a l-i-i-ar,' and then instructing the band to play 'FUCKING LOUD' on the concert's final song, 'Like a Rolling Stone'?[15]

It is not, I should say now, my purpose to argue here that Dylan has read and been influenced by Emerson, or that Ralph Waldo would have hailed *Highway 61 Revisited* as the answer to his prayers, but to explore some of the ways in which Dylan's development and personae might be seen as exemplifying a variety of American ideals. These ideals were first and most persuasively codified by Emerson, but have since come to underpin any number of the myths and genres that structure the foundation, expansion and future destiny of America. Numerous parallels can obviously be drawn between the non-conformism endlessly extolled by Emerson, Thoreau, and others associated with the Transcendentalist movement, and the spirit and activities of the counter-culture in America in the Sixties.[16] What, after all, were all those hippy communes but experiments in living loosely modelled on Brook Farm or Fruitlands? – but then, equally they can be seen as ultimately deriving from John Winthrop's vision of the first Puritan settlement as a 'Citty upon a Hill'.[17] To be a rebel or non-conformist is – as Sacvan Bercovitch for one never tires of pointing out[18] – the one sure way of proving you're a good American. '*Trust thyself*: every heart vibrates to that iron string,'[19] counsels Emerson in 'Self-Reliance' in 1841, a theme taken up most directly (and to very little effect, it must be said) in 'Trust Yourself', included on the uneven and disastrously over-produced *Empire Burlesque* of 1985.

The doctrine of self-reliance can, of course, be interpreted in widely varying ways: it can be used not only to justify the high-minded outsider who stands up for the truth of his or her principles, who determines as Dylan does in 'Restless Farewell', to 'make my stand / And remain as I am / And bid farewell and not give a damn,'[20] but also to underwrite laissez-faire capitalism, robber barons, the right to bear arms, the actions of any who – in the words of 'Foot of Pride' – 'look straight into the sun and say "Revenge is mine."'[21] 'And truly,' Emerson concedes, 'it demands something godlike in him who has cast off the common motives of humanity, and has ventured to trust himself for a taskmaster. High be his heart, faithful his will, clear his sight, that he may in good earnest be doctrine, society, law, to himself, that a simple purpose may be to him as strong as iron necessity is to others!'[22] Emerson's insistent, driving rhetoric cannot quite suppress the terrifying antithesis of his fantasy of utopian selfhood: 'How does it feel?', as the chorus of the song that began as 'this long piece of vomit about twenty pages long'[23] unanswerably asks, 'How does it feel?'[24]

In the context of the myths of America, the addressee of 'Like a Rolling Stone' really should 'have it made': having 'nothing to lose' is what links, say, Melville's Ishmael and Hawthorne's Pearl, Twain's Huckleberry Finn and Cooper's Natty Bumppo, whose freedom to be themselves depends on their remaining with no direction home, like complete unknowns. And in Emersonian terms there is no higher state than that of being relieved of one's social identity and the attendant inhibitions of self-consciousness: solitude is the catalyst of vision, as is most famously revealed in his account in 'Nature' (1836) of crossing a common at twilight in winter, and feeling 'glad to the brink of fear':

> Standing on the bare ground, – my head bathed by the blithe air, and uplifted into infinite space, – all mean egotism vanishes. I become a transparent eye-ball; I am nothing; I see all; the currents of the Universal Being circulate through me; I am part or particle of God.[25]

'Like a Rolling Stone' may have started out as a satirical description of the descent of an Edie Sedgwick-type poor little rich girl into despair and poverty, but its extraordinary charge derives from the extent to which, beneath its surface narrative, it seems a compulsive attempt to exorcise the speaker's own deepest fears. 'To live outside the law you must be honest,'[26] Dylan quips in one of his most Emersonian aphorisms on *Blonde on Blonde*'s 'Absolutely Sweet Marie'; but living outside the law also involves the possibility of being reduced to the nightmarish double of Emerson's transparent eye-ball – the opaque, unseeing, unresting nonentity of a rolling stone.

In his ecstatic trance Emerson claims the currents of the Universal Being circulate through him; at the same time he feels physically annihilated: 'I am nothing; I see all.' In the schizophrenic drama of the song, on the other hand, it is the addressee who is reduced to nothing and becomes 'invisible', but it is this destitution, we are subliminally aware, that makes possible the expressive powers or vision of the singer. Dylan has often called 'Like a Rolling Stone' his 'breakthrough', and it was one of course, not just for him, but for the history of rock music; he composed it at a point in his career when he himself felt he had 'nothing to lose', and was on the point of abandoning music altogether: 'I wrote that after I'd quit,' he revealed in an interview of 1966; 'I'd literally quit singing and playing, and I found myself writing this song.'[27]

Despite its appearing initially to be a vituperative, lower-Manhattan, score-settling song like, say, 'Positively 4th Street', it seems to me inspired – as much as Emerson's 'Nature' – by a kind of artistic exhilaration at the possibilities suddenly discovered within a seemingly exhausted genre. As Emerson found in the essay form he took up after abandoning the Unitarian church the perfect vehicle for all he'd wanted to say but couldn't in his weekly sermons, so Dylan discovered by fusing folk ('Once upon a time . . .' the song begins) and rock that at last he could find and sing the words he'd been looking for. 'As when the summer comes from the south; the snow-banks melt, and the face of the earth becomes green before it, so shall the advancing spirit create its ornaments along its path, and carry with it the beauty it visits, and the song which enchants it.'[28] It is Dylan's hypnotic rhymes – 'didn't you / kiddin' you', 'juiced in it/used to it' – which most dramatically embody an analogous spirit of self-regeneration, or as he himself put it, in hipster slang: 'It was something that I myself could dig.'[29]

Paradoxically, then, 'Like a Rolling Stone' seems to condemn the very ideal of freedom which is in fact its own life-blood. 'Do I contradict myself? / Very well then . . . I contradict myself; / I am large . . . I contain multitudes,'[30] Whitman declared with insouciance in 'Song of Myself' – an idea he borrowed directly from 'Self-Reliance': 'Suppose you should contradict yourself; what then? . . . With consistency a great soul has simply nothing to do.'[31] Dylan seems to have felt that 'Like a Rolling Stone' was the first song in which he fully staged the drama of his own self-divisions, and it is also the song which has become most obviously the badge of his own commitment to the troubadour lifestyle he has led for most of the thirty-five years since he wrote it. 'I'm not there,' he wails hauntingly in one of the most beautiful songs recorded during his sessions in the basement of Big Pink in Woodstock with The Band in 1967, 'I am gone'.[32] 'I take SPACE to be the central fact to man born in America,'[33] Charles Olson observed in his 1947 meditation on the writings of Melville, *Call Me Ishmael*, and in Dylan's œuvre the geography of the country comes to figure the refusal of his Muse to let him settle anywhere at all for long. Dylan often seems condemned, like Ishmael, to a life of wandering as a way of 'keeping one step ahead of the persecutor within',[34] of 'driving off the spleen, and regulating the circulation'.[35] For the American hero, as Emerson argued in 'Self-Reliance', 'power ceases in the instant of repose; it resides in the moment of transition from a past to a new state, in the shooting of the gulf, in the darting to an aim.'[36] In 'Tangled Up in Blue', to take the most obvious example, Dylan transforms the linear quest of the travel journal or road movie into a never-ending romance with America, a dreamy search for a lost past that also propels him remorselessly down the road into the future and the illusory attractions of 'another joint'[37]: the song spans the States as it does time, travelling east and west, from the Great North Woods to New Orleans and Delacroix, and then rounds back on itself as if to illustrate Emerson's assertion in 'Circles' (1841) that 'the life of man is a self-evolving circle, which, from a ring imperceptibly small, rushes on all sides outwards to new and larger circles, and that without end ... The way of life is wonderful; it is by abandonment.'[38]

Dylan's 'road maps for the soul'[39] tend, then, like Emerson's, to take the form of successive acts of self-invention, and yet both insist time and again on the inviolable unity underlying the continual process of metamorphosis by which genius extends and fulfils itself. 'A character,' Emerson notes, 'is like an acrostic or Alexandrian stanza; – read it forward, backward, or across, it spells the same thing.'[40] In his introduction to the only ever live performance – and it is a sublime one – of 'Caribbean Wind' at the Fox Warfield Stadium in San Francisco on 12 November 1980, Dylan alludes to the life and career of the blues singer Leadbelly, who made his name in the Thirties singing songs he'd written in and about prison, but then switched to recording children's songs: 'People said, "Oh, what, has Leadbelly changed?" Some people like the older ones, others liked the newer ones. But he didn't change,' Dylan adds to delighted cheers from the audience, 'he was the same man.'[41] In the context of the mainly Evangelical material he was performing during this tour, on which he was often jeered and booed, as in 1966, by disaffected fans, Dylan is clearly attempting to illustrate the kind of point often made by Emerson: 'For of one will, the actions will be harmonious, however unlike they seem. These varieties are lost sight of at a little distance, at a little height of thought. One tendency unites them all.' In 'Experience', composed in 1844, he insists more categorically still: 'Use what language we will, we can never say anything but what we are.'[42]

Yet however much we are supposed to read each provisionally

adopted persona in relation to some inescapable but indefinable core being – the 'man in me' to borrow a Dylan title – saying 'what we are' also inevitably involves confronting history and society, and, in particular, the phenomenon of America, often figured by both Dylan and Emerson as almost simultaneously ideal and degraded, utopian and apocalyptic. In the course of the economic chaos induced by the Panic of 1837, Emerson became convinced that 'Society has played out its last stake',[43] and in essays such as 'The American Scholar' of that year and 'The Divinity School Address' of 1838, he assumed the mantle of guide to an impending and corresponding revolution in consciousness which would confound, once and for all, the grubby materialist ethos of capitalist America. This new age, alas, never dawned, and, ironically, by the 1850s Emerson's resonant celebrations of the infinite potential of the self were beginning to be cited as morally justifying the laissez-faire economic system whose death knell he had felt confident they would help ring. But in this he merely anticipated nearly every American rebel-hero, whose early defiance and integrity all too often come finally to mean their agents can drive a harder bargain for the ads and product endorsements to which fame must, it seems, inevitably lead. Indeed, the advertising industry above all depends on peddling, as Dylan points out in 'It's Alright, Ma (I'm Only Bleeding)', an Emersonian vision of the individual's powers:

> Advertising signs they con you
> Into thinking you're the one
> That can do what's never been done
> That can win what's never been won
> Meantime life outside goes on
> All around you.[44]

Like 'Foot of Pride', 'Licence to Kill', 'Yonder Comes Sin' or 'Slow Train Coming', 'It's Alright, Ma' might be said to continue the tradition of the American Jeremiad, and its insistently rhyming, ballad-like short lines directly recall in particular one of the most famous and popular of these – Michael Wigglesworth's vision of the Second Coming and Judgement, 'The Day of Doom', published in 1662 and immediately a runaway bestseller:

> Wallowing in all kind of sin,
>   vile wretches lay secure:
> The best of men had scarcely then
>   their lamps kept in good ure.
> Virgins unwise, who through disguise
>   amongst the best were number'd,
> Had clos'd their eyes; yea, and the wise
>   through sloth and frailty slumber'd.[45]

Though he insists in the early 'Long Time Gone', composed in the summer of 1962, that he 'ain't no prophet / And ain't no prophet's son,'[46] Dylan's lyrics draw more heavily even than Emerson's essays on the Bible and traditions of biblical commentary, and both tend to represent America more or less within the parameters of the Puritans' dual conception of their mission into the wilderness: America is at once the New Canaan promised by God to his chosen people, and the site of such terrible backsliding that, almost any moment since the Founding Fathers landed at Plymouth Rock, His wrath might descend and obliterate the entire community for having irredeemably broken its covenant with the Lord. 'Ain't no man righteous, no not one,'[47] sings Dylan in the 1979 song of that title, but of course, as for Wigglesworth or Anne Bradstreet, it is precisely the strength of his sense of personal and universal corruption which proves his own fitness for heaven, and which, in a song like 'In the Summertime', allows him to recreate for a moment the early pantheistic landscapes of 'Lay Down Your Weary Tune' or 'Mr Tambourine Man', in which nature is presented as embodying a wild, high romantic harmony. 'When you gonna wake up?'[48] he demands in born-again preacher-mode on the first of his explicitly religious albums, *Slow Train Coming* (1979), echoing the key term in Jonathan Edwards's blood-curdling sermon of 1741, 'Sinners in the Hands of an Angry God', which was delivered in the hope of 'awakening'[49] to a recognition of their sins the unregenerate in the congregation.

In Emerson evil is also often figured as a kind of apathy. In the opening paragraph of 'Experience' he complains that

> the Genius which, according to the old belief, stands at the door by which we enter, and gives us the lethe to drink, that we may tell no tales, mixed the cup too strongly, and we cannot shake off the lethargy now at noonday. Sleep lingers all our lifetime about our eyes, as night hovers all day in the boughs of the fir-tree. All things swim and glitter.[50]

In this essay, written two years after the death from scarlet fever of his five-year-old son Waldo, Emerson powerfully articulates one of the most persistent of American themes – the loss of one's sense of reality. 'I seem to have lost a beautiful estate – no more,' he observes of himself dispassionately; 'It does not touch me ... I grieve that grief can teach me nothing, nor carry me one step into real nature.'[51] In 'Circles' he rejoiced in the conviction that 'there are no fixtures in nature. The universe is fluid and volatile. Permanence is but a word of degrees,'[52] but in the later essay he figures himself floundering in a miasma of false appearances and shadows, of 'scene-painting and counterfeit':

> Dream delivers us to dream, and there is no end to illusion. Life is a train of moods like a string of beads, and, as we pass through them, they prove to be many-colored lenses which paint the world from their own hue, and each shows only what lies in its focus.[53]

If Emersonian belief in the ultimate truth of one's subjectivity can render the universe infinitely malleable and potentially ideal, it can, equally, make it seem phantasmagoric or 'unreal', as his descendant and antagonist, T. S. Eliot, was to argue in *The Waste Land* (1922), which uses the adjective three times.

How to live in a world without narratives capable of persuading us of the meaning of experience also often appears to be the burden of Dylan's finest post-Evangelical songs, in which a drained, uncertain speaker either looks towards death ('There at least,' as Emerson grimly phrases it in 'Experience', 'is reality that will not dodge us'), or sifts through fragmented, unstable memories. In songs such as 'Series of Dreams', 'Dignity', 'Blind Willie McTell', 'Tryin' to Get to Heaven', the singer is like a survivor wandering through the rubble of America's history and myths, almost randomly recalling characters, events and images that once held purpose and meaning, but now no longer do. 'Gotta sleep down in the parlor,' he muses in 'Tryin' to Get to Heaven', 'and relive my dreams: / I close my eyes and I wonder / If everything is as hollow as it seems.' The apocalyptic fury that drives and holds together the dizzying poetry of 'Caribbean Wind' or 'Ain't Gonna go to Hell for Anybody' or 'The Groom's Still Waitin' at the Altar', gives way in Dylan's songs after

Infidels (1983) to a more puzzled, even paralysing awareness of reality's elusiveness, the way 'nothing', as he complains in 'Series of Dreams', 'comes up to the top: / Everything stays down where it's wounded, / And comes to a permanent stop.' The song embodies exactly the dilemma Emerson confronts in 'Experience'. 'Where,' he asks, 'do we find ourselves? In a series of which we do not know the extremes, and believe that it has none.'[54] As Dylan finds 'no good' the cards he is holding, so Emerson deplores above all 'this evanescence and lubricity of all objects, which lets them slip though our fingers then when we clutch hardest . . . Gladly we would anchor, but the anchorage is quicksand.'[55] 'People don't live or die,' Dylan notes in a similar vein in a song recorded, like 'Series of Dreams', in 1989, 'people just float'[56]: the woman who leaves in pursuit of a latter-day mystery tramp, the hellfire-breathing Man in the Long Black Coat, is admired for her determination to escape the unreality of our secular limbo.

The potent term with which Dylan attempts to sum up what such a character and the singer himself are ultimately seeking is 'dignity', which might be glossed as what survives of self-reliance as an ideal after the bitter casualties of experience. The song 'Dignity' (also first recorded in 1989[57]) accepts the quest can never end, as Emerson does in 'Experience': 'How easily,' he sighs, 'if fate would suffer it, we might keep forever these beautiful limits, and adjust ourselves, once for all, to the perfect calculation of the kingdom of known cause and effect . . . But ah! presently comes a day, or is it only a half-hour, with its angel-whispering, – which discomfits the conclusions of nations and of years!'[58] Dylan's personification of dignity incarnates a severely chastened form of such 'angel-whispering' – 'Heard the tongues of angels,' he asserts, 'and the tongues of men,/Wasn't any difference to me.' But while the song appears to aim for the sort of panoramic perspective on experience of 'Series of Dreams', the vignettes and mini-scenarios that crowd its sixteen verses have all the resonance and panache of classic mid-Sixties songs such as 'Tombstone Blues' or 'Highway 61 Revisited'. Dylan is not just peering, like his drinking man, into the 'lost forgotten years', but actively negotiating a carnival as unsettling and richly layered as that of 'Desolation Row'.

'What is the grass?' a child asks Whitman in 'Song of Myself', 'fetching it to me with full hands; / How could I answer the child? . . . I do not know what it is any more than he.'[59] Dylan's galaxy of nursery-rhyme archetypes – who include a Whitmanesque wise man 'lookin' in a blade of grass' – are equally at a loss to decipher their circumstances; and the decision to move on – Whitman and Dylan's favourite panacea – instead perversely hinders the attempt to recover a sense of self. 'I tramp a perpetual journey, / My signs are a rain-proof coat and good shoes and a staff cut from the woods,' Whitman boasts before departing 'as air'.[60] Dylan finds, on the contrary, that he's

> Got no place to fade, got no coat,
> I'm on the rollin' river in a jerkin' boat
> Tryin' to read a note somebody wrote
> About dignity.

The open road cruised by Whitman and Dylan or Ginsberg and Kerouac is an exhilarating experience of SPACE, but in 'Dignity' time's rolling river leads inexorably to 'the edge of the lake', and a recognition of what Emerson calls the 'poverty' that is 'the native of these bleak rocks'. 'We must hold hard to this poverty,' he counsels, 'however scandalous, and by more vigorous self-recoveries, after the sallies of action, possess

our axis more firmly.'[61] Here, proleptically, Emerson might
be said to provide his fullest response to Dylan's compelling,
endlessly resourceful search for what it's going 'to take / To
find dignity.'

8

DEATH'S HONESTY

Neil Corcoran

It could be called arsenic music, or perhaps phaedra music . . . I have to think of all of this as traditional music. Traditional music is based on hexagrams. It comes about from legends, Bibles, plagues, and it revolves around vegetables and death.

Bob Dylan, 1966[1]

> For them that think death's honesty
> Won't fall upon them naturally
> Life sometimes
> Must get lonely.
>
> 'It's Alright, Ma (I'm Only Bleeding)'

1

Life sometimes (at least) must get lonely for everyone, of course; and Dylan is a great writer of states of isolated self-enclosure, from 'One Too Many Mornings' in 1964, where the very acknowledgement of mutuality is irretrievably sucked into a vortex of abandonment – 'You're right from your side / And I'm right from mine / We're both just one too many mornings /

And a thousand miles behind' – to 'Not Dark Yet' in 1997, where the painful awkwardness of isolation is conveyed again, and now epigrammatically, as spatial distress: 'There's not even room enough to be anywhere'. But the collocation of loneliness and death in 'It's Alright, Ma' signals something permanently true about Dylan: that some of the most characteristic emotions and engagements of his art derive from a possession by the thought of death. He tells Ramona in 'To Ramona', in one of the very few self-reflexive moments in his work, that 'there's no use in tryin' / T' deal with the dyin', / Though I cannot explain that in lines'. But, despite this disclaimer, and the fact that he is explaining his explanation in these very lines, his songs continually deal with the dying, and the dead, and his lines are the place where that process is made to register: with force, intelligence, assiduity and, sometimes, wit, but also sometimes with a kind of excess which is as disturbing and distressing as it is, itself, patently 'honest'. I want to think about some instances of death's honesty in Bob Dylan's work – from the 1960s, when he was a young man, and from the 1990s, when he was not – and to suggest some of the ways in which I find them an inextricable element of the essential genius of his art. But first, a few moments from the life when Dylan behaves with his peculiar kind of honesty.

(i) In December 1963, three weeks after President Kennedy was shot, Bob Dylan was given the Tom Paine award by the Emergency Civil Liberties Committee in New York for his contribution to the civil rights struggle. In his in any case extraordinary acceptance speech, in front of a committee which included James Baldwin, he appalled his hosts by concluding with his reaction to the assassination:

I'll stand up and to get uncompromisable about it, which I

have to be to be honest, I just got to be, as I got to admit
that the man who shot President Kennedy, Lee Oswald, I
don't know exactly . . . what he thought he was doing, but
I got to admit honestly that I, too – I saw some of myself
in him. I don't think it would have gone – I don't think it
could go that far. But I got to stand up and say I saw things
that he felt in me . . . [Boos and hisses][2]

He subsequently wrote a clarification (not an apology) which
he circulated to members of the committee; and 'As I Went
Out One Morning' on *John Wesley Harding* (1968), which
opens 'As I went out one morning / To breathe the air around
Tom Paine's', may allegorise this event, in an oblique narrative in which it is Tom Paine who apologises to the singer.
Nevertheless, the thought of Kennedy's assassination prompts
from Dylan something unpredictable and, in his own coinage,
'uncompromisable' ('which I have to be to be honest'): the
platitudes of liberal outrage evaporate in the part-identification
with Oswald. Honest, unevasive, and desolating, this was not
calculated to appeal. Neither, I think, was it calculated to offend.
It was not calculated at all: it was a statement hardly including
the sense of an audience; and Dylan's subsequent 'performances'
in front of audiences have often followed suit. The poet's life,
said Keats, is a continual allegory: Dylan's, in public, where he
has spent a great deal of it, is so, while being also a continual
performance of an exceptional self.

(ii) Donn Pennebaker's movie of Dylan's British tour of 1965,
Dont Look Back, includes a press conference in which Dylan
reprimands a *Time* magazine journalist for the pointlessness of
his job. Michael Gray and John Bauldie have observed of the
Dylan of this movie that he 'wasn't a fraction as derailed by his

fame and fortune and hipness as most of us would have been', which is true; but here, although Dylan is playfully ironic as well as vituperative during the conversation (or monologue), he is certainly licensed by his status into a callowly aggressive arrogance.[3] Even so, the twenty-five-year-old's *memento mori* is startling in its intensity:

> I'm saying that you're going to die, and you're gonna go off the earth, you're gonna be dead. Man, it could be, you know, twenty years, it could be tomorrow, any time. So am I. I mean, we're just gonna be gone. The world's going to go on without us. All right: now you do your job in the face of that, and how seriously you take yourself, you decide for yourself, and I'll decide for myself.[4]

In one of its most central aspects Bob Dylan's work has always insisted this knowledge and this seriousness. Dylan is as permanently, unillusionedly certain that 'Most things may never happen: this one will' as Philip Larkin is in his poem 'Aubade'.

(iii) In 1991, in front of a television audience, Dylan was given a National Association of Recording Arts and Sciences Lifetime Achievement Award. This was the time of the Gulf War, and Dylan sang 'Masters of War', that song from 1963 which concludes with an address to the political architects of war:

> And I hope that you die
> And your death'll come soon
> I will follow your casket
> In the pale afternoon

And I'll watch while you're lowered
Down to your deathbed
And I'll stand o'er your grave
'Til I'm sure that you're dead

He sang it, however, in a rushed, almost indecipherable way. Mikal Gilmore tells us what happened next:

> . . . a deliriously amused Jack Nicholson presented Dylan with his Lifetime Achievement Award. Dylan, dressed in a lopsided dark suit, stood by, fumbling with his gray curl-brim fedora and occasionally applauding himself. When Nicholson passed the plaque to him, Dylan looked confused. 'Well, uh, all right,' he said, fumbling some more with his hat. 'Yeah. Well, my daddy, he didn't leave me too much. You know, he was a very simple man. But what he told me was this: He did say, "Son . . ."' And then Dylan paused, rubbing his mouth while silently reading what was written on the plaque, and then he shook his head. 'He said so many things, you know?' he said, and the audience tittered. 'He said, "Son, it's possible to become so defiled in this world that your own mother and father will abandon you. And if that happens, God will always believe in your own ability to mend your ways."'
>
> After that, nobody was laughing much. Dylan gave a final tip of his hat, spun on his heels, and was gone.[5]

Doing the unexpected once more, Dylan is possibly speaking here in self-disgust and self-rebuke; but he is also possibly rebuking his audience and, through them, the American nation which, arguably, is only self-interestedly pursuing its foreign policy in the Gulf. The reckless inappropriateness of the occasion must imply that no such occasion ever exists in a context-free zone, that the Gulf War is happening here as well as there, and that blame must be apportioned and guilt accepted. Dylan doesn't know what it means to let anyone off the hook, least of all himself. 'I look at him and I don't see a guy giving out leaflets, holding a banner,' said Patti Smith, 'I see a machine gun.'[6]

Such refusal to capitulate to expectation, an apparently autocratic resilience which seems fuelled, nevertheless, by deep vulnerability and an absence of the self-protective instinct, is also apparent in the experimental self-revisions of the work itself. But there is an exorbitance here too when Dylan confronts death. Death and rancour come together, as they sometimes do in Samuel Beckett. There is something intransigent and, it may be, even obsessive in Dylan, and it is responsible for some of his greatest strengths as a writer. It has, however, its disconcerting moments of what we might consider the Higher *Schadenfreude*: witness 'Masters of War', which gloats over a potential punishment by death, and presumes the knowledge that 'even Jesus will never forgive what you do', thereby making these deaths eternal damnations too. This is a *schadenfreude* made 'higher' only by the song's sense of the unspeakability of the crimes committed, which are not only against the living but also against the unborn: crimes that the punishment's endlessness may be thought to match. But the song is devastating in its judgement.

Dylan's *schadenfreude* is not confined to this song; and its connection with the deathly here, which prompts the aggression, may also lie behind the terrifying honesty we discover in such songs of personal relationship as 'Like A Rolling Stone' and 'Positively 4th Street'. Dylan's sympathy for the victim in some of his work is accompanied by an understanding of the motivation of the aggressor elsewhere; and this both saves his sympathy from sentimentality and impels his representation of an emotional complexity previously absent from popular song.

(iv) In 1987 Sam Shepard published *True Dylan*, describing it as 'a one-act play, as it really happened one afternoon in California'.[7] The description frustrates our desire to know whether the interview between 'Sam' and 'Bob' which the play records represents an actual conversation between Shepard and Dylan; and *True Dylan* has elements which encourage scepticism about whether we are getting anything like 'true Dylan' or not, in the way that Shepard's *True West* encourages scepticism about representations of the American West. However, the quoted speech of 'Bob' does sound very like Dylan in some of his interviews, with its characteristic compound of obliquity, insistence and sudden unidiomatic or quasi-surreal expression; and, in its central preoccupation, it does indeed log something 'true' about Dylan, because the conversation is almost entirely about the deaths of figures from American popular culture. Bob tells Sam that he has just visited the site of James Dean's death in Paso Robles, and he meditates also on Elvis Presley, Ricky Nelson, Woody Guthrie (to whose deathbed he says he came 'close'), and Hank Williams – all of whom died young. The play ends with Bob's recollection of his motorcycle accident in Woodstock in 1966, that accident in the real Bob Dylan's life which was widely thought at the time to have nearly, or actually, killed him. Is this 'true Dylan'? –

Sam: Who found you?
Bob: Sarah [*sic*]. She was following me in a car. She picked me up. Spent a week in the hospital, then they moved me to this doctor's house in town. In his attic. Had a bed up there in the attic with a window lookin' out. Sarah stayed

149

there with me. I just remember how bad I wanted to see my
kids. I started thinkin' about the short life of trouble. How
short life is. I'd just lay there listenin' to birds chirping.
Kids playing in the neighbor's yard or rain falling by the
window. I realized how much I'd missed. Then I'd hear
the fire engine roar, and I could feel the steady thrust of
death that had been constantly looking over its shoulder at
me. [Pause] Then I'd just go back to sleep.[8]

A fire engine figures also in the exquisitely sad 'Shooting Star'
on *Oh Mercy* (1989): 'Listen to the engine, listen to the bell / As
the last fire truck from hell / Goes rolling by, all good people
are praying'; and thoughts of death in Dylan are frequently
accompanied by thoughts of apocalypse too. What impresses
in these sentences from *True Dylan*, however, is their almost
abject simplicity and lack of self-pity. Unselfconsciously sealed
by the awkwardness of the mixed metaphor, Bob's recognition
of 'the steady thrust of death that had been constantly looking over its shoulder at me' informs Bob Dylan's work at
its deepest imaginative level. This steady thrust is what looks
over its shoulder at us, his listeners, in some of his finest
songs.

2

In the early work death is figured through versions and adaptations of blues music and through songs of political protest
during the civil rights campaigns of the 1960s; and blues, with
its affiliation to a poetics of death, persists deep into the most
recent Dylan. I shall not pursue this here, except to observe that
when Michael Gray claims that the first Dylan album, *Bob Dylan*

(1962), is 'enthralled with giddy delight in its use of the ancient bluesman's voice' and that 'its obsession with death is suffused with youth's sense of immortality', he is saying something true but insufficient.[9] In songs like 'Fixin' to Die' and 'See That My Grave Is Kept Clean' giddy delight in his own ventriloquial competence is, sure enough, an index of youthful self-approval; but that competence is also deeply inward with the conditions of imminent death being evoked. Dylan's ability to make both desperation and acceptance appear not ridiculous in one so young and so white is testimony to his brilliant exceptionality as a young white singer of black American blues and also to his inherently dramatic ability to repossess imaginatively, and with a difference, such traditional material.

In this way, the songs also persuade us to read them / hear them in congruence with those truly apocalyptic self-composed songs of the early 1960s, 'Let Me Die in My Footsteps', 'A Hard Rain's A-Gonna Fall', and, in a different register altogether, 'Talkin' World War III Blues', where the persona, who is indeed and necessarily a young man – a 'blue-eyed son', a 'darling young one' – is also, at this period preceding and during the Cuban missile crisis, haunted by the prospect of his own death in a nuclear catastrophe. In addition, Dylan is already capable, in the arrestingly lovely and generous 'Song to Woody', of that generalising historical conception, which carries a dejected apocalypticism along with it, of a contemporary world that 'Seems sick an' it's hungry, it's tired an' it's torn / It looks like it's a-dyin an' it's hardly been born'. For which the remedy eventually recommended in 'It's Alright, Ma' is to reverse the process: to be busy being born as a way of not being busy dying.

This all has its political dimension, but the politics is submerged in narratives of catastrophe which, for all their gloom, have a kind of brio too. The Dylan hero is a *picaro* of the last days: giving Whitmanian-Guthriesque democratic American patriotism a further outing as he footsteps through 'Nevada, New Mexico, Arizona, Idaho' in 'Let Me Die In My Footsteps'; heroically alone and defiant as he reflects from the mountain and stands on the ocean in 'A Hard Rain's A-Gonna Fall'; and jauntily whimsical and wittily insinuating in the New York sewer of 'Talkin' World War III Blues'. In the early protest songs, however, the political register is much stronger and more immediate, since these are songs about actual political murders which name and commemorate individuals ('The Death of Emmett Till', 'Only A Pawn in Their Game' – about Medgar Evers), or socially despairing suicides ('Ballad of Hollis Brown'). These songs are, literally, news that stays news: in them, as in no other songs of the genre and period, topicality transcends itself. One of the reasons for this is that they realise that protest is insufficient of itself, and must be subsumed in more complex reactions. One of the finest of them is 'The Lonesome Death of Hattie Carroll' on *The Times They Are A-Changin'* (1963).

The song is, famously, about the murder of a black servant by a white farm-owner at a social event in Baltimore, Maryland, in February 1963 (he beat her with his cane), and the consequent minimal sentence of six months that he was given under a corrupt, racist local judicial system.[10] Christopher Ricks has written penetratingly about the song, observing how it keeps indignation – 'a very good servant, and a very bad master' – in check; and one of the ways it does this is by never actually saying that Hattie is black.[11] The song knows that it is better not to protest too much about this, since not even to mention it, when every listener will nonetheless immediately understand it, is to indict more fundamentally a society which makes such implicit understandings possible.

When Dylan introduced the song during his concerts in 1965 he said, 'This is a true story. This was taken out of the newspapers. Nothing but the words have been changed.' This self-deprecatingly places primacy on the truth of the story, while also calling into question where the truth of any story might reside if, in order to tell it, you have to change the words: since, of course, in a newspaper there is nothing but the words to be changed. Dylan certainly tells the story in his song, beginning as plainly and declaratively as it is possible for any narrative to do: 'William Zanzinger killed poor Hattie Carroll'. However, the apparently unembroidered line in fact declares circumstance as well as sympathy. Hattie is said to be 'poor' presumably because the singer sympathises with the dreadful manner of her death; but she is also poor because she is economically deprived, and in this she is at the opposite end of the social scale from her killer: the song's second line tells us that Zanzinger killed her 'With a cane that he twirled around his diamond ring finger'. This is the murderous but still dandyish gesture of the pampered son of what the third verse calls 'rich wealthy parents', where the double epithet 'rich wealthy', itself an over-accumulation, is not so much an intensifier as a moving of them onto (for Hattie) an incomprehensibly remote plane or level. Indeed, the song is prominently about differences of level, which is a word it significantly repeats: Hattie cleans the ashtrays 'on a whole other level', and the judge in the final verse wants to give the – misleading – impression that 'the courts are on the level'. In Baltimore in 1963 such differences of level, such whole other levels, are also often differences in the colour of one's skin, and they may result in casual murder.[12] This song knows intimately what casual murder is: to kill by twirling a cane round your diamond ring finger is to kill as casually as it may be managed.

That opposition between different levels sustains the song

through four verses which accumulate material about the backgrounds of Hattie and Zanzinger and, as it were, eye-witness accounts of the murder and trial. Dylan has great instinctive rhetorical skills in some of his early songs, and syntactically these accumulations work by a subtly expressive use of what rhetoric calls polysyndeton: the repetition, in close succession, of the same conjunction – in this case, 'and' – to connect a number of co-ordinate clauses. (The antithetical figure of asyndeton is used to great effect in 'A Hard Rain's A-Gonna Fall'.) The conjunction is reiterated in the song like the blows of Zanzinger's cane, like the striking of the judge's gavel: 'And the cops were called in and his weapon took from him . . . And high office relations in the politics of Maryland . . . And swear words and sneering and his tongue it was snarling . . . And never sat once at the head of the table / And didn't even talk to the people at the table . . . And that the strings in the books ain't pulled and persuaded . . . And that the ladder of law had no top and no bottom . . . And handed out strongly for penalty and repentance'. Apart from its refrain, the song rhymes only intermittently, but we might regard this polysyndeton, which is often accompanied by strong alliteration, as a kind of rhyme, operating not at the end but at the beginning of lines and internally within them. It is reiterative and cumulative, and vehemently so. In fact, the word 'and' is contained in, and concludes, the word 'Maryland': so that the line 'And high office relations in the politics of Maryland' is a line that rhymes with itself (and with three other uses of the conjunction in the same verse), locking Hattie inescapably into the unjust social system of the place she inhabits.

If the song keeps indignation in check then – and it does – part of its strength derives from the fact that it only just manages to keep indignation in check. It does not do, when it is sung in the Greenwich Village of the 1960s, what Robert Lowell in 'Man and

Wife' in *Life Studies* (1959) tells us his wife did in the Greenwich Village of the 1950s – 'the shrill verve / of your invective scorched the traditional South': its only violent attack is Zanzinger's, not the violent attack in words that is invective. One of the ways in which it complicates the whole idea of 'protest', puts it on a whole other level, is the way the verses of the song themselves offer no explicit reaction to the narrative they retail. Only the repeated refrain carries rumination: but here too neither Zanzinger nor the false-hearted judge is referred to. The refrain instead addresses the song's own audience, by moving, with a corrective emphasis, from the repeated conjunction 'and' to the alternative conjunction 'But'. Three times – when Zanzinger is booked for first-degree murder; when he is speedily bailed nevertheless; and when Hattie's killing is described – we, the song's listeners, are advised like this:

But you who philosophize disgrace and criticize all fears,
Take the rag away from your face.
Now ain't the time for your tears.

Then finally (fourth time around), when the six-month sentence is handed out, the refrain is revised:

Oh, but you who philosophize disgrace and criticize all fears,
Bury the rag deep in your face
For now's the time for your tears.

These instructions, which are perhaps just a hair's breadth away from scorn – an effect enforced by the way the word 'rag' almost contemptuously replaces the more polite 'handkerchief' – caution us against placing sympathy where we might instinctively, and perhaps self-flatteringly, wish to. 'The Lonesome Death of Hattie Carroll' is a song written to correct response, in what might be a politically usable way: it is an elegy against elegy, an elegy that is at the same time a homily. The song's 'you' – who are by implication the armchair *philosophes* of the liberal-left, who will certainly have been its first, very appreciative audience – are advised away from the usual emotions of pathos and indignation and directed towards the only politically effective end of indignation: reparation. Instructing us to discriminate, the song itself, anti-pathetic in its motive and effect, discriminatingly leaves us not with the death itself but with the corrupt judicial system which, judging such crimes so lightly, permits or even encourages them. This assured ramification into the genuinely political lends weight to the gesture of contemporary crisis which is the title of the album on which it appears, *The Times They Are A-Changin'*. Listeners to 'The Lonesome Death of Hattie Carroll' are told three times that 'Now ain't the time', and are then finally told that 'Now's the time'. The implication is that to know when the time truly is is to be enabled to effect a change in the times. It was knowing the time, and the times, as well as this that made Dylan such an important political as well as cultural figure in the 1960s, whatever he has said subsequently about his earliest involvements and commitments.

Even if the song is an instruction in anti-pathos, however, its title is a piercing one. It is so because 'lonesome', with its American-English rather than British-English inflection, is the word Hattie would use herself, and also because, although OED tells us that 'lonesome' means 'all alone, without company or assistance', Hattie does not literally die alone but, perhaps even more dreadfully, 'at a Baltimore hotel society gatherin'': she is in company, without assistance. The verse describing the killing is pointedly delayed until we have witnessed Zanzinger's self-confidently indifferent reaction ('In a matter of minutes on bail was out walking'):

Hattie Carroll was a maid of the kitchen.
She was fifty-one years old and gave birth to ten children
Who carried the dishes and took out the garbage
And never sat once at the head of the table
And didn't even talk to the people at the table
Who just cleaned up all the food from the table
And emptied the ashtrays on a whole other level,
Got killed by a blow, lay slain by a cane
That sailed through the air and came down through the room,
Doomed and determined to destroy all the gentle.
And she never done nothing to William Zanzinger.

The first and final lines here suggest how carefully Dylan manages an appropriately hybrid language in this song. To call Hattie 'a maid of the kitchen' rather than a kitchen-maid or (what she in fact apparently was on the evening of her death) a barmaid, is to honour her with a tender archaism, while also drawing attention to the utter inappropriateness of the role inflicted on her by economic necessity, since to be a 'maid' of anything, or anyone, at fifty-one is demeaning, and no 'maid' ever 'gave birth to ten children'.[13] The genitive construction is matched by the phrase 'courtroom of honor' in the final verse: but here the effect is, in the song's feelingful irony, to dishonour the courtroom, since 'honor' is a missing commodity when such scant justice is done. In fact, a *tertium quid* between 'maid of the kitchen' and 'courtroom of honor' is the phrase 'maid of honour', and the song uses, at several points, very briefly, a language of almost courtly or ceremonial association which plays against the merely moneyed privilege of a 'society gatherin'': 'maid of the kitchen'; the cane aimed 'to destroy all the gentle'; and the class from which Zanzinger derives defined as 'the nobles', in the final verse.

'Gentle', OED tells us, was 'originally used synonymously

with *noble*', and the mark of such rank was to behave generously or courteously. The words, making an ethic congruent with a social ranking, are of course profoundly prejudiced ideologically, but Dylan's use of them in proximity here is a further discrimination made by the song. It is Hattie who is an instance of 'the gentle' – of true gentility as well as mildness – whereas the gentility themselves, the only nobles in this 'society', are murderers: the one courtesy Zanzinger extends Hattie is the courtesy of death.

In these little incisions Dylan may be regarded as intruding into this song about a racist slaying a hint of Southern genteel language and culture. The courtesies and rituals of the 'traditional South', which were all once sustained by black slavery, are now ('For now's the time') corrupted and, indeed, 'doomed'. Even so, in the present moment of the song, the murderous cane, 'doomed and determined', becomes a synecdoche for a violently racist and segregated society fated to destroy the powerless. 'Determined' carries connotations of programmed inscription as well as individual intent, and the cane appears to act almost without individual agency, as it 'sailed through the air and came down through the room'. The apparent serenity and dignity of the word 'sailed', so ironically unfitting to the action in fact being evoked, harmonises with the floating amplitude of the assonances of these lines (lay / slain / cane / sailed / air / came). Opposing the song's taut alliterations, these make the moment of the murder, suddenly seen from Hattie's perspective, a slow-motion one: it is the one point of the song, and the necessary one, at which her passivity co-opts auditory empathy.

The other element of the song's linguistic hybrid, which figures in the final line of this verse, as it does throughout, is the contemporary demotic: 'And she never done nothing to William Zanzinger'. This non-grammaticality is Dylan inhabiting the Guthrie persona, as he often does. Its naivety, innocence or, as it were, social non-contamination works wonderfully here, where the casual motivelessness of the murder is being evoked, because it asks us what moral universe anyone would inhabit who thought that if she had done something to Zanzinger, rather than nothing, then murder might be the merited punishment. Whose moral universe would this be? That of the judge who hands out a six-month sentence, perhaps. She never done nothing to William Zanzinger: but she has done everything for William Zanzinger. In the insistent incrementalism of this verse she carries; she does not sit; she doesn't even talk; she just cleans up; she empties. The circumscribed confinement of her life is sealed by the slamming gates of that triple identical rhyme, 'table / table / table', and its slant rhyme with 'level'. Hattie is little more than an active verb, functional and invisible; and, being so, she can then all too casually become passive, the Hattie Carroll who 'Got killed by a blow'.

There is in this verse, in the printed version, a little grammatical wobble. Since the first line ends with a full stop, the relative pronoun 'who' at the beginning of the third must refer to the children, whereas in fact it is not they, but she, who does all the things the verse says. The grammatical construction must be 'Hattie Carroll was a maid ... Who ... Got killed'; and if so the stop should be omitted, and the line 'She was fifty-one years old and gave birth to ten children' is a parenthesis. It is a very telling parenthesis indeed, giving us her age in the same gesture in which it reminds us that childbirth is another very strenuous and personally endangering activity (especially if you were black in Maryland between the 1930s and the 1950s, when Hattie must have had her ten children). But this relation of the pronoun to the children is certainly one way its listeners will hear the grammar of the song (since we cannot hear punctuation), and far from being a wobble on Dylan's part, it acts functionally and expressively, since it proposes that in this conditioned or 'determined' world Hattie's children can only share her doom of servitude and subjection, which is also still the lot of huge numbers of black Americans in the early 1960s. In one of the song's few verse rhymes, 'kitchen' slant-rhymes, or at least assonates, with 'children'.

It is a commonly reiterated paradox of elegy that it is usually self-preoccupied too. Gerard Manley Hopkins in 'Margaret, are you grieving' is insinuatingly alert to this when he decides of the grieving Margaret that 'It is the blight man was born for. / It is Margaret you mourn for.' A genuinely political elegy must be not at all self-preoccupied: its interest must lie all elsewhere. In 'The Lonesome Death of Hattie Carroll' Bob Dylan manages a selfless elegy, and one that instructs its audience in a comparable selflessness. This is the tribute Hattie Carroll deserves. It is Hattie the song mourns for. Nothing but the words have been changed.

3

> I have not painted the war . . . but I have no doubt that the war is in . . . these paintings I have done.
>
> Picasso, 1944

Highway 61 Revisited (1965) is one of those three astonishing mid-1960s albums – the others are *Bringing It All Back Home* and *Blonde on Blonde* – which Greil Marcus, understanding them as 'a single outburst', characterises as among 'the most intense outbreaks of twentieth-century modernism'.[14] I agree with the sentiment, even if I find 'outburst' and 'outbreaks' rather lurid metaphors; but this album is also locatable in a specific history as well as a specific aesthetic. Ezra Pound defines the epic as 'a poem including history'; *Highway 61 Revisited* is an album including Vietnam, although the word figures nowhere on it.[15] Not about Vietnam, but including Vietnam, it still extraordinarily gives of its period without being at all confined to it. Its musical and lyrical originality and verve are paradoxically often very death-inflected indeed. Opening with 'Like A Rolling Stone', one of the most aesthetically revolutionary songs of all time, it also opens, in the most traditional imaginable way, 'Once upon a time', only to tell a tale of *schadenfreude* so venomous, but also so exultant, as almost to create an entirely new emotion. Opening with its traditional 'Once upon a time', however, the album closes on 'Desolation Row'; and the fairy tale of *Highway 61 Revisited* is, like all great fairy tales, a very dark one indeed.

On Desolation Row, in the song's opening lines, 'They're selling postcards of the hanging / They're painting the passports brown'. The metamorphic, sexually ambivalent, violent, manipulative, coercively carnivalesque world created by the song is, in these lines, prominently a world framed by sadistic pornography and by the obliteration of normal identity. The pornography, commonly thought to be surreal, is in fact historically accurate. James Allen's *Without Sanctuary: Lynching Photography in America*, a collection of appalling photographs of lynchings of black men by whites in late nineteenth- and early twentieth-century America, makes it clear that the practice was not uncommon.[16] Many of the photographs were reproduced and sold as postcards: the 'spectacle' of the lynching was usually staged as a photographic spectacle too, with a view to subsequent commercial gain, and often the spectators themselves seek the camera's attention. 'In America, everything is for sale,' says Allen, 'including a national shame.' One aerial photograph shows a vast crowd at a lynching in Duluth, Minnesota, in 1920. As Dylan, who was born in Duluth in 1941, clearly knows, 'selling postcards of the hanging' is a fact of recent American history, not a surrealism.

As for the song's second line, there is bureaucratic Kafkaesque nightmare in having one's passport painted brown, since so much modern sense of identity is invested in the passport photograph and the protection and privilege it should provide; and the song is clearly allusive to Kafka subsequently (when 'the kerosene / Is brought down from the castles / By insurance men'). The minatory eeriness of these lines, however, seems also to acknowledge the flimsiness of any sense of identity actually provided by the passport. Paul Fussell has observed that 'the passport picture is perhaps the most egregious little modernism'; by which he means that, when it was introduced during the First World War, in 1915, it was an anxiety-inducing affront to people's sense of personal identity, since before that you did not have to present your certified image along with your face in order to cross a national border.[17] You were, in a new and startling way, manifestly under surveillance, subjected.

If the passport is the modernism, this song's painting of it brown may be a most egregious little post-modernism, and one appropriately introduced during another war, the war of 1960s America in Vietnam. I assume that we must read the place name Desolation Row as a metonym for the United States in 1965: the song title makes the kind of large claim for inclusiveness, authority and judgement that other such topographically metonymic titles make: *Bleak House*, *The Waste Land*, *Vineland*, *Underworld*. Since the album itself does not take the title of this, its longest song, and the one that brings it to conclusion, I think we should understand by its actual title that, when you revisit Highway 61 – that literal, not fictional, American highway, which bisects the entire United States, running from New Orleans in Louisiana to Thunder Bay in Ontario, and along which Dylan's birthplace of Duluth and hometown of Hibbing are situated – what you find in 1965 is Desolation Row: a place of transformation and instability where identities are misplaced, replaced, or forever lost in the ultimate loss that is death.

In the refrain of 'Tombstone Blues' the singer is characterised as the son in a dysfunctional family in which absence and loss are associated with the parents: the 'mama' has no shoes; the 'daddy' is 'lookin' for the fuse'. The singer-son does have something, but what he has he hardly wants: 'the tombstone blues'. The song moves through a surreal catalogue of historical, biblical and cinematic moments, in which various figures of American history and culture – from Paul Revere to Cecil B. DeMille and Ma Rainey – undergo nightmarish transformations and take part in bizarre little scenarios. This is what happens, we should understand, in the nightlife or unconscious of contemporary America when, as the opening line has it, 'The sweet pretty things are in bed now of course'.

The song's crazed comedy has, however, an insistent undertone of specific critique. The nightlife includes, for instance, John the Baptist:

Well, John the Baptist after torturing a thief
Looks up at his hero the Commander-in-Chief
Saying, 'Tell me, great hero, but please make it brief
Is there a hole for me to get sick in?'

The Commander-in-Chief answers him while chasing a fly
Saying, 'Death to all those who would whimper and cry'
And dropping a bar bell he points to the sky
Saying, 'The sun's not yellow, it's chicken'

The President of the United States is the Commander-in-Chief of the American Armed Forces, but John the Baptist's 'commander-in-chief' in the Gospels is, of course, Christ: so these lines have their blasphemous element. John the Baptist here is one of the several sadists who turn up on *Highway 61 Revisited*, a torturer apparently made sick by his own ingenuity, which he has perhaps perpetrated on one of the two thieves crucified with Christ. However sickened, though, he is obliged to take orders from a military commander who registers whimsical unconcern, while nevertheless letting it be known that death is the fate awaiting those who show cowardice. This macho aggressiveness is mocked both by John the Baptist's derisory, and camp, address to the 'great hero', and by the fact that the Commander is working out with bar bells which he cannot quite control. Yet it is also the force that rules this nightmare world, since, in that excellent joke, even the sun's colour, to one who sees the world so, is a register of its moral turpitude. Seeing a moral defect in a colour may be very much to the point here, as it is in 'The Lonesome Death of Hattie Carroll', since the next verse in the song continues the biblical and military *motif* like this:

> The king of the Philistines his soldiers to save
> Puts jawbones on their tombstones and flatters their graves
> Puts the pied pipers in prison and fattens the slaves
> Then sends them out to the jungle

It was of course black Americans who were once slaves, and it was also black Americans who died in a ratio far in excess of their percentage of the population in Vietnam's 'jungle'. This king of the Philistines – another presidential figure, like the Commander-in-Chief? – makes flattering speeches above the graves of the newly dead, but imprisons those who voice opposition – with a view to persuading others to do the same – and keeps in place an economic system which ensures the continuance of such servitude. 'Tombstone Blues' ransacks the formative texts of American culture in order to insinuate, rather than to make explicit, a judgement; and its satire is the more compelling for that. Outrage, and rage, are all in the ransack.[18]

In a song of 1965 called 'Tombstone Blues' such allegorical resonances are perhaps not so hard to overhear. Surely we should hear them too, though, in the portrayal of the 'graveyard woman' who is described and then addressed in 'From a Buick 6', a song whose rollicking, good-time blues sits extraordinarily uneasily with the grimness of its lyrics: so much so that Dylan should be regarded here as making irony virtually a principle of the formal relationship between music and lyrics:

> Well, you know I need a steam shovel mama to / keep
> away the dead
> I need a dump truck mama to / unload my head
> She brings me everything and more, and just like I said
> Well, if I go down dyin', you know she / bound to put a
> blanket on my bed.[19]

This could be the cry of a desolate urban junkie, I suppose, but surely it may also be the cry of a soldier anticipating an early death and praying for the bare minimum of comfort to accompany the moment (and, if so, the 'mama' might well be the actual mother rather than the lover). The strength of these lines is that they pit the minimal desire for a blanket on the dying bed against the overwhelming nature of the reality that must be coped with, which includes the hesitation about whether the blanket will actually be supplied: for to say that she is 'bound' to do it is not to be altogether convinced that she will; and that blanket assumes something of the pathos of the one that the Fool in *Lear* says has been uniquely 'reserved' for the outcast king – 'else we had all been shamed'.[20] The image of the dead so numerous that only a steam shovel might keep them away surely has, dreadfully, behind it those cinematic images of the Allies clearing the dead of Belsen into mass graves when they liberated the camp in 1945; and to have such a heavy load in one's head that only something as large as a dump truck can unload it is to be heavily burdened indeed. With what? With, we should presume, the deathly garbage, clutter and welter contained in the lyrics of *Highway 61 Revisited*, which at certain moments teeter into the utterly discomposed.

John the Baptist is about to get sick, and the woman addressed elsewhere on the album in 'Queen Jane Approximately' is imagined getting 'sick of all this repetition'. The cultural ransack that distinguishes *Highway 61 Revisited* is a kind of sick repetition too, revisiting characters, scenes and events and propelling them vertiginously into new combinations and modulations which carry oblique significance in relation to the contemporary American history that the singer is living through, and that many of his fellow American citizens are dying through. The title song itself is also a song sick of repetition and, specifically, of the repetition of the biblical narrative of Abraham and Isaac.[21]

In one of the great poems of the First World War, 'The Parable of the Old Man and the Young', Wilfred Owen makes a vitriolic parable out of the biblical story. In the original narrative in the book of Genesis (21: 1–19) God first instructs Abraham to slaughter his son but subsequently, proving it only a test of his obedience, tells him, through an angel, to leave Isaac alone and slaughter a lamb instead. For most of its course Owen's poem stays close to the biblical narrative, but in a devastating final couplet, spilling over the traditional fourteen lines of sonnet form, he has Abraham persist in his first instruction, disregarding God's new command. Abraham thereby becomes the representative of this son-slaying Europe in 1918: 'the old man would not so, but slew his son, / And half the seed of Europe, one by one.' 'Highway 61 Revisited' is another song in which, as in 'From a Buick 6', a kind of structural irony seems to operate in the discrepancy between the jaunty exhilaration of the music and the grimness of some of the lyrics.[22] It opens with Dylan's new transformation of the biblical tale:

> Oh God said to Abraham, 'Kill me a son'
> Abe says, 'Man, you must be puttin' me on'
> God say, 'No.' Abe say, 'What?'
> God say, 'You can do what you want Abe, but
> The next time you see me comin' you better run'
> Well Abe says, 'Where do you want this killin' done?'
> God says, 'Out on Highway 61.'

Dylan's dialogic wit here, making God a 'Man', makes him also a cross between a Mafia mobster addressing a minion and a careless farmer addressing a hand: 'kill me a son', not even 'your son' – as who should say, 'kill me a chicken', or, as the wacky farmer persona of 'Country Pie' on *Nashville Skyline* (1969) actually does say, 'Saddle me up a big white goose'. It also, perhaps, makes him a further presidential representative. Abe's demotic incredulity is quickly disciplined, however, into supine, self-protective capitulation by God's schoolyard threat, which is deliciously delayed across the enjambment ('but / The next time'), and God's tetchy aggression is also carried by the rhyming of 'what' and 'but' which, in Dylan's in-character pronunciation, is closer to a full- than to a half-rhyme. The capitulation, which is, we should remember, that of a father agreeing to kill his son –

and not just any old father (as though there were any such thing), but a biblical patriarch, *the* biblical patriarch – is insisted by the mildness of the question he asks: not why, which would be to ask for motivation and justification, but simply where. The effect is perfectly controlled formally by the way the verse rhymes, apart from its 'what/but' lines: a rhyme of *aaaaa* over five lines. This is a monotony or repetition indeed, in which mild demurral at the act of slaughtering your son already contains its own consent.[23]

This is a murderous Abraham morally depleted even beyond Wilfred Owen's. In Owen he is at least (as it were) satanically disobedient; in Dylan he is merely, and mechanically, servile. As is the culture itself in the song's final verse, where the blackness of the comedy satirises the capitulation of American political life to the collusion between commercial and military interest, but where the evocation of cynicism seems to go almost beyond satire into a kind of Swiftian or Popeian moral chaos:

> Now the rovin' gambler he was very bored
> He was tryin' to create a next world war
> He found a promoter who nearly fell off the floor
> He said I never engaged in this kind of thing before
> But yes I think it can be very easily done
> We'll just put some bleachers out in the sun
> And have it on Highway 61.

Throughout the song Dylan's ear for the patterns of American speech is very acute and his ability to convey them in dramatised verse dialogue is impressive. Here, the promoter's entrepreneurial speech opens into a chasm of amorality in which, whether you've engaged in it before or not, absolutely anything can be done – and, yes, very easily done. This is a nightmare of moral disengagement, and Dylan's satire has a very well-developed sense of what it wants to put an end to. Herbert Marcuse, in a remark he made in 1976, is alert to this element in Dylan but offers a more radical motive in it when he collocates Dylan and Brecht (we probably have to read the word 'revolution' more figuratively now than Marcuse intended):

> . . . we may find the meaning of revolution better expressed in Bertolt Brecht's most perfect lyrics than in his explicitly political polemics; or in Bob Dylan's most 'soulful' and deeply personal songs rather than in his propagandist mani-festos. Both Brecht and Dylan have one message: to make an end with things as they are. Even in the event of a total absence of political content, their works can invoke, for a vanishing moment, the image of a liberated world and the pain of an alienated one.[24]

'To make an end with things as they are' seems to me a good way of thinking about the intent of much of Dylan's work over its different phases. It may be particularly useful in thinking about *Highway 61 Revisited*, this most perfectly integrated of all his records, which wants to make an end of what America has made of itself in 1965. If we do indeed read the three albums of 1965 and 1966 as elements of a single creative trajectory, then we may also think that the pain of deathly alienation on *Highway 61 Revisited* is met 'for a vanishing moment' – the moment which is as long as the song lasts – by 'Mr Tambourine Man' on *Bringing It All Back Home* and 'Sad-Eyed Lady of the Lowlands' on *Blonde on Blonde*. The self-abandonment evoked as desire and possibility in the former and perhaps actually realised in the weird (even for Dylan) and in some ways hilarious, and never repeated, vocal styling of the latter are moments of rich ecstasy won only on the other side of a full contemplation of the poverty of things as they are. In those songs things as they are are changed on Bob Dylan's blue guitar.

4

Dylan's Christianity in the songs of the late 1970s and early 1980s is also inspired by the desire to make an end with things as they are; and his Christ is very much, if not exclusively, the eschatological Christ of Judgement and Apocalypse, the Christ of the Last Things. Nevertheless, it is to their credit that it is less the fear of death that appears the motivating factor for Dylan's conversion than his gratitude for life. 'Saving Grace' is explicit on the point in a way concrete enough to distress the faint-hearted ('By this time I'd a-thought that I would be sleeping / In a pine box for all eternity') and 'What Can I Do For You?' is a song of deeply acknowledging gratitude. Bryan Cheyette writes elsewhere in this collection about Dylan's religions, and I leave this aspect of my topic to him – with, I confess, some relief. Not that I am hostile to these songs: I am not, although I could wish for rather more of the gratitude and less of the reproof, which can seem merely self-righteous. However, I do find them less lyrically inventive and complex than the work of Dylan's that I most profoundly admire and return to. I want to close therefore with a glance at a recent song in which, as Dylan ages, thoughts of his own mortality increasingly preoccupy him, as they inevitably must all of us.

'Not Dark Yet' from *Time Out of Mind* (1997) has a beautifully plangent and elegant tune that allows the lyrics emphasis and space of a kind they richly merit. There is no ironic disproportion or discrepancy between words and music here, just a dedicated seriousness of address which is not, however, without its touches of humour; and Dylan's voice is deeply affecting: wise, tender and resigned. It is the appropriate mode for a contemplation, full-on, of that most personally distressing of all the things that an end must be made with: one's own mortal being. The song has a certain hymnal or anthemic quality, and is more solidly strophic in structure than some of Dylan's later songs, even though it is in fact written in verses of rhyming couplets. They work by setting up a metaphor in which life is the length of a day and the day is drawing to its close; and the metaphor has long traditional sanction, in poems which figure night and sleep as partners or images of death, as in, for instance, Shakespeare's sonnet 73 ('That time of year thou may'st in me behold'), where 'black night' is 'Death's second self'. In the day of 'Not Dark Yet', the singer records only a sense of constriction and desolation, an ultimately dejected disabusement, figured by the turning of his soul to steel, the carrying of scars that the sun won't heal, and the awkwardness of everywhere, as each of four verses, offering little epitomes of a life lived, culminates in the refrain 'It's not dark yet, but it's getting there'. A song about a heavy burden – 'Sometimes my burden seems more than I can bear' – it carries a heavy burden as its refrain. It is also a song deeply sick of all this repetition, and in this it reminds me of some of the late poems of Wallace Stevens, although the Dylan of 'Not Dark Yet' is of course younger than the Stevens who writes, for instance, 'It makes so little difference, at so much more / Than seventy, where one looks, one has been there before', in 'Long and Sluggish Lines'.

The song includes, in its second verse, an attenuated, oblique narrative of some particular distress in relationship, as many of Dylan's later songs do. This is evoked as the sending of a 'kind' letter to which the singer is nevertheless unable to respond feelingfully; and the song's generally contemplative melancholy is quickened by this poignancy. There are glimpses of earlier

Dylan songs in 'Not Dark Yet', as the singer reviews a life: the soul turned into steel, for instance, recalls the 'dreams . . . made of iron and steel' in 'Never Say Goodbye' on *Planet Waves* (1974); and this letter recalls other letters of a terminated relationship in Dylan, including the shipboard letter ending the affair in one of his most perfect songs, 'Boots of Spanish Leather':

> I got a letter on a lonesome day
> It was from her ship a-sailin'
> Saying I don't know when I'll be comin' back again,
> It depends on how I'm a-feelin' –

to which the singer responds with the probably self-deceivingly jaunty defiance of requesting from her, nevertheless, a pair of the eponymous boots. In 'Not Dark Yet' the singer is disconsolately far from such defiance: 'I just don't see why I should even care' is the register of a weariness beyond all effort or address, and isolatedly beyond any expectation of reciprocity. Even if it's not dark yet, the song is very dark indeed, and has certainly made an end with something vital. If human relationship has failed, so too, it appears, has a relationship with the divine. In fact, emphasising the lack of consolation available from prayer – even if Dylan's Christianity was never a religion much engaged in consolation – the song acts as a kind of anti-hymn:

> I was born here and I'll die here against my will
> I know it looks like I'm moving, but I'm standing still
> Every nerve in my body is so vacant and numb
> I can't even remember what it was I came here to get
>   away from
> Don't even hear a murmur of a prayer
> It's not dark yet, but it's getting there.

In this final verse it is really only the technical ingenuity with which Dylan delightfully, but very mournfully, manages the extremely long fourth line – a long and sluggish line, indeed – that keeps the song from the profoundest gloom. He can't even remember what it was, but experienced listeners to Dylan will certainly remember various other such instances of his ability to sustain, without faltering, extremely long lyrical lines against a melody: they are one of the hallmarks, one of the signatures. The technique always proposes that balance is being only very perilously maintained, and usually this is wittily or hilariously virtuoso: 'You know it balances on your head just like a mattress balances on a bottle of wine', for instance, in the buoyantly mimetic line of 'Leopard-Skin Pillbox Hat'. The long line in 'Not Dark Yet' has its lugubrious humour too, but the condition of both amnesia and anomie which it appears to describe suggests that balance is very close indeed to not being maintained at all; and the song thereby enacts performatively its strong sense of how hard it is to maintain poise in the face of mortality. The central metaphor and some of the imagery of 'Not Dark Yet' could be almost a writing against Newman's Victorian hymn 'Lead, Kindly Light':

> Lead, kindly Light, amid the encircling gloom,
> Lead thou me on!
> The night is dark, and I am far from home –
> Lead Thou me on!
> Keep Thou my feet; I do not ask to see
> The distant scene – one step enough for me.

Whereas some of Dylan's Christian songs, and some of what he said in interviews and from the stage around that time, seemed to constitute a sustained, rearguard assault on modernity, 'Not Dark

Yet' is profoundly in tune with modernity's anxieties, distresses and uncertainties in the face of death. It is not abject because its disillusionment is so certain as to constitute, itself, a kind of positive value: there is simply nothing that can be said in opposition to the feeling carried by the song, because the song deeply impresses on us the fact that this feeling cannot be other than it is. It is signed with a knowledge won from hard experience, and that experience constitutes this life and this writing. 'Not Dark Yet' is writing, and singing, in the face of death, under pressure but with what, for this listener, is, honestly, a fortifying honesty. And so the song is sung against death, and becomes a kind of company for its listeners, who might say to it, as 'Tears of Rage' from the Basement Tapes period says, with the honesty of complete simplicity:

> Come to me now, you know we're so alone
> And life is brief.

9

JOKERMAN

Susan Wheeler

Who came up with Alias? 'Alias what?' Kris Kristofferson as Billy the Kid asks, and Bob Dylan as butcher-turned-follower-of-the-man-who-was-so-free answers, 'Alias whatever you please.' The set of *Pat Garrett and Billy the Kid*[1] was chaotic under a stormy Peckinpah, and the writer, Rudolph Wurlitzer, saw much of his script hatcheted, after all. The moniker seems so apt for Dylan it's hard to believe he didn't propose it himself. He is the one who will write, 'You may call me Terry, you may call me Timmy, / You may call me Bobby, you may call me Zimmy, / You may call me R.J., you may call me Ray, / You may call me anything . . .'[2]

So I named my cat Alias. I vacuumed my mother's house in a state of empowered rage to, 'Well, she talks to all the servants / About man and God and law. / Everybody says / She's the brains behind pa. / She's sixty-eight but she says she's twenty-four.'[3] When the Commander-in-Chief pointed upward and said, 'The sun's not yellow it's chicken,'[4] I saw either George C. Scott in uniform or Katie Latoyah's dad. The sly jokes, the put-downs, the puns; the snarls, the goofs; the word riffs straight out of Dr Seuss: these were the pyrotechnics that cemented my Dylan allegiance for good. These were the evidence

175

of his trustworthiness; in the ballads and the love songs and the phantasmagoric indictments, the humor cemented the integrity.

For when Dylan makes jokes, they are not jokes *for* us or *on* us, but conjured for his own benefit. Humor seems to serve him as it does most of us, as a way of at once looking at, and not caving under, the worst. Many of Dylan's lyric jokes appear in the songs like private, giddy moments. 'Lonesome and blue,' a man calls the 'time operator / Just to hear a voice of some kind. / "When you hear the beep / It will be three o'clock." / She said that for over an hour / And I hung up.'[5] Son of the 'poor boy' in the traditional blues 'Poor Boy a Long Way from Home,' Dylan's 'Po' boy in the palace of gloom / Called down to room service, said "send up a room."'[6]

In writing about any aspect of Dylan, a fan runs the risk of becoming his *Tarantula* character, Scholar, 'his body held together by chiclets ... not even talking to anybody,'[7] and of course this is magnified when the subject is Dylan's *jokes*. 'What are your songs about?' *Playboy* magazine asked him in 1966. 'Oh, some are about four minutes; some are about five, and some, believe it or not, are about eleven or twelve.'[8]

Most of the jokes, and particularly the goofiest, are nothing on the page – little flecks in an absurdist cup of coffee. With Dylan's delivery, drawled or keened or barked, they're knee-slappers. Their sly tenor – their half-dumb, half-funny quality – gives us that glimpse of the riffing mind at work, like Sonny Rollins' improvised glissandos through the canon or Lenny Bruce's standup leaps. They also preserve a space for him to riff in; in the classic operation of a joke, they say *you expect oranges? I'll give you hammers*. For over forty years, they have helped him avoid any characterization of his work, even self-definition, which would limit in any way his arena.

Refusing to answer a Swedish journalist's question about

protest songs, moments later he notes that his new 'Rainy Day Women #12 & 35' was 'sort of a Mexican kind of thing, very protest, very, very protest and [one] of the pro-testiest of all things I've protested against in the protest years.'[9] A reporter in California asked him what was most important in his life. 'Well, I've got a monkey wrench collection,' he answered, 'and I'm very interested in that.'[10]

The standup humor he wielded, particularly early on, in press conferences and interviews – the 'dance' part, perhaps, of his self-description as 'song & dance man,' the white-face minstrel – set him up from the get-go as a slippery fellow: just when a journalist would get him on a line, he'd slip away. 'Wiggle to the front, wiggle to the rear, / Wiggle 'til you wiggle right out of here.'[11]

He was, by all reports, goofy from the beginning. He and his childhood friend, John Bucklen, invented a game they called *Glissendorf*. Around unsuspecting others, they enacted a kind of shaggy-dog conversation only to watch the bystanders' confusion. Dylan might say, for example, '"Say a word." Whatever answer Bucklen gave, Dylan replied: "Wrong word. I won."'[12]

He liked jokes and card tricks, and he named his first band – with his summer-camp cohorts Larry Kagan and Howard Rutman – *The Jokers*; his mother made them each sleeveless cardigans with the name embroidered on their chests. He played practical jokes. David Crosby and Dylan once spun an elaborate prank on P. F. Sloan, a lead-footed Dylan imitator and author of the song, 'Eve of Destruction.' Sloan was summoned to Dylan's hotel room where Dylan casually played for him the new acetates of *Highway 61 Revisited*. Suddenly David Crosby entered the suite, and Crosby and Dylan disappeared into the bedroom. Moments later, two topless women emerged from the bedroom, and sat silently on either end of the couch; they were followed by a man in a Zorro outfit swinging in through the window on a rope, who settled between them and stared at Sloan. Finally, after a quarter of an hour of silence, Zorro and the girls left the suite through the front door, and Dylan and Crosby came out of the bedroom as though nothing had happened.[13]

Anecdotes may resemble what actually happened, much as Dylan's mother's memory of his singing for the relatives at age five and finishing with a poised and funny quip may, too[14]; anyone who has seen recordings of his press conferences and interviews can be forgiven for thinking them fact. Just off the plane in the spring of 1965, in London, Dylan was greeted with a journalist's 'What is your message?' Putting a gigantic gag light bulb on the floor beside him, he grinned and answered, 'Always have a good head and carry a light bulb.'[15] *Dont Look Back* chronicles Dylan's evolution into a less genial subject; by the time he meets with a reporter for *Time* magazine, his frustration at misquotes and mischaracterizations results in a taunting interrogation. When he does answer a question, he can't not joke: 'I'm just as good a singer as Caruso,' Dylan says, 'and I can hold my breath three times as long.' Gag to scrappin' boast: put-on to put-down.

By December of the same year,[16] he had become adept at this improv comedy, both entertaining and putting his interlocutors in their place. It preserved that space around him in which he would not be restricted by definition or fixity, where he could maintain self-contradiction, a bit of Keats's negative capability. In this interview, among others, his infectious giddiness seems to spring from a sudden sense that he *could* control the pressures on him of an imposed reputation – that simply by joking and 'wiggling' he could in fact wiggle out of the noose (or, at least, collar) of a fixed aesthetic. Each answer, punctuated by an ebullient grin:

Q: Have you sold out to commercial interests by going electric?

A: [No.]

Q: If you *were* going to sell out to a commercial interest, which one would you choose?

A: Ladies' garments ...

Q: For those of us over thirty, what would you label yourself, and what do you see as your role?

A: I label myself as well under thirty, and my role is just to stay here as long as I can ...

Q: Who's Mr Jones?

A: I'm not going to tell you his first name, I'd get sued.

Q: What does he do?

A: He's a pinboy, he also wears suspenders ...

Q: What are your hopes for the future and what do you want to change?

A: I hope to have enough boots in order to change them.

The rimshot's audible at each turn. As a comedian in his interviews, his style was perhaps closest to Lenny Bruce, about whom he later wrote a tribute song, and who said, in Dylan fashion, 'I am not a comedian' and 'I am what I am.' With his own interlocutors, Bruce could also deflect what he considered extraneous or hackneyed questions. 'I get my inspiration from wheat germ,' he replied to Steve Allen. 'A bowl in the morning?' 'No, I smoke it.'[17]

But Bruce died, as the comedian Phil Spector put it, 'from an overdose of police.'[18] Dylan neither took on, nor – like Bruce – was he forced into, a crusade that would align him with one side of a particular policy issue (excepting Hurricane Carter's release). A San Francisco interviewer asked Dylan if he was planning any demonstrations. Yes, he said, getting excited. He was planning one in which a group of protesters would carry cards that he would have made up, cards with pictures of, say, 'the jack of diamonds, the ace of spades, mules ...' and some with just words, 'words like camera, microphone, loose – just words. I'd have thousands printed up and we'd just picket.' There was something of the merry prankster in the glee.

The jokes in his songs have used satire (the John Bircher 'investigated all the people that I knowed / Ninety-eight percent of 'em gotta go'[19]); wordplay and puns (naked, he's 'huntin' bare',[20] and Brigitte Bardot would 'make the country grow'[21]); pastiches of rhetorical forms (advice, for example, in 'Walk on your tip toes / Don't try "No Doz"'[22]); slapstick ('I took a deep breath / I fell down, I could not stand.'[23]); understatement ('The man was ravin' about how he loved m' sound; / Dollar a day's worth.'[24]) and hyperbole ('You cut me like a jigsaw puzzle, / You made me to a walkin' wreck, / Then you pushed my heart through my backbone, / Then you knocked my head off of my neck.'[25]); plays on clichés ('Somebody could freeze right to the bone. / I froze right to the bone.'[26]); sly jokes ('You say my eyes are pretty and my smile is nice / Well, I'll sell it to ya at a reduced price'[27]); sarcasm ('Why would I want to take your life? / You've only murdered my father, raped his wife, / Tattooed my babies with a poison pen, / Mocked my God, humiliated my friends.'[28]); and slurs-by-rhyme ('you're way wrong' and 'Erica Jong'[29]). There's a nod to standup, too, in jokes like 'Summer Days'' 'Well, my back has been to the wall for so long,' – and we hear *how long*? – 'it seems like it's stuck.'

Some of the jokes are straight out of Robert Johnson and Charley Patton, out of the blues, what Constance Rourke called the 'smothered satire' of the 'Negro tradition,' drawn upon by nineteenth-century minstrelsy.[30] The conceit of an airplane unfurls in Robert Johnson's 'Terraplane Blues':

I even flash my lights, mama
this horn won't even blow
Got a short in this connection
hoo-well, babe, it's way down below . . .

Now, you know the coils ain't even buzzin'
little generator won't get the spark
Motor's in bad condition, you gotta have
these batteries charged
But I'm cryin', please
please don't do me wrong
Who been drivin' my Terraplane now for
you since I been gone[31]

For the hard-livin' man's man, Dylan moves from car to construction:

I got eight carburetors, boys I'm using 'em all
Well, I got eight carburetors and boys, I'm using 'em all
I'm short on gas, my motor's starting to stall

My dogs are barking, there must be someone around
My dogs are barking, there must be someone around
I got my hammer ringin', pretty baby, but the nails ain't
    goin' down[32]

The boll weevil's sly retorts to farmers' questions identify
the sly worker with the singer in Charley Patton's 'Mississippi
Boweavil Blues,' and elsewhere Patton has to 'hitch up my
buggy and saddle up my black mare.' Little Walter Jacobs,
in a word-happy and a mighty misogynist punning, sings, 'I
thought I'd treated my baby fair, / Now she's getting up in

my hair. / If I get her in my sights / Boom, boom, out go the lights.'[33] O. V. Wright brags, 'Ace of spades, baby that's me' but sheepishly demurs with 'ace of diamonds is something every woman craves.'[34]

Dylan, listening in Minnesota to his scrounged recordings and late-night Little Rock broadcasts, got that these jokes were not for 'The Tonight Show' or the Catskills, but rather slid in their sly ways under the pop culture's wire to reach a *local* audience. If any aspect of Dylan's humor works to undermine the glib comedy of television it is this vernacular, made oppositional only by its lack of interest in the dominant culture.

Deadpan is an aspect of Yankee drollery, in Rourke's terms, but it also plays a role in the 'smothered satire' of the blues. (Rourke's work, known as the foundation text of cultural studies, identified three archetypes of American humor: the western backwoodsman and his hyperbolic yarns; the Yankee, who used figural language and an understated delivery in his monologues; and the black face of the white man in minstrelsy, a practice – as Sean Wilentz discusses elsewhere in this volume – risen out of both racism and envy.) 'The humorous story is American, the comic story is English, the witty story is French. The humorous story depends for its effect upon the *manner* of telling; the comic story and the witty story upon the matter,' Mark Twain wrote.

The humorous story is told gravely; the teller does his best to conceal the fact that he even dimly suspects that there is anything funny about it. The humorous story is strictly a work of art, high and delicate art, and only an artist can tell it; but no art is necessary in telling the comic and witty story, anybody can do it.[35]

Dylan's deadpan makes mock-praise like 'Well, if I go down

dyin', you know she bound to put a blanket on my bed'[36] funny. The eternal return of the gum in 'Fourth Time Around'[37] – first as adolescent (or Chaplinesque) gallantry, then as shaggy-dog corker, always deadpanned – makes the lover's quarrel funny. Just as Bukka White could sing about the greasy pillowcase he saves as a fetish after the 'Vaseline Head Woman' leaves, Dylan can take on any role and play it for laughs as long as he stays in character.

These characters catch the American idiom with an ear akin to Robert Frost's or James Tate's. Masquerade, in Rourke's schema, came naturally to the Yankee peddler as well as to the minstrel, and took on anthropomorphic dimensions with the earthy backwoodsman. Mimicry provides the destabilizing thrill of seeing or hearing the familiar evoked in the strange, and Dylan's portraits can be immediate and full, like red-haired Ruby on Henry Porter's wrecking lot outside of Amarillo, 'in the backyard hanging clothes'; it is her speech that gives us *Ruby*. '"Welcome to the land of the living dead,"' Ruby says. '"Even the swap meets around here are getting pretty corrupt."'[38]

In 'Highway 61 Revisited,' as Neil Corcoran has pointed out elsewhere in this volume, by his diction alone God is characterized as a cross between a mobster and a farmer. Throughout the song, every character gets his or her particular timbre, each moment of vocal mimicry following in swift succession on the last, until one sleazy pile-up in the person of the 'promoter.' The thief Mack the Finger (rimshot) enumerates his haul, and asks Louie the King (Louis XIV? – or if God with Abe is the mobster, is this God incarnate?), 'Do you know where I can get rid of these things?' Louie the King evokes the *patron* with: 'Let me think for a minute son.'

The fussily aligned 'fifth daughter on the twelfth night' confides to her 'first father' her troubles in perfectly enunciated elocution. 'My complexion is much too white.' The paternal voice here is domestic: 'Come here and step into the light ... Hmm you're right.' Georgia Sam, vagrant on the lam, urges 'poor Howard' to hurry up and give him directions: 'Tell me quick man I got to run,' the lingo of a small-time hustler. Finally, the 'promoter' recovers his shock at being asked to promote 'a next world war' with the silky language of a business deal: 'I never engaged in this kind of thing before, / But yes, I think it can be very easily done. / We'll just ...' Drawn here as types, the characters manifest their differences by way of their speech in as few as six words, and the quick-change artistry of the song's mimicry gives the parodies a frenetic hilarity. Elsewhere, Dylan is able to capture duplicity in a suffix, with a gladhander's claiming he loves 'all kinds-a people.[39] And even Jesus gets to use an American vernacular: 'Well, I'm gonna baptize you in fire so you can sin no more.'[40]

In songs like 'Tiny Montgomery' and 'Ballad of Donald White,' Dylan developed more extended personae; on the recent '*Love and Theft*' (2001), the device suffuses the collection. The persona of 'Po' Boy'[41] is a down-on-his-luck simple fellow, and to him Dylan gives sweet, almost child-like jokes. There is the 'Palace of Gloom / send up a room' joke, but also the knock-knock joke ('Knockin' on Heaven's Door?'):

Knockin' on the door. I say, 'Who is it and where are you from?'
Man says, 'Freddy!' I say, 'Freddy who?' He says, 'Freddy or not here I come.'

The 'Poor boy' refrains seem to be spoken by a more worldly benefactor, and this may be the voice that tells this joke, its cynicism foregrounding the simplicity of the others:

Othello told Desdemona, 'I'm cold, cover me with a blanket.
By the way, what happened to that poison wine?'
She said, 'I gave it to you, you drank it.'

In addition to his economy with mimicry, some lines are
packed with hidden narratives that burst from their confines
like jacks-in-the-box. 'I moved in with two girls from South
Dakota in a two-room apartment for two nights,' the unrecorded
'poem,' 'My Life in a Stolen Moment,'[42] goes. 'Rita May, Rita
May, You got your body in the way,' he sings on the flip side
of the single 'Stuck Inside of Mobile with the Memphis Blues
Again.'[43]

His verbal play finds antecedents in other kinds of popular
song. The verbal pyrotechnics of Cole Porter and Ira Gershwin
haunt passages like this one from 'Tiny Montgomery':

> Scratch your dad
> Do that bird
> Suck that pig
> And bring it on home
> Pick that drip
> And bake that dough
> Tell 'em all
> That Tiny says hello[44]

Compare this with a passage from 'Here Come the Drum
Majorettes!' by another poet drawing on musical theater, James
Fenton:

> Gleb meet Glubb.
> Glubb meet Glob.

God that's glum, that glib Glob dig.
'Dig that bog!'
'Frag that frog.'
'Stap that chap, he snuck that sig.'[45]

In 'Tiny Montgomery,' the lightness inherent in a two-beat line and the vowel-rhyming fashion a minstrel's performance, much as the giants of musical theater drew on their own apprehensions of black popular song. But both Dylan's and Fenton's lyrics turn the elegant, urbane phrasing of Gershwin or Fry on its head, resulting in the disruption of the standard form. Charles Bernstein describes this operation as:

acting out . . . the insincerity of form as much as content. Such poetic play does not open into a neat opposition of dry high irony and wet lyric expressiveness but, in contrast, collapses into a more destabilizing field of pathos, the ludicrous, shtick, sarcasm; a multidimensional textual field that is congenitally unable to maintain an evenness of surface tension or a flatness of affect . . .[46]

Historically, the tradition of the 'Talking Blues' mixes the kit and the kaboodle: the 'ludicrous, shtick, sarcasm,' but also the tall tale of Rourke's backwoodsman, and her Yank's fables. In Woody Guthrie's 'Talking Dust Bowl,' the slapstick and the tall tale depend upon the timing.

Way up yonder on a mountain road,
I had a hot motor and a heavy load.
I was going pretty fast, I wasn't even stopping,
A-bouncing up and down like a popcorn popping.
Had a breakdown, a sort of nervous bustdown of some kind.

> There was a fellow there, a mechanic fellow, said it was
> engine trouble.[47]

The unrhymed, halting speech of the last run-on line uses under-statement to anchor the hyperbole of that speedy, hyperbolic 'like popcorn popping.' The misnamed intensifiers, 'pretty' and 'even,' keep the assertions from being wholly fixed, wholly final. (The lack of American words' finality is a distinction of the American vernacular, according to Christopher Ricks in his essay, 'American English and the Inherently Transitory,' in which he discusses Dylan in the context of Ed Dorn's assertion that 'No particular word is apt to be final.'[48]) The speaker in 'Talking Dust Bowl' gives

> . . . that rolling Ford a shove,
> And I was going to coast as far as I could.
> Commenced coasting; picking up speed; was a hairpin
> turn; I . . . didn't make it.

Although the comic – the events, and how they happened – seems to be the emphasis in this tale, the way the tale is told is crucial: the short phrases that ratchet up the apprehension, and the caesura before the outcome is released. Then the hyperbole takes over:

> Man alive, I'm a-telling you
> The fiddles and the guitars really flew.
> That Ford took off like a flying squirrel
> And it flew halfway around the world.
> Scattered wives and childrens all over the side of that mountain.

In his first appearances and albums, Dylan used talking blues to target the funnybone, and he learned from Guthrie's mix of hyperbole and deflation just how to keep the ball in the air. In 'Talking Bear Mountain Picnic Massacre Blues' (1962), based on an event in the news, Dylan describes the huckstering of a picnic up-river, the boat overselling and overflowing its capacity:

> That old ship sinkin' down in the water,
> Six thousand people tryin' t'kill each other,
> Dogs a-barkin', cats a-meowin', [pastiche on the clichéd
>   use of a- as verb prefix]
> Women screamin', fists a-flyin', babies cryin',
> Cops a-comin', me a-runnin'.
> Maybe we just better call off the picnic.

A forerunner of Po' Boy, he has his 'head busted, stomach cracked, / Feet splintered, I was bald, naked . . . [pause: *timing*] / Quite lucky to be alive though.'

In 'Talkin' World War III Blues,' his speaker propositions a girl, but the rube, often a talking blues' protagonist, is done in by the logic of the *chick*:

> 'Let's go play Adam and Eve.'
> I took her by the hand and my heart it was thumpin'
> When she said, 'Hey man, you crazy or sumpin'
> You see what happened last time they started.'

A song that seems to grow out of talking blues, 'Motorpsycho Nitemare' (1964), spins its own tall tale about finding lodging at a farmhouse where he is warned from touching the farmer's daughter. When she comes on to him, he finds the only way out is to yell, 'I like Fidel Castro and his beard,' bringing the wrath of the farmer down on him. In a slapstick scene, the farmer lobs a

Reader's Digest (that quintessential American middlebrow read) at his head and goes for his rifle; the giddy speaker is 'thankful as I romp / Without freedom of speech, I might be in the swamp.' His arrival in America, with Captain Ahab, in 'Bob Dylan's 115th Dream,' launches a sea of absurd events that career between the rube's seventeenth-century expectations and the mid-twentieth-century world he finds. Ahab wants to '"set up a fort and start buying the place with beads"' when suddenly a cop jails them 'for carryin' harpoons'.

Dylan allows the John Bircher in 'Talkin' John Birch Paranoid Blues' to portray paranoia so comically and with such sympathetic pluck that we find the indicted has already given himself his just desserts. As his fear over Communists coming overtakes him, the speaker looks for them high and low, finds Eisenhower to be 'a Russian spy' as well as Lincoln, Jefferson and 'that Roosevelt guy.' By the song's end he's confined to investigating himself. 'Hope I don't find out anything . . . hmm, great God!' The speaker being as fallible as the next person figured both in minstrelsy and burlesque, and some of Dylan's best jokes implicate himself:

> Well, lookit here buddy
> You want to be like me
> Pull out your six-shooter
> And rob every bank you can see
> Tell the judge I said it was all right.
> Yes![49]

Acknowledging he is fallible, however, doesn't mean the sin of pride in others needs go unacknowledged. It's in his vitriol, his Catullan slurs, that Dylan's humor is perhaps most important, coming as it did before punk, or heavy metal, or even The

Beatles had put a musical stamp on anger. Worthy targets are the high-handed, the self-serving, the self-deluded, and the insincere. Maggie's brother patronizes you with small change and small talk, but 'he fines you every time you slam the door.'

The 'Man of Peace' (1983), like the corrupt sweet-talker in 'Moonlight' is

> . . . a great humanitarian, he's a great philanthropist,
> He knows just where to touch you, honey, and how you
>   like to be kissed.
> He'll put both his arms around you,
> You can feel the tender touch of the beast.

By contrast, the Mr Joneses are portrayed more as buffoons than deserving of venom. In 'Don't Fall Apart on Me Tonight' (1983),

> What about that millionaire with the drumsticks in his pants?
> He looked so baffled and bewildered
> When he played and we didn't dance.

Those that need a weathervane can still look at those who don't with envy. Dylan acknowledges this with some sympathy. But with those who cannot recognize a universe alternate to their own, and who have sewn up the good deeds in it to boot, Dylan is merciless. The hypocritical bring out rancor, and good jokes:

> Yes, I wish that for just one time
> You could stand inside my shoes
> You'd know what a drag it is
> To see you.[50]

A special scorn is reserved for his protagonists' ex-lovers. The 'gal' in 'Hero Blues' (1966) wants him to 'walk out running' and 'crawl back dead,' just so long as he is a hero, and there's a giddy snarl in 'Leopard-Skin Pillbox Hat' (1966):

> Well, I see you got a new boyfriend
> You know, I never seen him before
> Well, I saw him
> Makin' love to you
> You forgot to close the garage door

Rancor is the apt response to the ennui of their new beaux: 'Yes, you, you just sit around and ask for ashtrays, can't you reach?'[51]

The vitriolic jokes give us pleasure; they transgress, as Lenny Bruce's jokes transgressed; they articulate the responses we do not articulate because of our fear, our speed, our courtesy; they claim a freedom in their making of hatred and anger a *quip*. And they entertain. Mo, Hardy, Groucho – each of them could wither with a quip, and the comedian that is Dylan balances the sly humor in 'I been in trouble ever since I set my suitcase down,' in 'Mississippi' with a word to Missus Henry in the men's room: 'Now don't crowd me, lady, or I'll fill up your shoe.'

10

HIGHWAY 61 AND OTHER AMERICAN STATES OF MIND

Richard Brown

Is anything central?
Orchards flung out on the land,
Urban forests, rustic plantations, knee-high hills?
Are place names central?

John Ashbery, 'The One Thing That Can Save America'

The American mystery deepens.

Don DeLillo, *White Noise*

In an *oeuvre* as extensive, diverse and axiomatically self-contradictory as Bob Dylan's, the naïve readerly search for reductive kinds of significance or 'message' has typically been frustrated by a series of playful enigmatic turns which define the authorial intention as provocatively evasive or perverse. As Aidan Day has pointed out in his readings of 'Mr Tambourine Man' and 'Jokerman', Dylan's lyrics construct an author-reader relation posited on the model of an irresolvable enigma which is both the incitement to and the perpetual frustration of readerly desire.[1] Both the increasing proliferation and the celebrated indeterminacy of Dylan's lyrics seem to insist that 'something is happening' in a bohemian counter-cultural sense even though the 'Mr Jones' who may want to track this 'something' is, presumably, by now terminally condemned to the fixed condition of not knowing 'what it is'.

Deprived of stabilities or of consistencies, readers of Dylan often work to construct narratives of his stylistic trajectory characterised by a series of revivals interspersed with unexpected swerves or even reversals of certain intellectual positions, manners of performance and audience expectation. The paradigm begins with the shift in gears from the protest folk song acoustic mode to the three more contemporary, more performative electric albums of the middle 1960s (*Bringing It All Back Home*, *Highway 61 Revisited* and *Blonde on Blonde*), and (after the 1966 motorcycle accident) to the slower, apparently less energetically self-deconstructive mode of *John Wesley Harding*, *Nashville Skyline* and *Self-Portrait*, then to the intense emotional upheaval in the Seventies revival of *Planet Waves*, *Blood on the Tracks*, *Desire* and *Street-Legal*, veering again in the conversion phase of the later Seventies, before backing into the Eighties revivals of *Infidels*, *Knocked Out Loaded* and the designer Dylan of *Oh Mercy*, the digressions of the early Nineties folk and children's song covers and the latest revival to date that we may find in *Time Out of Mind* (1997) and '*Love and Theft*' (2001). It is however in the very nature of the complex paradoxical discourse of Dylan's lyrics for such narratives to be unstable, for their implied oppositions to be at least apparently already resolved and for their projected future movements or conclusions to have already been anticipated or (as Jacques Derrida has said of James Joyce) 'signed in advance' by Dylan.

Since the Sixties, Dylan's work has grown up with and partially outgrown the procrustean bed of mass popular musical culture and spread easily across the collapsing borders between supposedly 'high' and 'low' cultural forms, from 'The Times They Are

A-Changin'' (1965) to 'Things Have Changed' (1999). The struggle of the critical reader to celebrate and somehow accommodate – let alone communicate – this flood of symptomatic cultural indeterminacy can itself become a defining intellectual pursuit of the contemporary. Boundaries of cultural legitimation have changed to the extent that (as his audience of the Sixties and Seventies become the poets and professors of the Nineties and 00s) those who are attacked in Dylan's early work as figures of cultural authority can now become increasingly exhausted travellers in his polysemantic wake.

I want to argue that an exploration of the represented spaces of Dylan's lyrics (of which his naming of particular American places forms a part) can lead us into and through these phases (selecting from the 1960s, the 1970s and then some more recent work) in a way that may avoid at least some of the worst pitfalls of narrative reductionism. In Dylan's lyrics we can see space as a territorial marker and as an aspect of the symbolic language in which reference to specific geographical place is accompanied by a more metaphorical idiom that speaks as much to subjective states as to physical ones, in a discourse that lodges legitimately within the defining cultural and political discourses of modern American literature.[2] His songs mark places that can also be a time or times in history: a landscape of the 1960s, for example,[3] or of the whole of the later part of the last century with several of its typical intellectual concerns. They also map a landscape of the self and a landscape of desire.

Dylan's lyrics draw what is inevitably a social and political space and so they can also be approached through the work of such French theorists of social space as Henri Lefèbvre, Michel Foucault and Michel de Certeau.[4] They construct an implicit representation of the American polis of the modern or post-modern world that is itself already partly a national and partly an international space. His cultural production, it may be argued, 'polices' the experiences of political subjectivity in this national and international space and the 'edges', borders or faultlines between the legitimate and the illegitimate that it inscribes. In this it works as assiduously as (and perhaps even more insidiously than) the cops or guards or figures of authority or else the many outlawed or morally ambiguous figures who populate his work. His songs deploy symbolic locations that serve to define the northern, eastern, western and southern borders of that imaginary polis and its characteristic conditions of perpetual motion as a mode of being. They mark the borders between freedom and constraint and between reason and unreason that it continually maps and re-maps.

Dylan's 'roadmaps for the soul' typically mark conditions of transition and becoming as well as points of location, and these conditions are independently observed in his work and yet can also be seen to be mediated by an extensive literary and cinematic cultural inheritance or intertextuality. In this they don't sacrifice originality or authenticity so much as enter a critical dialogue with the post-modern world and its phenomena of mediatedness by spectacle and simulacrum.

The lyrics speak universally but create a representation of the American polis in the second half of the twentieth century whose freshness, comedy and mimetic viability rival that of almost any literary contemporary. Despite Michael Gray's suggestion that Dylan's songs proliferate with place names less, for instance, than those of Chuck Berry,[5] they resonate with the distinctive toponomastic poetry of the United States with its distinctive blend of borrowed European and Native American vocabularies and with its sweeping distances 'from the Golden Gate / To Rockefeller Plaza 'n' the Empire State' and not just in those songs (like 'Dusty Old Fairgrounds' or 'Wanted Man') which attempt to reflect the plethora of American places with a list. Dylan's work is both distinctively American and distinctively global in its remit and in its points of departure. He speaks out of an 'Okie' (jokey and then increasingly croakey) middle American vernacular voice but lodges with Tennyson on the Isle of Wight, complains of the 'neighbourhood' bullying of the Middle East, may be an Ambassador to England or France, has a belt buckle from the Amazon, dances cheek to cheek in Mozambique and comes live from Budokan.

If, as my title and opening explanation suggest, I focus here on this Americanness, it is not just to ground him within a particular nation – albeit one of the most global of modern nations – or even to lock him within the imaginary museum of twentieth-century Americana. Post-modern America can itself be seen to be a primary site of semantic instability, an inner as well as an outer journey, and this is neatly suggested in Dylan's own jokey narrative *fab*ulation (in part a lyric squib on the national epic *Moby Dick*), 'Bob Dylan's 115th Dream', where the narrator, arriving on the *Mayflower* to find a very contemporary urban chaos, announces: 'I think I'll call it America' and departs just as Columbus makes his anachronistic arrival.[6]

Dylan's lyrics both name and re-name America as a national, political, psychological and historical space in ways that are as richly polysemic as the place and the times they name; and I choose the American motif not least as an attempt to celebrate the fact (to borrow Samuel Beckett on James Joyce) that in another way they *are* that America itself.

TALKIN' NEW YORK

In songs of the early and mid-1960s Dylan's lyric idiom mixes with the predominantly rural setting of the folk and protest song a new urban location that talks in and of New York. This rural–urban mixture grows towards the rich and complex poetic idiom of certain key songs that chart a surreal beat-inspired landscape of the Sixties and which can be especially interesting as we see their represented locations mediated through an intertextual frame.

Of *The Times They Are A-Changin'* Dylan has said, 'These songs were all written in the New York atmosphere.'[7] He refers to 'the cafés and all the talk in the dingy parlours' that made up the music scene of the Greenwich Village of the 1960s of which he briefly became the best-known product and symbol. However, in strictly numeric terms, the majority of the songs released on the first four albums and the larger repertoire he could perform at the time don't feature the New York urban landscape anything like so much as they do a variety of actual or symbolic Southern, Northern, Wild West (or occasionally West Coast), but more typically non-specific rural American locations that are identified with their social protest themes. These include the landscape of Dylan's youth, of Hibbing and Minnesota in 'North Country Blues', the South Dakota farm of Hollis Brown, the racially divided South of the 'poor white' who has shot Medgar Evers, though he is only a 'pawn' in the game of privileged whites like William Zanzinger of 'The Lonesome Death of Hattie Carroll'. This is the insular and self-justified small-town America of the period whose prejudices Dylan so powerfully satirises in 'With God on Our Side', an America whose attitudes are in the process of overdue change, a place of many old prejudices to be challenged and overturned; but it is also the location of an authentic America that the songs seek partly to endorse and reveal. In 'Bob Dylan's Blues' on *The Freewheelin' Bob Dylan* he invokes the country/city distinction as a way of legitimating the song because it was not written 'uptown' in Tin Pan Alley but in an unnamed non-specific location 'somewhere down in the United States'.

Freewheelin' has a similar mix of locations. There is Oxford Town (where the first black student attempted to gain entry to the University of Mississippi), Hibbing again as the north country of 'The Girl from the North Country'. There is the surreal urban space of 'Talkin' World War III Blues', but also the symbolic locations visited by the 'blue-eyed son' of 'A Hard Rain's A-Gonna Fall' and the symbolic landscape of roads and seas and the moving air which links and transcends them in 'Blowin' in the Wind'. On *Bob Dylan* the authenticating rural locations include that of 'Gospel Plow' and the three death-centred blues songs, the Colorado of 'Man of Constant Sorrow', the 'boomer shack' in Dixie of 'Freight Train Blues', and intriguingly in 'Pretty-Peggy-O' a place called Fenario, the place that Dylan admits is a place he's 'been around this whole country' but never yet found. Fenario may be a symbolic mask or analogy for the relative anonymity of his own home town but at any rate neatly confirms the suggestion of the symbolic role of the non-specific rural place as a type of the nation. Another recurrent location of the period is New Orleans in 'The House of the Rising Sun' and in 'Bob Dylan's New Orleans Rag', where it appears as a site of Bakhtinian carnival as well as sexual exploitation and spiritual waste or despair.

As interesting are the songs on these albums which begin to define a characteristic location that isn't so much a place of stasis as a state of motion. This seems to chime in not just with the life of the itinerant worker or musician but, increasingly, with the condition of the newly leisured, newly mobile rootless beat generation of the 1950s and 60s. In the key text of the era, Jack Kerouac's *On the Road*, the narrator Sal Paradise and his friend Dean Moriarty 'cross and re-cross' (east and west, north and south) the spaces of the nation, linking up its listed place names in a journey that becomes its own bohemian *zeitgeist* and *raison d'être*.[8] There are, of course, trains whose noises recur in the discourse of the blues song but it is the highways that predominate. Dylan's explicit 'highway' songs on these albums include 'Standing on the Highway', 'Down the Highway' and 'Highway 51', though the songs are typically full of roads, streets and highways and of journeys to and from that give the impression of perpetual motion from place to place and from relationship to relationship as a condition of being.

In Dylan's developing lyric discourse, 'roads' often stand for symbolic journeys, 'streets' are entrapping urban thoroughfares and 'highways' are long-distance routes that are places of relative freedom linking towns and cities physically distant from one another but often uncanny reproductions of each other in character and typical of American space. According to de Certeau, who is amused to find that in modern Athens buses and trains are called *metaphorai*, all writings are journeys. The highways form a dominant spatial metaphor in Dylan's lyric discourse at this stage and the whole population, it seems, is moving onto them; he says 'Your streets are gettin' empty, Lord/ Your highways gettin' filled'. In *My Life in a Stolen Moment*, Dylan frames himself in a Kerouacian tour of the nation repeatedly escaping from Hibbing (the 'town' of his upbringing) at '10, 12, 13, 15, 15$^{1/2}$, 17 an' 18' to the highways of America '61–51–75–169–37–66–22'.[10]

Though they may be in the numerical minority, it was the addition of material set in New York as well as Dylan's special modernistic persona of self-presentation that helped make his early songs more than the expectations of their genre. These songs represented the physical spaces of New York and the city seems almost to speak itself in their talking blues idiom. As Robert Shelton's acute liner notes explain, the novelty of Dylan's juxtaposition of his predominantly rural folk and protest song discourse with this urban location and the hinted performativity of the singer's comic Chaplinesque immigrant persona work together to produce the effect here.[11] 'Talkin' New York' is given pride of place on the first album, *Bob Dylan*. It dramatises the plight of the dead-beat singer, recently arrived from the 'wild West', who soon despairs of the exploitative city and is now leaving to go back West. The humour of the song emerges from the simplicity of its observations – 'People goin' down to the ground / Buildings goin' up to the sky' – and its ironic contrast between mystification and reality: '*New York Times* said it was the coldest winter in seventeen years; / I didn't feel so cold then' and 'The man there said he loved m' sound … Dollar a day's worth' and the hint of surreality in overworked performance: 'I blowed inside out an' upside down'. It also has a strikingly sharp underside in its social protest: 'they got a lot of forks 'n' knives, / And they gotta cut somethin'.'[12] This is in turn ironically undercut with a simple place name as the singer's bold gesture of flight back to the West founders in the humbling contingency of New Jersey: 'So long, New York, / Howdy, East Orange.' New Jersey is a wrong-side-of-the-tracks location he returns to, memorably, for instance, in 'Hurricane' and in 'Tweeter and the Monkey Man'.

New York songs from the early period include 'Hard Times in New York Town', 'Talkin' World War III Blues' (where the singer pauses to light a cigarette on a burning post-nuclear parking meter), the Chaplinesque 'Bob Dylan's Blues', 'Spanish Harlem Incident' and above all 'Subterranean Homesick Blues', which announces the new electronic Dylan of *Bringing It All Back Home* with a symptomatically urban, fast-talking and elusive picture of life in an alternative or underground society. This song, especially as performed by the singer in an urban scene with punning accompanying captions in *Dont Look Back*, seems to have much in common with the Bakhtinian notion of the carnivalesque or Michel Foucault's idea of a 'heterotopia' where the orders of syntax that govern reality are temporarily suspended in new forms of discourse.[13]

The sharpness of these observations of the urban location and the democratic, resistive quality of Dylan's comedy of satiric vulnerability gradually takes over from the more sober issue-based protest idiom and begins to speak more widely to the alienation of the young and the suburbs. What's more, Dylan's comic voice, especially, for instance, in 'I Shall Be Free' and 'I Shall Be Free No. 10', speaks of the new suburban world of the 1960s with its 'average, common' strained consumer affluence and anonymity and its weird compensating media icons of political and cultural significance such as John F. Kennedy, Brigitte Bardot, Cassius Clay and Barry Goldwater. It is a world governed by advertising and also by the cross-over between image and reality where the singer talks to the media image of Kennedy on the telephone, makes love to the screen persona of Elizabeth Taylor and shadow-boxes, at least in rhyme, with the good-looking boxer of the television age Cassius Clay, and where the logic of the media image (Mr Clean) produces the madness of reality (his great granddaughter, the 'funniest woman I ever seen'). The *ingénu* is excluded from the tennis club but parades his alternative lifestyle at the Omaha country club and golf course as if these symbols of middle-class affluence are all there is to be freed from or into. Entitling the second song 'I Shall Be Free No. 10' suggests not so much eight missing intervening songs as a discourse of complaint that is endlessly revisitable. In the gospel manner the singer's demand for freedom can be endlessly repeated because it is never fully attainable. It names a permanent condition of the 1960s that is mitigated only by the mixture of the celebratory in its satirical comedy.

Fascinating symbolic spaces which map out psychic or ideological reality such as the 'edges' of 'My Back Pages' occur in the songs on *Another Side of Bob Dylan*. On the other hand, what distinguishes the return of the representative non-specific rural location in its comic version in 'Motorpsycho Nitemare' on this album is not just the comedy but also the fact that the symbolic space is mediated through a comic parody of the Hitchcock film. In a sense then, Dylan's America can be approached as already having something of the quality of what Don DeLillo calls (in his novel of that name) *Americana* – places whose significance is second-hand in the sense that they are places that have become interesting because they have been thought to be interesting. DeLillo's classic example of this is the tourists who line up to photograph 'the most photographed barn in America' in *White Noise*.[14]

THE LANDSCAPE OF THE SIXTIES

This mix of symbolic mapping and mediation is already embedded in Dylan's mature lyric discourse by the time of the songs on *Bringing It All Back Home*, *Highway 61 Revisited* and *Blonde on Blonde*. The subtly figured psychic places of 'My Back Pages' are translated into the artistic mental journey in 'Mr Tambourine Man' and the spatial metaphors for the ambiguously welcomed fallen condition that we get in 'Gates of Eden': a condition of dreams that resist recuperation 'into the ditch of what each one means'. The state of being an outlaw in 'Outlaw Blues' or on the road in 'On the Road Again' is one of restless desiring that has taken on a sexual flavour. The 'frogs inside my socks', which take the singer away from a constraining family environment, presumably suggest the love-sick frog of the nonsense song to which Dylan has subsequently returned. 'California', an early version of 'Outlaw Blues' recorded but not released at the time, glimpses a place beyond the 'wild West' that is the usual fourth cardinal point in the compass of Dylan's American geography, perhaps surprisingly appearing not as a place of indeterminacy but as a place where one might complain about the very consistency of its weather, especially in an implied contrast with the promised unpredictability of the New Orleans carnival: 'I'm used to four seasons,/California's got but one'. (One might contrast the line 'so long as there's an "if" in California' in Paul Muldoon's rather Dylanesque surreal narrative quest poem 'Immram' in this respect.) On this album, urban dwellers haunt the marginal spaces of the 'dime stores and bus stations' and talk of 'situations' in contrast with the presumed fullness of being, presence, sensual warmth and vulnerability associated with the loved object of the singer's sexual desire.

By the time of *Highway 61 Revisited* the blues melancholy of the train and the surreal comedy of the city have been mixed so that 'It Takes a Lot to Laugh, It Takes a Train to Cry'. Life is seen from the speedily moving perspective of the individual on the highway 'From a Buick 6'. Urban settings mark emotional states: for instance in 'Positively 4th Street' we are given a street address for a very urban kind of personal frustration. Mediated spaces include the melancholic Edgar Allan Poe mood 'down on Rue Morgue Avenue' with the hungry women in 'Just Like Tom Thumb's Blues'.

The movement of 'revisiting' or revision that leads from the

'Highway 51' of *Bob Dylan* to 'Highway 61' charts not just a movement from place to place but from place to displacement. It is a movement between decades, from the 1950s to the 1960s and from one mode of critical discourse to another. It is a movement from the conventional complaint of the blues to the voicing of a more complex social and generational uncertainty and uneasiness that crosses boundaries of social class and race. Rather than the abandonment of politics, the new discourse inaugurates a more contemporary politics.[15] The symbolic highway offers less potential for escape and more sense of cultural entrapment. Its symbolic value representing the condition of being as motion and place as no-place enables the song to map a surreal landscape of the junkyard of consumer waste and alienation, through an allegory of child sacrifice drawn from the biblical intertext. Children are being sacrificed all over Dylan's 1960s ('It's all right ma, I'm only bleeding') and the anthemic demand 'How does it feel?' to be alone and without direction is a question asked both of the condemning and condemned.

With the strong dependence on biblical subtext for the construction of its narrative 'Highway 61' also provides an extremely clear example of the way in which Dylan's American places can be both strongly original to him and yet deeply mediated by previous cultural productions. The Old Testament material (like so much in American culture) belies the reality of the lower-middle-class suburban reality it frequently disguises or masks. The singer's initial refusal to sacrifice the child to a social compromise which has apparently already been accepted by the parents forms a necessary political posture, and it is one that underlines the key thematic opposition throughout the album of the competing claims of individual self-liberation and integrity against the apparently inevitable self-abnegation and compromise required by the parental law, the symbolic code and society.

It was a feature of 1950s beat idiom to use place names to describe emotional states that Dylan takes to extreme lengths in 'Desolation Row' (in American English a 'Row' even more than a 'street' is a place of entrapment rather than liberation). The song imagines a strange spatial mixture that has traces of Dylan's depressive carnivalesque New Orleans as well as his alienated New York and is at the same time not so very far from Steinbeck's social realist novel of a Californian carnivalised ethnic mixture, *Cannery Row*, to which he is still alluding on the next album. It's not easy to find a single answer to the question of what kind of place Dylan's 'Desolation Row' is, since it is a place inhabited by so many different kinds of symbolically-named character-grotesques and is capable of sustaining so many different levels of interpretation.

If 'desolate' is the condition of Eve after the introduction of sin and death into Paradise according to Milton in *Paradise Lost* Book X, then Dylan's 'Desolation Row' is also a place of enabling cultural production and freedom, a place from whose carnivalesque perspective traditional lovers like Romeo may seem 'in the wrong place', preposterously outdated stereotypes, because attached to what may have seemed like archaic notions of sexual possession. Here even such powerful modernistic cultural icons for the 1960s as T. S. Eliot and Ezra Pound seem to be 'fighting' in a 'captain's tower', to be engaged, that is, in an apparently futile struggle in a place of disabling isolation and aloofness.

The play of desolation and consolation at the stoic recognition of the human fallen state is present in the song in its play with ambiguities. Dylan's is a negatively inflected location, yet it may also be a bohemian place of creative licence and diversity, evocative of the alternative society imagined and in part produced by the young people of the 1950s and 1960s. If it's recognisable as an infernal place then it's not a hell avoidable by the avoidance of disobedience or sin. It seems rather to be one that is either universal to the human condition and therefore inescapable or else a place whose honesty is such that society has to employ menacing 'insurance men' in order to prevent people from throwing off the myths and deceptions of conventional 'straight' society and escaping there.

It is important to remember that, in America, where place names proliferate with the speed of population expansion and carry many different kinds of cultural and semantic association, even 'Tombstone' can be a place name – in this case, of course, a place in southern Arizona, close to Tucson and as close to the Mexican border. In association with the death and burial songs of *Bob Dylan*, the title 'Tombstone Blues' might seem to translate as a rather doomy or morbid joke, an existential melancholy produced by an awareness of the inescapable condition of human mortality. Indeed much of the body of the song can be read as a critique of the structures of urban, medical and legal authority that (by comparison with the terminality of the human condition) may especially seem to be, in Dylan's redundantly emphatic words, both 'pointless *and* useless knowledge'. Then again, the awareness of Tombstone as a place in Arizona and moreover as a place richly mediated by its representation in American popular culture immediately conjures additional levels of potential meaning of a relevant kind, even if the song's opening allusions to the American patriot Paul Revere of the Boston Tea Party (made famous by Longfellow in 'Paul Revere's Ride'), point initially to a quite different American cultural border that is both historically and geographically distant.

Tombstone is the location and title of a famous 1942 Western film (based on the story by Albert Shelby Le Vino) which recast the pervasive Western myth of Wyatt Earp and his taming of the lawless West in the gunfight with the Clanton Gang at the O.K. Corral. That is the title given to the story in the even more famous 1957 film version starring Burt Lancaster and Kirk Douglas. The 1947 film is remembered for its eminently quotable line: 'Good men (and women) live in Tombstone – but not for long.' The line foregrounds the primary issue on which this kind of Western myth is grounded: the relation between order and disorder, legitimacy and illegitimacy, the unrestrained desires of the individual and the obligations and constraints associated with society. Seen in this light the song (and the album) becomes readable as one which polices the southern border of the American state of mind, between law and lawlessness, reason and irrationality, though in some ways, as in the case of 'Desolation Row', it may be made deliberately unclear on which if either side of the border Dylan's narrating persona has set up camp.

In celebrating these intertextualities and mediations the aim is not to complain about some supposed failure of sincerity or authenticity or some loss of a critical grasp on the real. On the contrary we might say that the folk protest mode of 'authenticity' loses its power when it is seen as a style or mode of discourse among others and that Dylan's supposed break from it should rather be welcomed in its ability to imagine (in sympathy with contemporary critical social theorists from Guy Debord to Jean Baudrillard) that we live in a society governed by spectacles and simulacra, by mediations and by the production of images in which critical access to reality is only gained by the recognition of such mediation.

In the carnival atmosphere of *Blonde on Blonde*, with its sense of being as motion and of everywhere being everywhere else – in what sometimes seems an extended translation of the surreal image of the New Orleans of the earlier songs – place quickly becomes displacement and location dislocation. Places both of the outer and the inner journey of the singer temporarily vanish in favour of the serial catalogue of sexual relationships that unfolds. However, the relationship to the loved object can easily be translated into the symbolic forms of domestic space; the windows, doors, ceilings, hallways and alleyways of 'Temporary Like Achilles' and the emotional state of the loved object herself may be definable with a spatial metaphor, most notably in 'Sad Eyed Lady of the Lowlands'. The 'street' and even the 'breakfast table' where the 'rainy day women' may 'stone' you are partly realistic locations but the landscape of the love songs is 'lost' in symbolic spaces that map emotional states such as the 'gate', the 'alley', and the 'honky-tonk lagoon'. Almost as literally as in the line 'I'll take you where you want to go' of 'Pledging My Time', they map a landscape of desire.

I've elsewhere argued that the representation of libidinally driven, impermanent sexual liaisons (their characteristic intensities, emotional vulnerabilities and even their painful but potentially liberating ruptures) is energising to Dylan's creativity – adding, of course, the further ambivalence that Dylan's lyric discourse is frequently ambivalent enough to be unfaithful even to its idea of infidelity.[16] These relationships also have their symbolic spaces definable as a mixture of repetition and difference, stasis and movement, so it is perhaps especially appropriate that the condition of desiring and of waiting should be locatable as being 'stuck' inside of a place punningly called 'Mobile' with the Memphis blues which, in the surreal language of the title, may be named here because they are named after a place that is somewhere else.

In contemporary American popular musical discourse certain kinds of music (like Handy's 'Memphis Blues'), are named after the places where they are produced, and it seems appropriate enough that Dylan's next unlikely move was one that took him to Nashville, one of the most prominent of these and somewhere, as Dylan has said, with 'more space' than New York.[17]

THE LANDSCAPES OF DESIRE

Turning to the symbolic Western, fantasy and dream landscapes of *John Wesley Harding*, we may well ask what is apparently absent from the lyric idiom of this album. There is no comic surreal or nightmare urban location, not so much comedy (not even in the comic surreal Western narrative 'The Ballad of Frankie Lee and Judas Priest'), no directly invoked threat of nuclear war, no anger against religion, no complaint against the absurd junk yard of consumerist society drowning in its own wastage, no states of extreme abjection and alienated despair, no love songs that offer raw and acute vernacular articulations of masculine emotional vulnerability and sexual need or which lament or even slyly celebrate the passing of a fleeting relationship. Yet in some ways it also has all of these things. The assumed power of these messages by the end of the Sixties was such that a song like 'All Along the Watchtower' with its Tolkienian fantasy landscape became Dylan's most familiar roadside anthem and, performed by him or by Jimi Hendrix or by a thousand buskers around the world, could say all of these things and more. There's a deeper investment in the symbolic landscape of the inner journey and in the Western myth and landscape of the symbolic outlaw and, as with all Dylan's changes in style, something has been gained along with whatever may have been lost along the way.

Since his Isle of Wight reference to Tennyson, Dylan's readers have been on the lookout for unlikely allusions to the English Victorian poet. Tennyson's best-known poem, the elegy *In*

Memoriam, is made up of a series of lyrics that are sometimes linked by recurrent images like hands and trees and, perhaps most relevant, doors which signify the absent presence of his lost companion. Dylan's anthem of the Western condition of the period, thanks to its recurrent use in *Pat Garrett and Billy the Kid*, places him in the definitively liminal condition: 'Knock, knock, knockin' on Heaven's door' and doors and windows and hallways and gates frame countless of his songs.

Planet Waves is one of Dylan's most cheerful albums in mood despite or perhaps because of the naming of such extreme locations as that marked in the song 'Dirge', in which the speaker seems untroubled by ethical ambiguity (or even good manners) in his declaration to the rejected lover that 'You were just a painted face on a trip down Suicide Road'. Most of the other songs are more optimistic love songs in which the character of the physical spaces described is aesthetically coloured by the emotional intensity the singer feels for the beloved, from the domestic interior of the 'old cabin door' of 'On A Night Like This' to the Romantic outdoor landscape of 'Twilight on the frozen lake' in 'Never Say Goodbye'. Extreme liminal or borderline spaces are invoked, but with a certain comic carelessness and a humorous acceptance of limitation: 'I've been walkin' the road/ I've been livin' on the edge, / Now I've just got to go/ Before I get to the ledge' ('Going, Going, Gone'). Lines such as 'There's not much more to be said/ It's the top of the end' seem to voice a sense of resignation at the permanently extreme liminal conditioning of the singer.

However, on *Blood on the Tracks* we are given a darker and more fascinating re-negotiation of these kinds of emotional state in terms of their stability and instability, the security or comfort that they may offer as opposed to their chaotic capacity for emotional upheaval and displacement. The album is one whose disrupted sense of time was a deliberate strategy on Dylan's part,[18] and this brings place into the foreground in different ways. In 'You're Gonna Make Me Lonesome When You Go', the lovers' tryst is defined by an agreed specific location mapped by the rational grid system of American urban street geography: 'Meet me in the morning, 56th and Wabasha'. Such an agreement bounded by precise physical space is necessary to plan the outlaw lovers' shared escape: 'we could be in Kansas by the time the snow begins to thaw'.

The lover is spatially defined by absence and loss. 'If', the singer requests, 'you see her say hello / She might be in Tangiers' – a place that seems to have been chosen as much for its surreal-sounding unlikelihood as for its contemporary resonance as a bohemian location of extreme cultural freedom for the William Burroughs and Joe Orton generation. Chance accumulations of cash and disaster characterise the existential weather forecast of 'Idiot Wind'. The lover can offer a quasi-maternal kind of welcome and 'Shelter from the Storm' but can also be so invaded and inflected by the idiot wind of uncontainable desire, chance and change that she takes on the character of the wind herself, becoming an 'idiot babe'. Her selfhood is dispersed in a trajectory across the political or infrastructural nation linked by hidden pun from the Grand Coulee Dam (Washington State) to the Capitol (Washington DC). Places from Honolulu to San Francisco to Ashtabula can be made equivalent by the absence or presence of the desired object, connected by distance and sameness as the comic coincidence of rhyme suggests. The relationship in 'Tangled Up In Blue' is spread across and recalled in terms of named locations that once again form the four cardinal points of the north, south, east and west of the United States.

The songs on the 1975 album *Desire* (perhaps with the help of their collaborator Jaques Lévy) string together an unusually rich range of locations from the American urban realism of 'Hurricane' and the Italian American gangster New York Brooklyn of 'Joey' (captured instantly in the reference to and performed strain of accordion music in the opening of the song) to the exotic Mexican-American flavoured 'Romance in Durango'. This song has a 'romance' which speaks atmospherically, almost stereotypically, of its place and vice versa and uses as location the stage-set Western landscape of Colorado where Dylan had already traced the absent-presence of the fugitive figure of Billy the Kid in the song 'Billy' from the film. The scene shifts to the African coastal republic of Mozambique which Dylan had visited on the eve of its revolution in the early Seventies ('we have relations in Mozambique' he says on the liner notes). The song 'Sara' charts a nostalgic retrospect in the form of a diary of significant locations (children on the beach, Portugal and Jamaica, the Chelsea Hotel), in stark contrast with 'Isis' which names places – 'high place of darkness and light' and 'pyramids all embedded in ice' – which once again have the character of a Gothic or medievalised Tolkienian landscape of fantasy.

The most interesting setting on the album may be that of 'Black Diamond Bay', another borderland location which is mediated inasmuch as it is ingeniously translated from the 1915 South Seas novel *Victory* by Joseph Conrad (who is pictured on the album cover), a tragically serious and deeply ironic work. Dylan's emphasis on the name of the place may be related to Conrad's opening line identifying coal and diamonds as made from the same base substance in carbon and suggesting the instability of surface appearances as a guide to what lies inside. It was none other than D. H. Lawrence who was to identify these 'allotropic states' as a feature of the modernist conception of literary character, and Dylan's song begins with a comparable image of the girl's passport photo 'face/From another time and place'. On the first page of his novel, Conrad styles modernity in a Dylanesque way as 'the age in which we are camped like bewildered travellers in a garish, unrestful hotel', and the action in Dylan's song all takes place in an hotel. The mood catches Conradian opacity, though with a more blackly comic or surreal twist (coming in part from the figure of the suicidal Greek). Both novel and song have a love tangle and gamblers and, in both, the action takes place under the shadow of a volcano, which erupts at the close. 'Black Diamond Bay' lacks a central tragic character like Conrad's Heyst but at the close introduces the typical Conradian device of a framing 'I' narrator, who (with a post-modern twist), pops up at the close having watched the action on TV and disavows any interest in what he has just narrated. Colonialism (the album notes mention Guam, which houses a US naval base) may be a theme of both, and the surreal events of the song (a wrangle between gamblers and the perverse logic of desire on the eve of an eruption) suggest something of our contemporary Pompeii as described, for instance, by Baudrillard in 'Fatal Strategies'.

REDEEMING SPACE THROUGH TIME

When Dylan's complex poetic idiom returns around the period of *Infidels* (1983) so too does his desire to write American space as history in the pop music vernacular mode, and this ambitious creative goal is for many fans of his work most nearly achieved in the elegy for the blues singer 'Blind Willie McTell'. This began as an outtake from the album and was not performed for many years but has since become one of the most admired of his mature songs. Again, it seems to me, the powerful contemporary significance of the song falls into place when we recognise the paradoxical character of its mediatedness – the basis of which can be seen to emerge from the discourse of poetic elegy within the literary tradition (in Shelley on Keats or Auden on Yeats). Dylan sings about the places that McTell has sung about or could have sung about and, as readers have commented, in his very claim that 'nobody can sing the blues like Blind Willie McTell' he legitimates the possibility that perhaps he himself can and is doing so in so saying.

The representative American space mapped out in the lyric requires the poetic treatment of the melancholy blues idiom because it is unredeemed and unredeemable space.[19] The song begins with a roadsign (or is it a Passover image?) announcing 'that this land is condemned', a gesture that is a declaration of its semantic independence and irrecuperablity and yet opens the way towards its semiotic renewal. The work of the song is to name a series of representative places and thereby offer a species of cultural redemption in the very act of denying its possibility. Reviewing a history of war and loss, of rebellion, the legacy of slavery, gender relations and other social change, it paradoxically revindicates not only what is signed but also the agency that signs it and the manner in which it is signed through articulations of the echoes of desire and loss that the blues may be said to voice.

Michael Gray, in a full analysis, has pointed out that the song employs a 'double' narrative perspective,[20] and it may be helpful to go a little beyond this and suggest that it is Dylan's ability to keep this doubleness in doubt or suspension that makes it work so effectively in the song. For us to remain *unclear* whether the scenes from American landscape and history are articulated by McTell or by the narratorial persona or by both (or by the narratorial persona as an interpretation of the performer) makes for part of its success precisely because it refuses either to relegate the voice of McTell to the place of an other or else to appropriate that voice to itself. It is therefore neither an act of denial nor of dispossession. Though the song allows us to glimpse the experiences and think we know the tragic struggles of American history, all it directly tells us, or that the singer feels he can ever really know, is the fact of this story's mediation: that 'nobody can sing the blues like Blind Willie McTell'. The song maps a nation through the spirit of the singer dispersed throughout and now embodied in the land, like the present–absent lovers of *Desire* or the spirit of Woody Guthrie, that is imagined as being located in the Grand Canyon at sunset in Dylan's eloquent prose-poem 'Last Thoughts on Woody Guthrie'.[21]

The other strikingly substantial song of the 1980s is 'Brownsville Girl', originally called 'New Danville Girl', which was evidently retitled to name the Southern border town that might thereby name a range of overlapping borderline states of mind. The song scintillates with Sam Shepard desert landscapes of the American South that the lovers scorch through in their flight that apparently tracks an eastward course from Arizona across Texas (though the sun comes up over the Rockies oddly enough). Meanwhile the singer crosses in and out of the virtual space of 'this movie I seen one time' from which he only hazily recalls the dying words of the gunfighter played by Gregory Peck which seem to speak to him as much of the actor's trials of celebrity as of the character's dangerous life with a gun. An additional level builds the backing singers into a comic dialogue with the singer's self-dramatising concerns.

Along with such ambitious acts of historical and cultural mapping, the Dylan of the Nineties and 00s seems to display an increasing sense of the necessary interinvolvement of space and time. This we can easily see in the modest revisiting he self-consciously makes to 'Knockin' On Heaven's Door' in 'Tryin' to Get to Heaven Before They Close the Door'. The latter song is especially interesting for the way in which it seems to validate the contingent named or suggestive locations ('muddy water', 'middle of nowhere', 'Missouri', 'lonesome valley', 'platforms', 'down the road', 'New Orleans', 'Baltimore', 'all around the world', 'in the parlour', 'Sugartown') however digressively they may be visited on the way.

Time Out of Mind is a collection of songs with as much symbolic location as content, or where the content frequently is the symbolic location. The choice of the geographical location of the 'Highlands', the longest song on the album, is something of a mystery, suggesting the reworking of a Burns original in which an ideal vision of the Scottish Highlands is celebrated, and therefore suggesting an emotional place that is, perhaps, meant as a direct counterpoint to the 'lowlands' of 'Sad-Eyed Lady of the Lowlands' of 1966. Dylan's 'highlands' are a Romantic alternative to the life of strained and exhausted celebrity he describes but also perhaps an indication of its condition of alienation ('a prisoner in a world of mystery') and of the inevitable erosions of the temporal.

A sub-theme of the album seems to be to confirm a continuing sense of desiring as a state of being that is perhaps also a performance of the character of the 'Dirt Road' or 'lonesome valley' of a desire of maturer years. The condition of being 'lovesick' in the De Chirico-like 'streets that are dead' of the opening song is a place where there are other lovers 'in the meadow'; for the singer himself desire is a Platonic dystopia of 'shadows'. The deep grumbling croak of the song has an effect (Gray tells us) which was engineered by Lanois to resemble the sound of the harmonica. The croak presumably also develops the quasi-comic persona of the lovesick frog of the nonsense song 'Froggy Went A-Courtin'' that he included on *Good as I Been to You*, now not just lovesick but sick of being lovesick too. Perhaps in this sense the 'highlands' are to be understood as a strange emotional condition of being beyond the desire that outstrips its available objects in the earlier songs and approaching a lonelier 'long-sighted' condition in which objects are not so easily attained or even desired as such. This dry destiny seems foreshadowed in the awkward un-flirtatious sparring that is captured with great vividness in the story of the singer's meeting with a waitress in a restaurant 'in Boston town' that the song narrates, where he has 'no idea what I want,' and hopes that the waitress will be able to suggest something. The lover is trying to get close but is 'still a million miles from you'.

The majority of the songs on *Time Out of Mind* confirm the picture of an alienated observer locked into his own obsessive pattern of social withdrawal. It has been argued that the later songs 'disclose a deepening pessimism over the efficacy of social and political action', though that in them Dylan 'valorises artistic endeavour and in particular the aesthetic power of traditional songs'.[22] The reading of 'Highlands' in Gray focuses on the debt to Burns and on the botanical inaccuracies of the song rather than exploring the subjective states it may represent. Taken in these terms it surely has something of the quality of the physical spaces that come to be characteristic of the work of the later Samuel Beckett. Beckett's spaces are increasingly abstract, geometrical, confined or sensually deprived, and they map increasingly extreme spiritual states of entrapment and incapacity and alienation evoked by such titles as 'Still', 'Closed Space', 'Enough', 'Lessness', 'Imagination Dead Imagine'. They tell of an increasingly sharply perceived failure of imaginative grasp of anything at all outside the experiencing self, let alone a fully fleshed and differentially imaginable other. The mood is defined spatially in the refrain to the song 'Cold Irons Bound' as a paradoxical state: being both exiled from the margins of community ('twenty miles out of town') and yet also still incarcerated within some constraints. Perhaps the singer is imprisoned, as it were, in an existential freedom of his own making, one strangely anticipated as early as the 'chains of the skyway' that Dylan had noted as confining even the freedom of birds in 'Ballad in Plain D'.

'*Love and Theft*', Dylan's first post-millennial album (though it celebrates 'a place where there's still something goin' on' and in 'Po' Boy' has one of Dylan's funniest songs ever), develops aspects of the detached or confined and lovesick persona with a variety of songs which imagine spaces, especially Southern spaces, associated with rivers and water. These include the digressive *apologia* 'Mississippi', in which the singer says there's only one thing he's done wrong and that is having been 'in Mississippi way too long'. In earlier Dylan Mississippi has been the Southern place of prejudice and protest, but it is here rather a place of hot weather and lazy days, of dissipation and waste, not to mention the huge mysteriously eddying river that has marked the middle of the American self since Twain. Vicksburg, Clarksdale, moonlight 'along the levee': these songs are flooded by and almost drowning in the American river.

We do, to be sure, also get glimpses of places from 'gay Paree' to Florida and Ducktown (Tennessee? whose ladies 'do the ducktown strut') and a dynamic picture of 'the city that never sleeps' in 'Honest With Me'. The biblically inflected landscape of those resigned to a fallen or condemned condition that we saw in 'Gates of Eden' and 'Desolation Row' can also be seen in 'Tweedle Dum and Tweedle Dee', who are 'living in the land of Nod' (Cain's place of exile) though they are still 'trusting their fate to the hands of God'. This strange pair of Lewis Carroll outlaws are also mediated through the allusion to Tennessee Williams that has been waiting to be used throughout Dylan's representation of American space to date. They are, of course, 'taking the streetcar named Desire'. Meanwhile the bells of Thomas Gray's elegy can be heard on this album too.

The relatively stable places from which the persona sings in the albums of the later Nineties and 00s betray a distance that may either suggest a wise detachment or else a bitter alienation. It is increasingly a place of which he can say that its paradoxes of fixity and fluidity, of being and becoming, were 'stuck inside of Mobile' all along – 'I know it looks like I'm moving, but I'm standing still' – and this is perhaps to be understood in the context of the idea of a journey which is as much temporal as spatial, that is 'Not Dark Yet' but is 'getting there'. Yet these recent songs can also impress with the renewed urgency and confidence of their expressions of passion, from the knowing 'You're gonna need me baby, you can't make love all by yourself' to the committed 'I'll make you see just how loyal and true man can be'.

As I began by arguing, it is hard to trace anything that can be clearly or unequivocally defined as a development or progression in an *oeuvre* as diverse and as ambiguous as Dylan's, but we can, surely, still celebrate the energy with which he has been able to find new ways of maintaining the significant structuring ambivalences on which his lyric discourse is constructed. Nevertheless the symbolic spaces of *Time Out of Mind* and '*Love and Theft*' have all their other associations suggestively coloured with the patina of Dylan's imaginative encounter with ageing, in which space increasingly becomes conflated with ideas of time.

11

ON THE 'D' TRAIN: BOB DYLAN'S CONVERSIONS

Bryan Cheyette

This is an account of Bob Dylan's many journeys, primarily by train, both real and imagined, literal and spiritual. I have characterised Dylan's many references to the railroads in his songs according to the schema of Wolfgang Schivelbusch, the cultural historian of train travel, who has suggested that 'the railroad knows only points of departure and destination'.[1] Dylan's preoccupation with the railroads, which as we will see directly follows Woody Guthrie, is intimately bound up with his initial departure away from his Jewish self. The Christian 'slow train' is both the furthest possible point from his origins and is also, as I will show, imagined specifically in opposition to an unrestrained 'carnival train'. Most writers on Dylan have focused teleologically on the 'slow train' to Christianity, as if it were the inevitable destination of his many other possible journeys. For this reason, I spend a section of the essay exploring Dylan's restless wanderings on the 'carnival train' where he embraces the very fears and passions which he attempted to expunge in his Christian songs.

Following Dylan's train of thought, his many rail-hoppings in his songs help me to make sense of one kind of conversion – from, say, folk-blues to folk-rock or from rock 'n' roll to country blues and back to rhythm and blues – which have distinguished Dylan's breathtakingly various performances. His refusal to settle on any one style or identity means that he constantly reinterprets his songs both musically and lyrically in the concert hall and studio. This unwavering provisionality is also found most obviously in his best albums, which are characteristically transient snapshots of his work rather than, with the notable exception of his 'Christian' albums, polished and definitive studio versions. This constant restlessness and ambivalence is, paradoxically, utterly consistent throughout Dylan's long career. There is, then, a sense of absolute certainty in his own vision of continual and all-embracing uncertainty, especially in relation to his audience's fixed expectations.

For this reason, I speak crucially of two kinds of conversion with regard to Dylan. On the one hand, his many conversions are a form of freewheeling self-reinvention, which makes everything heterodox and provisional. On the other hand, we have his absolute transfiguration during his 'Christian' period which, in orthodox religious terms, divides the self into old and new, before and after, sick and redeemed. As we will see, in the face of such extreme heterodoxy and orthodoxy, both in the name of conversion, the endlessly mobile and immobile world of the train is a resonant metaphor for Dylan's many selves and transformations.

This essay is also a personal journey back into the world of Bob Dylan which I left as a teenager more than two decades ago. At one time I used to listen religiously to Dylan's music and, like many of his fans, thought that I was communing directly with his honest and authentic voice. After all, like Dylan, I was the son of a Jewish shopkeeper and I was also from a smallish town, albeit in the British Midlands as opposed to the American Midwest. But, like many fans of my generation, I stopped listening to Dylan in disbelief when he followed one of his best albums, *Street-Legal* (1978), with what I then regarded as one of his worst, *Slow Train*

Coming (1979). I now realise that Dylan's profound exploration of his many selves, both orthodox and heterodox, converted and unconverted, helps us to re-evaluate his Christian albums and enables us to go beyond the logic of their fundamentalist revivalism. This is then, finally, an argument about re-embracing one's origins without succumbing to the all-American game of identity politics. After all, Dylan has managed to write a great deal about death and suffering in boxcars with the minimum of reference to the Holocaust. But this is a specifically American story of self-invention, rebirth and self-forgiveness, and is a life-giving rejoinder, biblical in its scope, to those who insist on digging up 'Mengele's bones'.[2] As we will now see, this story begins with a twenty-year-old Dylan born again as a 'young Woody Guthrie'.

'THE VERY LAST THING I'D WANT TO DO'

In his career-making *New York Times* review of the 1961 concert at Gerde's Folk City, which enabled Dylan to obtain a record contract with Columbia Records, Robert Shelton wrote devotedly: 'Mr Dylan is both comedian and tragedian. Like a vaudeville actor on the rural circuit, he offers a variety of droll musical monologues . . . "Talking Havah Nagilah" burlesques the folk-music craze and the singer himself.'[3] 'Talking Havah Nagilah Blues' was one of a number of Talkin' Blues goofs, which were a characteristic part of Dylan's performances at the time, and also included the more accomplished 'Talkin' Bear Mountain Picnic Massacre Blues' and 'Talkin' New York'. The rather slight 'Talking Havah Nagilah Blues' is mentioned because, as Shelton implies in his review, it indicates something about Dylan's mysterious antecedents: 'Mr Dylan is vague about his antecedents and birthplace, but it matters less where he has been than where he is going, and that would seem to be straight up.' These comments are remarkably prophetic, as Dylan's future-oriented perspective and absolute refusal to be limited by his past – 'deep in our soul we have no past' – has proved to be one of his most consistent features.[4]

Although it is less than a minute long, probably his shortest performed song, 'Talking Havah Nagilah Blues' says a great deal about Dylan's ingrained antipathy towards any single, fixed identity which, as is widely recognised, distinguishes his career as a whole: 'I don't think of myself as Bob Dylan. It's like Rimbaud said, "I is another."'[5] As Shelton rightly notes, his self-conscious ditty is a double parody of both the folk-blues tradition, which Dylan was wary of too easily appropriating, as well as his own conventional lower-middle-class Jewish background. The spoof is introduced by Dylan in his most pronounced Midwestern drawl as a 'foreign song' which he had 'learned in Utah'. After a brief snort on his harmonica and with a gentle regular beat on the guitar, he sings slowly and tunelessly the first line of the commonplace Hebrew song, 'Havah Nagilah' (literally 'let's celebrate'). In doing so, he wrenches each syllable out of shape, 'h-a – v-a – na-geeee-lah', until, with much relief that the musical torture is over, he switches seemlessly into a perfect prairie holler and yodels masterfully, 'yodel-ay-hee-hoo'. Here the folk-blues tradition, which he would soon transform and individualise, comically supersedes the kitschy Hebrew folk tune (heard amusingly in unJewish Utah) which was part of his adolescence and would have certainly been played at his lavish Bar Mitzvah.[6]

It is doubtful whether Dylan read Richard Wagner's notoriously anti-Semitic *Judaism in Music* (1850) in the early 1960s, although one is constantly surprised by the breadth and eccentricity of Dylan's reading at the time. In this tract Wagner argues that Jews are so unmusical – with no aesthetic taste whatsoever – that all they can do is gurgle, yodel and cackle:

> We are repelled . . . by the purely aural aspect of Jewish
> speech . . . The shrill, sibilant buzzing of [the Jew's] . . . voice
> falls strangely and unpleasantly on our ears . . . Who has not
> had feelings of repulsion, horror and amusement on hearing
> that nonsensical gurgling, yodelling and cackling which no
> attempt at caricature can render more absurd than it is?[7]

Dylan seems uncannily to take Wagner at his word and creates
an ideal comic mixture of garbled Hebrew and stunningly pitched
yodelling. His gloriously imperfect and constantly mobile singing
voice, and his boundless ability to mix musical styles, eerily
correspond to Wagner's stereotype of 'the Jew' as aesthetically
and culturally impure. In these terms, there is much about Bob
Dylan's musical career which conforms to Zygmunt Bauman's
description of Jews in relation to an ordering modernity as
'ambivalence incarnate'.[8]

While this is clearly a flagrant over-reading of this brief spoof,
it is worth noting in general the extent to which this moment, at
the genesis of Dylan's career, indicates the double displacement
of both his Jewish and folkish identity. Shelton, in his concert
review, maintains from personal experience that in 1961 the
prodigious Dylan had been 'sopping up influences like a sponge',
although, it should be stressed, Dylan only assimilated musical
forms provisionally. The very last thing that he wanted to do
was to celebrate unequivocally any one tradition; a single set of
conventions was bound to constrain his creativity and limitless
sense of self. It may not be a coincidence in this regard that
Woody Guthrie's son, Arlo Guthrie (his other musical heir),
had a 'hootenanny Bar Mitzvah' in New York in 1961.[9]

One way of thinking of Dylan's many transformations is as a
response to his all-pervading ambivalence. His serial conversions
can be thought of as either partial resolutions or short-lived

imagined communities which enable him to locate his wandering self within certain, fixed boundaries. The first and foremost of these imagined communities was undoubtedly the blues-folk tradition of the Depression era, elements of which continue to pervade his work. It is well known that Dylan discovered folk music in the bohemian district of Minneapolis in 1959, when he was enrolled at the University of Minnesota and living in the Jewish fraternity house, Sigma Alpha Mu. Dylan, who changed his name from Robert Allen Zimmerman at about this time, finally moved away from his first love, rock 'n' roll, and devoured enthusiastically Guthrie's autobiographical *Bound for Glory* (1943). By all accounts he became utterly obsessed with Guthrie: 'Dylan decided to remake himself in Woody's image. He learned all the songs, and held his guitar the way Woody did in the pictures ... and invented a rambling past.' Significantly, Dylan's Guthrie-obsession had been prefigured a decade earlier by Ramblin' Jack Elliott, born Elliott Adnopoz, the son of a successful Brooklyn doctor, who was to make a guest appearance in Dylan's Rolling Thunder tour. Dylan's intense amusement at discovering his Jewish doppelgänger, with regard to his would-be surrogate father, has been recorded by Anthony Scaduto.[10]

As Michael Alexander has contended, there is a long twentieth-century history of 'outsider identification' by socially successful American Jews. Dylan can most certainly be situated in this cultural tradition, not least in his use of African-American influenced blues and gospel music which continues to be heard in his latest album, *'Love and Theft'* (2001). As Sean Wilentz has noted, this album's title is taken from Eric Lott's book on the origins and character of American blackface minstrelsy during the Civil War.[11] This tradition reached a mass audience when Al Jolson put on his blackface on film, which, according to Alexander, was also crucial to American Jewry's sense of identity during the Jazz Age:

To a people who imagined itself fundamentally as Other, a Jew painted as an African American was an image of magisterial striking power. To the Jews in America, its symbolic power must be compared to the prophet Ezra . . . The people of the book have also become the people of the fringe. Marginalization has become a core component of American Jewish identity.[12]

While Alexander's argument is confined to the prewar period, it can be usefully applied to Dylan. Woody Guthrie obviously enabled Dylan to instigate a lifelong preoccupation with the socially and politically deprived, especially the rural poor, although it would be wrong to assume that this was a straightforward identification even at the beginning of Dylan's career. A crucial part of Dylan's self-mythology is that he travelled east primarily to visit Guthrie, who was in the Greystone Hospital in New Jersey suffering from Huntington's Disease. Dylan, at this point, is described as a 'young Woody Guthrie', and even wore one of Guthrie's old suits when he performed in the 1961 concert at Gerde's Folk City.[13] While he began to assume Guthrie's mantle as spokesman for the poor and oppressed of America, especially in his next two albums, this was not as unproblematic or cynical as many have assumed. In an extension of Alexander's argument, E. Anthony Rotundo, with reference to American folk-rock, notes the shattering contrast between Dylan's 'restrained, civilized past', which privileged the printed word, and his invented Okie persona as 'the son of grassroots America . . . something wild and primitive':

Few singers have railed against words, rationality, and formal education with the bitterness of Bob Dylan. His lyrics mocked schooling and intellectual analysis. The only true knowledge to Dylan was the knowledge that came from life experience and personal feeling. This escape from meaning, this flight from rational to intuitive knowledge was central to the ways in which many Jewish rock figures submerged their own cultural identities.[14]

Both Rotundo and Alexander place Dylan's multiple conversions in a broad cultural context which includes most American 'Jewish rock figures' as well as other key cultural icons such as Al Jolson, whom Dylan refers to as 'somebody whose life I can feel' in the booklet which accompanies *Biograph* (1985).[15] This is a useful corrective to those commentators who treat Dylan's routine transfigurations as if they are merely a product of his particular brand of Romanticism coupled with his individual genius.

Dylan's manifold conversions are particularly resonant with reference to the postwar American-Jewish literary novel. One key example of this genre is the career of Philip Roth, another distinctive product of the 1960s, who also points to a lifelong rewriting of a 'restrained, civilized' American-Jewish upbringing. More explicitly than Dylan's work, much of Roth's is a prolonged exploration of Jewish 'appetite and renunciation', most famously in the character of Alexander Portnoy. By the 1980s, Roth was to locate the endless play of Jewish identity specifically in *The Counterlife* (1987) and *Zuckerman Bound* (1989), as signified by Nathan Zuckerman's various splits and myriad mutations.[16] At the same time, as Mark Shechner has argued, Roth is one of a significant number of American-Jewish postwar novelists and critics, including Saul Bellow, Norman Mailer, Bernard Malamud, Isaac Rosenfeld and Lionel Trilling, who are all 'converts of one variety or another and their writing is a testament to their conversion'. Shechner's conversions take place mainly in the political and linguistic arena but also include crucially, as in the case of Malamud, the Christianised tropes of death and rebirth or what Leslie Fiedler has called 'The Christian-ness of the Jewish American Writer'.[17]

While it is true to point to the explicitly Christian roots of his folk-rock and blues influences – located especially in the rural Midwest and the deep South and strongly influenced by black gospel music – it is wrong to assume that Dylan was uniquely aberrant in his assimilation of these Christian tropes. What is more, not unlike his literary counterparts, Dylan's absorption of Guthrie's Dust Bowl Ballads is acknowledged, from the beginning, as a highly self-conscious and constructed act. Dylan was well aware that writing from a Guthrie-like 'life experience' was patently a fiction. The last two stanzas of his 'Song to Woody' (1961), for instance, make clear the contradictions inherent in too easy an embrace of Guthrie and his extended connection with the history of the Depression era:

> Here's to Cisco an' Sonny an' Leadbelly too,
> An' to all the good people that traveled with you.
> Here's to the hearts and the hands of the men
> That come with the dust and are gone with the wind.
>
> I'm a-leavin' tomorrow, but I could leave today,
> Somewhere down the road someday.
> The very last thing that I'd want to do
> Is to say I've been hittin' some hard travelin' too.

At first Dylan is claiming an allegiance with a group of folksingers and fellow travellers (in all senses) who sang regularly with Guthrie during the Second World War, which included Gilbert 'Cisco' Houston (who was dying of cancer in 1961), Huddie 'Leadbelly' Ledbetter and 'Blind' Sonny Terry. But, given Dylan's lack of any actual connection with this group, apart from his abiding love of their music, it is not surprising to find an uneasy blend of identification and differentiation in 'Song to Woody'. Dylan is 'a thousand miles from my home' and 'seein' [Guthrie's] world' but, at the same time, he admits that 'I know that you know/ All the things that I'm sayin' an' a-many times more'. He was well aware that it would be utterly phoney – and this is stressed in his performance of the last two lines of the song – to claim a part of the history of those who have 'gone with the wind'. The 'very last thing [he'd] want to do' is to declare too easy an affinity with those whose 'hard travelin' was forced on them by extreme impoverishment, segregationist racism and the economic dispossession of the Dust Bowl years.

As Greil Marcus has shown, Dylan from the beginning was laying claim to a folk tradition that valued above all the immediacy of the spoken word, the power of community and the purity of native traditionalism:

> [Dylan] symbolized a scale of values that placed, say, the country over the city, labour over capital, sincerity over education, the unspoiled nobility of the common man and woman over the businessman and the politician, or the natural expressiveness of the folk over the self-interest of the artist.[18]

In embracing this resonant version of authenticity, Dylan also knew that the 'natural expressiveness of the folk' was something that was essentially inauthentic, as he could all too easily construct and manufacture his own version of the American folk. Hibbing, where Dylan lived from the age of six, was brutally transformed by the iron ore industry during his youth. Nonetheless, there was a world of difference between the vicissitudes of American capitalism, as experienced by his immediate family, and the complete displacement of tens of thousands of his fellow Midwesterners in the 1930s.[19] But if this lack of historical authenticity meant that Dylan had to see the world through Guthrie's eyes, as he puts it in 'Song to Woody', then he would as a result also have to deny his own artistic individuality and freedom. To resolve the tension between 'the folk over ... self-interest', in Marcus's formulation, Dylan gradually shifted his 'hard travelin' from the realm of actuality to that of metaphor. His picaresque version of the 'hard traveller', especially with reference to the hobos who once rode the rails, is particularly relevant in this regard. As Michael Gray has rightly shown, the chimerical train journeys in Dylan's songs were often somewhere between dream and reality.[20] For this reason, I want to begin by noting the multifaceted origins of Dylan's carnivalesque rail-hopping before focusing on the final destination of his one-track 'slow train'.

'AROUND WITH THE CARNIVAL TRAINS'

In 'Long Time Gone' (1963), an early song, Dylan imagines the eternal rambler from the Judaicly symbolic age of 'twelve and one' until his death:

> I remember when I's ramblin'
> Around with the carnival trains,
> Different towns, different people,
> Somehow they're all the same.
> I remember children's faces best,
> I remember travelin' on.
> I'm a long time a-comin',
> I'll be a long time gone.

As Aidan Day has shown, 'the vagabond ... is one of the troupe of irregular and carnivalesque figures that processes through Dylan's work' or, in terms of this essay, boards Dylan's 'carnival trains'. It is also worth noting that Dylan, from the beginning, is at pains to give the vagabond figure a mythic and self-consciously over-determined personal genesis: 'I ran away . . . when I was 10, 12, 13, 15, 15½, 17 an' 18/ I been caught an' brought back all but once'.[21] Given Dylan's propensity, at this early stage in his career, to multiply many different versions of the Midwestern youthful rambler, it is not surprising that he characterises this figure in 'Long Time Gone' as caught between sameness and difference: 'Different towns, different people, /Somehow they're all the same'. After all, as Gray has noted, the 'Railroad Theme' is something of an American cliché: 'the railroad meant, or was at least seen to mean, freedom, opportunity, rebirth'. While Dylan has always directly confronted clichés in his songs, there is a growing sense of unease between his creative individualism and the fact that, in his earliest songs and poems, he was merely following the same old 'folk tradition' in writing about the hobo or rambler or vagabond.[22]

Leo Marx has argued influentially in his *The Machine in the Garden* (1972) that the American railroads were commonly conceived as creative forces which could realise the potential of the country's natural resources. In stark opposition to the destructive character of the industrial revolution in Europe, industrialisation in the United States coincided with the beginnings of modern American nation-building and so, in the nineteenth century, modernisation appeared popularly as a 'railway journey in the direction of nature'. It is in these terms that trains in the United States were thought to have an 'immediate relationship to nature' and that, because of this popular perception, the naturalisation of the railroads became synonymous with a quintessentially American form of mobility.[23] It is in the light of this cultural history that both Guthrie and Dylan were able to construct the railroads as a resonant point of genesis and change for the

American folk as well as for their vagabond selves. After all, in 'Hard Times in New York Town' (1962), the Guthriesque Dylan imagines riding into New York on a 'one-way track', a favourite phrase in his early songs, to reinforce a sense of inevitability and determinism in his future destination.

A sustained and original example of the conjunction between Dylan's origins and the railroads can be found in his 1963 poetic sleeve notes to 'Joan Baez in Concert, Part 2'.[24] At the beginning of this rambling poem (in all senses) Dylan explicitly refashions the iron ore freight trains in relation to his childhood in Hibbing:

> In my youngest years I used t' kneel
> By my aunt's house on a railroad field
> An' yank the grass outa the ground
> An' rip savagely at its roots
> An' pass the hours countin' strands
> An' stains a green grew on my hands
> As I waited I heard the sound
> A the iron ore cars rollin' down
> The tracks would hum an' I'd bite my lip
>
> . . .
>
> It's then that my eyes'd turn
> Back t' my hands with stains a green
> That lined my palms like blood that tells
> I'd taken an' not given in return

This estranged account of Dylan's childhood melds together the experience of waiting for a freight train with a heartfelt sense of betrayal, 'I'd taken and not given in return'. It is the adolescent Robert Allen Zimmerman, as opposed to the iron ore works, who is deemed oddly to have 'savagely' destroyed the landscape, ripping out its 'roots' which look 'like blood' on his hands. Dylan, in the extremity of this moment (which he soon moderates), is all too conscious of not having roots in nature, of the landscape not being part of his family's 'blood'. This abiding sense of disconnection with nature might possibly account for the otherwise inexplicable anger towards the upwardly mobile immigrant in 'I Pity the Poor Immigrant' (1968).

The feeling of an outsider betraying the folk, the supposedly authentic product of rural America, has already been hinted at with regard to Dylan's appropriation of Guthrie's hobo identity. As Stephen Scobie has argued, there is often a repressed self-identification in Dylan's work with the figure of Judas, as can be seen at the end of the first section of 'Joan Baez in Concert':[25]

> An' I'd wipe my hand t'wash the stain
>
> . . .
>
> In the dawn a t'morrow's rain
> An' I asked myself t' be my friend
> An' I walked my road like a frightened fox
> An' I sung my song like a demon child
> With a kick an' a curse
> From inside my mother's womb

As Dylan wanders the landscape like a 'frightened fox', he is re-enacting the mythological origins of the Wandering Jew who, in his Judas-like rejection of Christ, is also an accursed and timid figure who is made to wander the earth for all time. The 'demon child' remains uncleansed until after tomorrow's rain and instead receives, frighteningly, a 'kick an' a curse' from inside his 'mother's womb'. While this elemental 'curse' might refer to the Christian doctrine of Original Sin, it is also worth noting that Dylan was considered Jewish through his maternal blood-line, which seems not unrelated to his conscious self-loathing: 'An' I asked myself t' be my friend'. At the same time, as virtually every British Romantic poet has recognised, the Wandering Jew is a strangely attractive outsider for the Romantic writer.[26]

Dylan's curse is also his blessing, as by becoming a 'demon child' of nature he is able to develop and authenticate his all-important persona as a wild and primitive folksinger. By the second section of the poem, therefore, it is not his emotions but his intellect which betrays the American folk. In this section, an older Dylan boasts quite openly about stealing the 'voice' of his 'idols':

> But I learned t'choose my idols well
> T' be my voice an' tell my tale
> An' help me fight my phantom brawl
> An' my first idol was Hank Williams
> For he sang about the railroad lines
> An' the iron bars an' rattlin' wheels
> Left no doubt that they were real

Only when he hears the 'railroad lines' in a Hank Williams song does Dylan believe that his experiences as a child are 'real'. That the transfiguration of 'phantom' words into a song is more 'real' than reality can be said to be the paradox at the heart of all forms of imaginative writing. The fact that he could channel his adolescent experiences of the iron ore rail trains through Williams's and Guthrie's songs indicates above all that Dylan is acting like a poet, even though he might not yet know it. In his 'Last Thoughts on Woody Guthrie' (1963), the one and only time he has performed one of his poems, Dylan literally turns the chronically ill Guthrie into a fantasy train. When your 'train engine fire needs a new spark to catch it':

> . . . you need something special
> Yeah, you need something special all right
> You need a fast flyin' train on a tornado track

To shoot you someplace and shoot you back
You need a cyclone wind on a steam engine howler
That's been banging and booming and blowing forever
That knows your troubles a hundred times over

Here Guthrie is conceived of as a 'fast flyin' train' who is a natural force, a tornado or cyclone, which can transport his audience away from the mundane and familiar, but who is, at the same time, also understanding and knowledgeable.

This fusion of extreme movement and stillness can be said to characterise rail travel in general, as it combines, according to Michel de Certeau's description, the simultaneous experience of mobility and immobility. Sigmund Freud, in these terms, famously compared 'free association' to the accidental juxtapositioning of words that might come from a 'traveller sitting next to the window of a railway carriage and describing to someone inside the carriage the changing views which you see outside'.[27] Such a Freudian traveller is also the implied narrator of Scholem Aleichem's Yiddish *Railway Stories* (1911), whose 'moods change like scenes a traveller sees from a train'. As Sidra Dekoven Ezrahi has noted, all of Aleichem's stories are recited on a train and provide the narrator with a 'uniquely intermediate space' somewhere between inner and outer, fixity and randomness, nature and modernity. Such modernist indeterminacy might be said to prefigure Dylan's railway-influenced songs which, like Aleichem, tell 'the story of the road as opposed to home, of the transitory as opposed to the permanent, of passing as opposed to ongoing human encounters'.[28]

Once Dylan stopped figuring himself as a representative American rambler, the individualised men who ride the rails in his songs are transported, in all senses, by various uncontrollable appetites: 'Honey, just allow me one more chance/ To ride your passenger train'.[29] Dylan's personae – from 'Bob Dylan's Dream' (1963) to 'Where Are You Tonight? (Journey Through Dark Heat)' (1978) – either write or dream on a train and, in doing so, reflect on the ever-moving grounds of their creativity. In the opening lines of 'Where Are You Tonight?', for example, we have the following image of the songwriter:

> There's a long-distance train rolling through the rain,
>   tears on the letter I write.
> There's a woman I long to touch and I miss her so much
>   but she's drifting like a satellite.

The movement of the train blurs inner and outer, rain and tears, which makes it impossible to have a firm grasp on anything: 'she's drifting like a satellite'. No wonder, in this song, Dylan's lyric speaker later states that: 'The truth was obscure, too profound and too pure, to live it you have to explode'. Even when it is the female figure who is making her escape, as in the refrain to the co-written 'Walk Out In The Rain' (1978), dreaming and drifting are equally opposed:

> Walk out in the rain,
> Walk out of your dreams,
> Walk out of my life
>   . . .
> And catch the next train.

Dylan's male lovers are invariably transported to an other-place: 'If dogs run free, then why not we . . . ? /My ears hear a symphony/ Of two mules, trains and rain'.[30] By the time of *Blonde on Blonde* (1966), the displaced characters in his songs are never quite where they want to be, and are dreaming of past female encounters or remembering unfulfilled erotic desires.

In 'Absolutely Sweet Marie' (1966), the ex-convict (a common character in Dylan's songs) cannot jump her 'railroad gate' and is left standing 'lookin' at your yellow railroad/ In the ruins of your balcony/ Wond'ring where you are tonight, sweet Marie'. This moment of unrequited longing is repeated powerfully in the later co-written 'Brownsville Girl' (1986) when 'The memory of you keeps callin' after me like a rollin' train'. Such memories can even inspire the making of art as a whole in 'When I Paint My Masterpiece' (1971), when the singer's thoughts are transformed into: 'Train wheels runnin' through the back of my memory'.

But one should not underestimate the power of these carnivalesque desires, especially when they move from contemplative longing to a nightmarish dream-world. Above all, it is the women in Dylan's songs who understand the dangers and attractions of such transportations, as in the third verse of 'Stuck Inside of Mobile with the Memphis Blues Again' (1966):

> Mona tried to tell me
> To stay away from the train line.
> She said that all the railroad men
> Just drink up your blood like wine.
> An' I said, 'Oh, I didn't know that,
> But then again, there's only one I've met
> An' he just smoked my eyelids
> An' punched my cigarette.'

The world of the 'demon child' is writ large in this song, with the railroad men occupying the monstrous role of 'the Jew' within anti-Semitic discourse who, for centuries, has also drunk 'your [Christian] blood like wine'. This is a phantasmagoric world where dark fantasies are partially transformed into surreal reality:

'he just smoked my eyelids/ An' punched my cigarette.' Dylan's use of the reassuring 'just' here highlights the masculine sangfroid in the song as opposed to Mona's uncontrolled forebodings which surround 'all the railroad men'. Mona's identification with the railroads and irrational forces of all kinds is, however, taken from the earlier 'Train A-Travelin' (1963). In this song, Dylan's male singer was to utilise the 'iron train a-travelin'' as an extended metaphor for an unrestrained world made up of a 'firebox of hatred and furnace full of fears'.

But the distinction between reason and unreason is not quite so starkly made in 'Stuck Inside of Mobile'. After all, the difference between female fantasies and masculine realities revolves, in the end, around the transposition of two verbs, 'punched' rather than 'smoked', so that we have the image of smoking 'eyelids' instead of 'cigarettes'. It is as if the male figure, made impotent by his immobility in Mobile, is merely pandering to Mona's anxieties. And yet there is an ambivalence at the heart of 'Stuck Inside of Mobile' which dramatises the extent to which the 'iron train a-travelin'' is both part of and opposed to the feminine realm. On the one hand, rail-lines most obviously reinforce a phallocentric linearity and, in its origins, a form of escape from and betrayal of the maternal sphere. At the same time, trains are associated in virtually all of Dylan's lyrics with the memory, desire and dreams which, together with his female muses, inspire his songs.

This tension can be seen most clearly in the contrast between a normative masculinity and a playful and imaginative femininity in the second verse of 'Visions of Johanna' (1966):

> In the empty lot where the ladies play blindman's bluff
>   with the key chain
> And the all-night girls they whisper of escapades out on
>   the 'D' train

We can hear the night watchman click his flashlight
Ask himself if it's him or them that's really insane

The confusion of the night watchman attempting to illuminate
the night, and make sense of the carnivalesque world on the '"D"
train', illustrates the dangers of riotous emotion which Dylan
was to find increasingly difficult to order. On the one hand,
the D(ylan) train has the authorial imprimatur as a dream-space
of absolute freedom and game-playing where one can go off
the rails even if this was to leave 'blood on the tracks'. Here
Dylan's carnival train so far transcends the ordinary that the
song's alternative masculine voice seems to ask tautologically
if going off the rails isn't a 'really insane' thing to do. The
unresolved tension between transcendence and order in 'Visions
of Johanna' is anticipated in the earlier song, 'Chimes of Freedom'
(1964), where Dylan declares himself to be: 'Trapped by no track
of hours for they hang suspended'. Dylan's voice is 'suspended'
between what Aidan Day rightly calls 'freedom and constraint' as
it is both liberated and yet trapped within the ordered temporal
sphere.[31] Here we have the contradictions between the immobility
and fixity of the 'track of hours' and the endless mobility and
plenitude of the inner world of artistic creation, sexual freedom
and escape. As we will now see, such ambivalences are finally
and starkly resolved in Dylan's period of salvation where his
'Christian' songs attempt to end such drifting uncertainties and
unbridled game-playing.

'ON THE SLOW TRAIN TIME DOES NOT INTERFERE'

As early as *Highway 61 Revisited* (1965), Dylan began his freely
associative sleeve notes with 'On the slow train time does not

interfere' so as to take his 'hard travelin'' out of the temporal realm. He also ends the main section of his notes with a reference to 'the holy slow train' which evokes the gospel tradition of the 'freedom train' as a symbol of historical emancipation from slavery which is underpinned by the language of Christian salvation.[32] The doubleness of 'the holy slow train' is captured perfectly in Guthrie's autobiographical *Bound for Glory*, whose title is taken from the gospel-inspired song 'This Train Is Bound for Glory', which contains the line: 'Don't ride nothin' but the righteous an' the holy'. In the book's opening and closing chapters, Guthrie describes himself playing the song in a boxcar full of homeless and lawless men who, in their common suffering, transcend race, creed and colour.[33] This redemptive moment is repeated in many of Dylan's early Guthrie pastiches such as 'Only a Pawn in Their Game' (1963) and 'Ain't A-Gonna Grieve No More' (1963):

> Brown and blue and white and black,
> All one color on the one-way track,
> We got this far and ain't a-goin' back
> And ain't a-gonna grieve no more.

As Paul Williams has reported, 'This Train Is Bound for Glory' was played near the beginning of the concerts to promote *Slow Train Coming*, Dylan's first 'Christian' album. The song, however, was rewritten so as to purify it of its original double message and was reduced to mere religious exaltation: 'This train is a clean train, this train' and 'I was lost in sin/ I had no peace within/ Until I met my Jesus on this train'.[34]

All of Dylan's concerts at this time began with a story about an old woman barred from boarding a train to see her dying son as she had no money for a ticket. She prays to the Lord for help as the conductor starts the train. But the train does not move and, as a result, the conductor lets her on board with the following refrain: 'Old woman, Jesus got your ticket, now come on this train.' This story is taken from the gospel tradition but, as John Schad has demonstrated, Jesus travelling on a train has deep roots in much nineteenth-century European culture which can be summarised by the philosopher Kierkegaard who writes of: 'Christian understanding [as] . . . a steam engine going down a railway track'.[35]

That Dylan's 'slow train' ushering in a new Christian age spans Kierkegaard, Guthrie and the gospel tradition gives a strong sense of its multiple resonances. The immediate antecedents for the gospel 'slow train' can be found in Dylan's debut album, which included adaptations of 'Freight Train Blues' (1962) and 'Man of Constant Sorrow' (1962) which both evoke, as can be seen from the latter song, righteous suffering on the slow train:

> Through this open world I'm bound to ramble
> Through the ice and snow, sleet and rain
> I'm bound to ride that mornin' railroad
> P'raps I'll die on that train.

Redemptive death on the railroads is such a common feature of these early songs that it is pastiched joyously in 'It Takes a Lot to Laugh, It Takes a Train to Cry' (1965). The 'lone soldier on the cross, smoke pourin' out of a boxcar door' is a powerful reworking of this motif in 'Idiot Wind' (1975) which, most notably, became a central image in the film *Renaldo and Clara* (1978).

Dylan has always played with Guthrie's version of the Christ-figure as a 'socialist outlaw' who promises in the song 'Jesus Christ' that 'the poor would one day win this world'.[36] The sixty-nine men who illegally occupy the freight boxcar at the beginning of *Bound for Glory* are being chased from state to state by the police and are all economic migrants: 'I set down with my back against the wall looking all through the troubled, tangled, messed-up men. Traveling the hard way. Dressed the hard way. Hitting the long old lonesome go . . . A crazy boxcar on a wild track. Headed sixty miles an hour . . . due straight to nowhere'.[37] When Guthrie sings 'This Train Is Bound for Glory' he momentarily redeems and contains the overwrought emotion of the 'crazy boxcar', albeit as part of his class politics. Dylan's earlier versions of this fleeting salvation differ greatly from 'Slow Train Coming'. In 'Train A-Travelin'', most incisively, we have the lone 'voice' of Dylan juxtaposed with the uncontrollable passions of the boxcar with its 'blood-red broken frame':

Did you ever stop to wonder 'bout the hatred that it holds?
Did you ever see its passengers, its crazy mixed-up souls?
Did you ever start a-thinkin' that you gotta stop that train?
Then you heard my voice a-singin' and you know my name.

This is Guthrie's inglorious train going 'nowhere' which Dylan, the 'protest' singer, wishes to 'stop' by showing his audience the nature of an historical injustice. By associating Guthrie with the high point of his Christian fervour, Dylan is encouraging a sense of determinism, beyond his mere 'voice', that the born-again Guthrie leads inevitably to the born-again Dylan. This teleology is the reason why so many of the songs in the 'Christian' albums, *Slow Train Coming*, *Saved* (1980) and *Shot of Love* (1981), return Dylan to the generalised world of social critique of his 1960s songs. As Scobie and Gray have maintained, the world is no less corrupt in the 1970s and 80s than when Dylan first sang his Guthrie-inspired 'protest' songs. His earlier songs were similarly characterised by an apocalyptic fear – 'before the flood' – that the world was coming to an end, albeit in the 'secular form of nuclear war'.[38] Dylan's fundamentalist brand of Christianity, taken from the Vineyard Fellowship, was quite specific about predicting the time and place of Armageddon, which would come to pass 'West of the Jordan, East of the Rock of Gibraltar' as he put it in 'The Groom's Still Waiting at the Altar' (1981). And yet, while time is refashioned on the Christian 'slow train', his voice is minimised next to the God-given prophecy that a new messianic era is imminent.

The continuities between Dylan's converted and unconverted selves have been exhaustively rehearsed in a range of commentaries which have traced his use of biblical, moralising and prophetic language, his self-identification with the suffering Christ-figure, and the redemptive role of women in his songs. This argument can be summed up by the contention that there is a straightforward journey from 'Song to Woody' to 'Slow Train Coming'.[39] It is as if Dylan's absolute investment in teleology, which is fundamental to his orthodox religious sense of being 'saved' from a corrupt past, has been transferred to his critics. But if we return to the other key point of continuity between his unconverted and converted selves, and once again rail-hop with Dylan, we can see the limitations in this teleological train of thought.

The problem with focusing on the end-point of Dylan's temporary salvation, as opposed to the many points of departure of his real and imagined rail-hopping, is that it reduces his carnival journey to a single destination. There is, I believe, a clear and unresolved tension in Dylan's 'Christian' phase between his orthodox religious conversion – which splits the self into old and new, before and after, pure and impure – and his previous heterodox transformations which deliberately confuse his various selves. The quest for continuity between Dylan's transient and volatile heterodox selves, and his absolute and redeemed orthodox self, fails to account for the radical difference between these two modes of conversion. The shift from his inner creative resources (on the carnival train) to an external authority (watching the slow train coming) especially indicates this marked dissonance. After all, the logic of his conversionist orthodoxy meant that Dylan in his 'Slow Train Coming' and 'Saved' concerts refused to play any of his previous music and denied, even more completely than usual, his past selves.[40]

One way of reading Dylan's Christian songs is as a response to his unbounded self, which could always potentially, as Aidan Day has argued, confuse the forces of 'alienation' with those of 'carnival'.[41] Dylan's Christian songs are precisely distinguished by their desire to order and master his unconverted self so as to resolve all ambivalences and uncertainties. As he states in 'Precious Angel' (1979), 'Ya either got faith or ya got unbelief and there ain't no neutral ground'. This refusal of any neutral space, a provisionality which had hitherto characterised his best songs, above all defines his Christian Manicheanism. This can be seen especially in 'Gonna Change My Way of Thinking' (1979), where in markedly Dylanesque and unChristian terms the singer states that: '[Jesus] said, "He who is not for Me is against Me", / Just so you know where He's coming from'. It was in exactly this polemical language that Dylan spent an unusual amount of time in the concerts of this period haranguing his audience for refusing to take sides with regard to the coming messianic age.[42]

This quest for certainty did not merely take a moral form, as is often assumed, but involved a fundamental remaking of the self in a bid to expunge inauthenticities and impurities of all kinds. In 'When He Returns' (1979) Dylan asks both himself and his audience to 'Surrender your crown on this blood-stained ground, take off your mask'. Once the game-playing has stopped, a purified self will come into being to replace a graceless self-hatred: 'How long can you hate yourself for the weakness you conceal?' The 'you' in this song is a means of gaining an external perspective on an unconverted self which, both Scobie and Day have contended, is a division which remains unresolved in these songs. By continuing to focus exclusively on the slipperiness of Dylan's lyric identity, however, both of these commentators miss the main point of the Christian songs. All of these songs, that is, radically rewrite his previous work as they introduce an alternative set of values which are specifically designed to resolve a lack of a fixed identity and an abiding sense of homelessness.[43]

At the same time, one should not underestimate the level of unredeemed self-disgust in Dylan's supposedly redemptive songs. After all, 'Slow Train Coming' begins with: 'Sometimes I feel so low-down and disgusted', which transports us back to the world of 'Joan Baez in Concert' where Dylan asks himself 't' be my friend'. As is indicated in a 1991 observation from the stage, the transcendence of self-loathing is the subject of many of his God-centred songs: '. . . it is possible for you to become so defiled in this world that your own mother and father will abandon you. If that happens, God will believe in your ability to mend your ways.'[44] In this mood of self-disgust, Dylan imagines himself as alien to those closest to him, 'saved' by a transcendent force. Whereas such self-hatred leads in the first place to the 'demon child', who was quickly to become the wild and primitive folksinger, his Christian songs embrace such passivity and thereby deny the grounds of his own 'savage' creativity.

In the fourth verse of 'Trouble' (1981), on the *Shot of Love* album, Dylan's lyric speaker is no longer aboard the 'carnival train'. He succumbs instead to an external knowledge that it is not only himself who is 'cursed', as in the earlier song, but humankind as a whole. The tortured double negatives concerning his solitariness in the following verse give a sense of how difficult it is for Dylan to go beyond the earlier Romantic ideals of inner creativity. By viewing the coming of the slow train from afar, his persona indicates finally that the railroads have ceased to be a self-reflexive dream-world and are merely a means of delivering a message:

> Put your ear to the train tracks, put your ear to the
>   ground,
> You ever feel like you're never alone even when there's
>   nobody else around?
> Since the beginning of the universe man's been cursed by
>   trouble.

In 'Heart of Mine' (1981), Dylan advises unequivocally, 'Heart of mine go home, /You got no reason to wander, you got no reason to roam', and thereby completely rejects his Guthriesque rambling persona. Once he has stopped travelling in disguise, his dream-songs turn out to be circumscribed by a higher authority, as in the opening lines of 'When You Gonna Wake Up' (1979): 'God don't make no promises that He don't keep. /You got some big dreams, baby, but in order to dream you gotta still be asleep'. What is more, the 'carnival train' is now more like a 'ghetto' than a place of liberation:

> The glamour and the bright lights and the politics of sin,
> The ghetto that you build for me is the one you end up in,
> The race of the engine that overrules your heart,
> Ooh, I can't stand it, I can't stand it,
> Pretending that you're so smart.

Whereas the railway 'engine' and 'the heart' were once united, they are now considered to be radically at odds with each other.

Dylan's heart must now find its way 'home' and stop wandering or racing. His heart must, quite literally, be still. But this is the only possible response to someone who has completely gone off the rails and let his own creative will, in the name of his heart and dreams, determine reality. As the singer asks his redeemer in 'In the Summertime' (1981): 'Did I lose my mind when I tried to get rid of everything you see?' Instead of such unrestrained creativity, we have in 'When He Returns' (1979) the 'iron hand' of God who replaces the metaphorical 'iron train a-travelin'' with the all too literal 'iron rod, /The strongest wall will crumble and fall to a mighty God'. In 'Never Say Goodbye' (1973), Dylan's lyric speaker tells us that 'My dreams are made of iron and steel' which are ruthlessly disciplined in his new guise as a supplicant. As he puts it in 'When You Gonna Wake Up?' (1979):

> Do you ever wonder just what God requires?
> You think He's just an errand boy to satisfy your wandering
>   desires?

Just as Dylan once located his unconverted wandering Jewish self in the pure and authentic world of the folk, he has now situated his converted self in the equally pure and authentic domain of God-given prophecy. But, as we will now see, Dylan finally returns to the foundational ambivalences of his Jewishness by bringing together his converted and unconverted selves in the imagined homeland of the Bible.

'I'M EXILED BUT YOU CAN'T CONVERT ME'

As Allen Ginsberg has noted, one of the key indications that Dylan's Christian orthodoxy was beginning to wane by the time of *Shot of Love* is that this album contains the heartfelt lament for Lenny Bruce. By highlighting the 'outlaw' Lenny Bruce as well as Guthrie as our 'brother', Dylan is evoking another key early influence from the beginning of his career. Bruce becomes a troubling and uncontained 'ghost' in the song as he is somewhere between a righteous victim and the 'spirit' of impure carnival: 'Lenny Bruce was bad, he was the brother that you never had'. By using the black street vernacular 'bad', which actually means good, Dylan is highlighting a disruptively amoral black American culture as an alternative to the virtuous Christian gospel tradition. As Lenny Bruce could not have been more outrageously Jewish in his comedy, there is a clear rapprochement in the song with Dylan's unconverted and 'exiled' self.[45]

That the gloriously unredeemed self – in the guise of Lenny Bruce – might be once again sanctified is hinted at in 'Gotta Serve Somebody' (1979), where we have a plethora of possible identities all contained by a higher power which they will have to 'serve':

> You may call me Terry, you may call me Timmy
> You may call me Bobby, you may call me Zimmy,
> You may call me R.J., you may call me Ray,
> You may call me anything . . .

But there is a profound difference between linguistic game-playing – Terry/Timmy, R.J./Ray – and Dylan's actual name changes, Bobby/Zimmy. While Bobby/Zimmy is just another arbitrary signifier in this song it is also clearly loaded with a great deal of historical and biographical baggage which Dylan can no longer easily transfigure. In his post-Christian 'I and I' (1983), Dylan explicitly comes face to face with the origins of his identityless identity in the guise of the Hebrew God who states 'I am that I am' to Moses on Mount Sinai.[46] Dylan's divided persona is both

Jewish and Christian, converted and unconverted, and is no longer waiting for the slow train to come. He is instead watching those on the platform, as if they were an adult version of his demon child, who see the reconversion of the 'holy slow train' back into the cyclical world of nature:

> Outside of two men on a train platform there's nobody
>   in sight,
> They're waiting for spring to come, smoking down
>   the track.
> The world could come to an end tonight, but that's
>   all right.
> She should still be there sleepin' when I get back.

At this point Dylan is once again the sceptical poet trying to understand his divided selves, 'two men on a train platform', whose insouciance at the potential end of the world, the non-arrival of the slow train, is made clear when placed next to his 'sleepin'' female redeemer: 'Took a stranger to teach me, to look into justice's beautiful face/ And to see an eye for an eye and a tooth for a tooth'. Such is his non-redemption that he no longer rejects his unconverted self in disgust but instead unites his converted and unconverted selves in a delightfully savage pun: 'an eye for an eye'. It is, paradoxically, the vengeful law of the Hebrew Bible which enables Dylan to re-imagine himself as a Guthriesque 'outlaw' in the context of ancient Israel. Such is his fantasy in the *Biograph* interview with Cameron Crowe:

> As far as the sixties go, it wasn't any big deal. Time marches on. I mean if I had the choice I would rather have lived at the time of King David, when he was the high King of Israel,

I'd love to have been riding with him or hiding in the caves with him when he was a hunted outlaw.[47]

Dylan also wrote in 'Precious Angel' about his African-American saviour: 'We are covered in blood, girl, you know our forefathers were slaves .../ On the way out of Egypt, through Ethiopia, to the judgement hall of Christ'. By the time of *Infidels* and 'I and I', however, the uncertainties and ambivalences inherent in Dylan's Jewish identityless identity are no longer resolved in the 'judgement hall of Christ'. By figuring himself as a Hebraic outlaw, or a 'slave' from Egypt, he is able to bring together both his Jewish and Guthriesque selves. Most crucially, by again embracing his own provisionality and vagrancy in 'I and I', he has stepped outside the logic of a redemptive Christianity which, to achieve its necessary transcendence, splits the self irrevocably in two.

At its best, his abiding sense of Jewish difference and otherness enables Dylan to continue to re-engage as an 'insider-outsider' with the musical histories of the poor and oppressed of America as in his latest album, '*Love and Theft*'. At its worst, as in 'Neighborhood Bully' (1983), it results in a righteous refusal to discern the unbounded power which can be gained by those who were once 'exiled' and 'wandered the earth'.[48] What is clear, however, is that a 'shot of love' in its redemptive purity is no longer enough to transform Dylan, who has finally stopped travelling on the road to Armageddon. In his music he remains a 'thief', a betrayer, someone who continues to appropriate the 'hunted outlaw' or 'slave' through his restless and carnivalesque imagination. The devotedly impure Dylan now rides equally on the carnival and slow trains as Judas and Jesus, Jew and Christian. That is why by the time of his late song, 'Tryin' To Get to Heaven' (1997), he can still 'hear' the 'hearts a-beatin'' of the 'people on the platforms/ waiting for the trains'. After spending so many years communing with the hopes and sufferings of the wandering folk of America, he seems to be no longer sure in 'Things Have Changed' (2000) whether he is interpreting God-given prophecy or whether he is merely arguing with himself in a man-made wilderness:

> I've been walking forty miles of bad road
> If the bible is right, the world will explode
> I've been trying to get as far away from myself as I can
> Some things are too hot to touch
> The human mind can only stand so much
> You can't win with a losing hand

12

'A DIFFERENT BABY BLUE'

Pamela Thurschwell

Joyce Carol Oates's short story 'Where Are You Going, Where Have You Been?' was first published in the literary magazine *Epoch* in 1966.[1] The story concerns fifteen-year-old Connie, whose mind is filled with what her mother calls 'trashy day-dreams' inspired by the pop music that seeps through the portals of teenage girls' lives and radios in the early Sixties.[2] In rebellion against the constraint and boredom of her suburban American home Connie wanders through the shopping plaza with her friends, exuding a prematurely knowing, yet simultaneously innocent sexuality that is refracted through the story's incessant pop music soundtrack. In Oates's world pop music stirs up desire through its driving beat, but masks the physical truth of sex through euphemistic clichéd lyrics. For Connie and her friends, music pulses through every aspect of their interior and exterior lives. It is sacred and mundane as well as sacred and profane: 'They sat at the counter and crossed their legs at the ankles, their thin shoulders rigid with excitement, and listened to the music that made everything so good: the music was always there in the background like music at a church service, it was something to depend upon'.

The music that Connie hears continually, in the drive-in restaurant, in her house, in her head, eventually takes human form in the menacing figure of Arnold Friend, who turns up at her door to woo her into taking a drive with him and his friend Ellie in his gold jalopy. Arnold Friend initially resembles all the other teenage boys with whom Connie necks in alleys. He dresses 'the way all of them dressed; tight faded jeans stuffed into black, scuffed boots, a belt that pulled his waist in and showed how lean he was, and a white pullover shirt'. He establishes common ground with Connie by pointing out that they've both been listening to the same radio program; she in the safety of her house, he in his car on Ellie's transistor radio. The show is the XYZ Sunday Jamboree, DJ Bobby King, a substitute for the church which 'none of [her family] bothered with'. But the story soon exposes Arnold Friend's teenage credentials as fraudulent – he's clearly not like all the other boys. Connie realises that he's much older than he claims, that the slang he uses is last year's slang, that he's wearing a wig, and has stuffed his boots with something to appear taller.

Alternately seducing and threatening her through the screen door, but always making it explicit that he intends to rape her, Friend mesmerizes Connie with his rhetoric until the familiar surroundings of her parents' house seem to dissolve around her: '"The place where you came from ain't there any more, and where you had in mind to go is canceled out. This place you are now – inside your daddy's house – is nothing but a cardboard box I can knock down any time. You know that and you always did. You hear me?"' But like Dracula, who can't come in unless invited over the threshold, Friend tells her he won't enter her house; Connie must choose to come out to him. The story ends with Connie pulling herself up off the kitchen floor where she has been crouching terrified, and, as if in a trance, going towards him: 'she put her hand against the screen. She watched herself push the door slowly open as if she were safe back somewhere in the other doorway, watching this body and this head of long hair moving out into the sunlight where Arnold Friend waited.'

Like the clothes, hairstyle and tan that don't quite fit him, Arnold Friend's relationship to pop music is also uneasy. He ventriloquizes but does not inhabit the music that marks the limits of Connie's worldview. Rather he uses it; if on the one hand he seems to represent the sexual menace hidden under the friendly surface of early Sixties pop, on the other hand he doesn't necessarily care for the music itself – it's all a part of his act. The story ends with him proffering generic or vaguely misremembered lyrical sweet talk which is completely unrelated to Connie herself:

'My sweet little blue-eyed girl,' he said, in a half-sung sigh that had nothing to do with her brown eyes but was taken up just the same by the vast sunlit reaches of the land behind him and on all sides of him, so much land that Connie had never seen before and did not recognize except to know that she was going to it.

In this newly unfamiliar environment Friend's recycled pop lyrics seem to become co-extensive with the landscape, as if nothing is to be trusted now that Connie's house of cards has tumbled around her, not even the natural world.

What are we to make of these 'vast sunlit reaches'? Do they represent the promised land or a graveyard? When 'Where Are You Going, Where Have You Been?' was republished Oates added a dedication, 'For Bob Dylan'. In an interview she explained the double inspiration of the story and the reason for the dedication:

After hearing for some weeks Dylan's song 'It's All Over

Now, Baby Blue,' and after having read about a killer in
some Southwestern state, and after having thought about
the old legends and folk songs of Death and the Maiden,
the story came to me more or less in a piece. Dylan's song
is very beautiful, very disturbing.[3]

The meaning of this dedication, and Oates's story's relationship
to Dylan's 'Baby Blue', has vexed subsequent readers. Is Friend
finally a positive force, a representative of some kind of alternative value system espoused by Dylan? In which case then is
Connie's choice, if a terrifying one, still the only one she can
make because it is 'all over' for her in her parents' house, as it is
politically 'all over' for the conformist attitudes of early Sixties
suburbia? (Friend himself says, 'It's all over for you here'.) Mike
Tierce and John Michael Crafton maintain that this is the case:
'The story is dedicated to Bob Dylan, the troubadour, the artist.
Friend is the artist, the actor, the rhetorician, the teacher'.[4] They
point out Friend's physical similarities to Dylan; he has shaggy
hair, a long and hawklike nose, and his outfit resembles Dylan's
look of the early Sixties. Their reading disputes earlier readings
of the story that equate Friend with the Devil and see him as
a figure of absolute and mysterious evil. Tierce and Crafton
see him as the Devil only insofar as he is like the attractive,
freewheeling Satan that Blake discerned in *Paradise Lost*. In
their views, Friend is a positive influence come to explode a
stagnant suburban wasteland. He expands the mind and world
of the confined teenage girl:

Arnold is the personification of popular music, particularly
Bob Dylan's music; and as such, Connie's interaction with
him is a musically induced fantasy, a kind of 'magic carpet
ride' in 'a convertible jalopy painted gold.' Rising out of
Connie's radio, Arnold Friend/Bob Dylan is a magical,

musical messiah; he persuades Connie to abandon her father's house. As a manifestation of her own desires, he frees her from the limitations of a fifteen-year-old girl, assisting her maturation by stripping her of her childlike vision.[5]

Even if Arnold Friend is finally a projection of Connie's imagination, with this reading we are still left with the troubling implication that Connie's pop mindset conjures up an attacker as saviour. Most other readers of Oates's story have assumed that Connie will wind up not so much 'assisted to mature' as raped; not so much stripped of childlike vision as an unclothed corpse. If Arnold Friend really resembles Bob Dylan then there is clearly something horrifically menacing in this version of Dylan's message, particularly for the girl on the brink of adulthood.

But we also know that Arnold Friend's outfit is a masquerade; nothing fits. It seems unlikely that he is a 'magical musical messiah' if for him the music is really a sham. Furthermore, the musical content of Connie's world simply doesn't support the equivalence between Friend and Dylan. If Arnold Friend is the personification of the pop music in the story then it is quite clear that he is not the personification of Bob Dylan's music. The music that Arnold Friend is associated with is the same music that Connie loves. He's not Connie's Tambourine Man, playing her a mind-expanding new song. Rather, he's exploiting the ambiguities of the old ones – the promise of raw sex dressed up in pretty language and what Oates portrays as a dangerous trance-inducing beat. Young girls such as Connie are vulnerable, the story suggests, because the lyrics that wash over her and float her through life give her nothing to think about. In fact the lyrics may make no difference at all – all she knows is contained in that sexy hypnotic sound.

As previous critics have pointed out, the title questions, 'Where are you going? Where have you been?' sound like the type of questions that would be asked by Connie's exasperated mother and left unanswered as Connie heads out for another night at the drive-in. The title resembles a typical frustrated parental lament. But the story also suggests that these are questions that are specifically unanswerable in the early Sixties because, once they are out of the house, there's no particular place for young women like Connie to go. In this case Oates's dedication to Dylan takes on tremendous significance; Dylan becomes Connie's missing guide. It was the lyrical sophistication of Dylan's music, his infusion of politics into pop music, that offered girls like Connie a direction other than into the arms of an Arnold Friend.[6] As James Healey puts it:

> Oates rightfully dedicates this story to Dylan . . . because Dylan, more than any other popular singer/songwriter in the early sixties, did more to expand the range of subject matter of pop music. With the appearance of Dylan and his songs on the musical scene, American pop music lost an element of innocence . . . Through Dylan's lyrics the threat of nuclear war, the injustices of race inequality, and the desperation of everyday American life drew the attention of a generation of teenagers away from puppy love, going to the prom, holding hands, and first kisses.[7]

Here we see Dylan representing an alternative to Arnold Friend – he offers the prophylactic larger picture, the political and cultural overview that might have protected Connie from invasion by dumb and dangerous music and men.

In the first interpretation of the story (Dylan as Arnold Friend), the social and political upheavals of the Sixties are played out as a violent sexual awakening for the teenage girl initiate. In the second interpretation (Dylan as anti-Friend), the social and political upheavals of the Sixties, if only they had been experienced by Connie through the music of Dylan, might have protected her from the threat of Friend, and this experience would itself have been the metaphorical equivalent of a sexual awakening, forcing the teenage girl to 'lose her innocence', forget puppy love, and confront a new world. Both versions of the story's dedication portray Dylan's music confronting the naïve teenage girl with frightening, difficult, potentially freeing truths; but in so doing, both readings conflate sexual and political sophistication, and place Dylan in the role of teacher/troubador. Both also suggest that teenage girls need guides – someone, some pop star, dj, or pied piper substitute to show them the light.

So what does the dedication to Dylan indicate? Is Dylan good for young girls or demonic? The answer may be that this is simply the wrong question. The relationship between the dedication and the story is not so cut and dried. The first interpretation of Arnold Friend as Connie's true 'friend' lands the reader in the familiar double-bind for women of Sixties radicalism out of which late Sixties feminism emerges. When sexual freedom stands in for other kinds of political and social freedom, women are faced with the same old imperative voiced by some male leaders of radical groups such as the Weathermen and Black Panthers: join the revolution, make the tea, go on the pill, spread your legs. The second interpretation, in which Dylan is the anti-Friend, the man whose intelligent, politically engaged music might have saved Connie from following the pop music pied piper with the transistor radio to oblivion, seems to be, initially, a much more inviting one. Yet it doesn't hold up either if we take into consideration what Oates says about the story in her interview.[8] She talks about the power of 'Baby Blue' to haunt, not to save: 'Dylan's song is very beautiful, very disturbing.' Like the competing and contradictory images of women in Dylan's songs, the reverberations of Oates's story should not be reduced to either a feminist or a misogynist message. 'Where Are You Going, Where Have You Been?', along with the Dylan songs I'm about to explore in more detail, chart continuing disturbances in the interaction between the realms of the sexual and the socio-political; they don't consolidate a single image of woman as victim or object.

It's significant that the song in question for Oates is 'Baby Blue', not 'The Times They Are A-Changin'' or 'A Hard Rain's A-Gonna Fall' or another of those songs of Dylan's that became political anthems for a generation.[9] 'It's All Over Now, Baby Blue' is, on the face of it, one of Dylan's moody, personal songs with vaguely apocalyptic imagery not easily adapted for political purposes. Where critics have seen it as proffering some kind of social message that message is usually Dylan's renunciation of his uncomfortable position as the voice of his generation; in it he confounds the expectation that he will continue to write the political folk songs that initially made him so popular. By ending *Another Side of Bob Dylan* (1964) with the savage 'It Ain't Me, Babe' Dylan rejects both women who expect too much from him and a culture that was doing the same. When he ends his next album *Bringing It All Back Home* (1965) with 'It's All Over Now, Baby Blue' the terms of the dismissal have shifted. Still claiming that something (the relationship, Dylan's 'folksinger' period, or perhaps, as the Oates story might have it, an earlier pre-Sixties moment) is over, 'It's All Over Now, Baby Blue' also presses for a new beginning: 'Strike another match, go start anew'. If Dylan vehemently denies his ability to save or prophesy in 'It Ain't Me, Babe', then by the time of 'Baby Blue' he's occupying a version of that prophetic position again. He surveys the apocalyptic landscape and tells Baby Blue what she needs to do now. It was an acoustic version of 'Baby Blue' that Dylan chose to play when he was finally persuaded to come back on stage after being booed off for going electric at the Newport Folk Festival in 1965. 'Baby Blue' can be seen as Dylan's part poignant, part patronising, goodbye/fuck you to the folk revival.[10]

Like 'Where Are You Going, Where Have You Been?', 'Baby Blue' tells the story of the disintegration of a woman's world, but instead of doing so through the arrival of a potentially death-bringing, world-shattering lover, it does so in the wake of a departing one. The apocalyptic landscape of 'Baby Blue' signifies paradoxically both the approach of death and the promise of revelation: 'Look out the saints are comin' through ... This sky, too, is folding under you,'[11] and the imperative to leave the dead behind: 'Leave your stepping stones behind, something calls for you./Forget the dead you've left, they will not follow you.' Aidan Day finds that 'there is something disconcerting about the usurpation of the known in "It's All Over Now, Baby Blue"' but that the song simultaneously 'emphasize(s) the creative and positive potential of abandonment to spaces of unmapped, unwritten possibility'.[12] The tension between the exhortation to participate in these creative active abandonments and the apparently passive abandoned woman who is addressed in the song is suggested by lines such as 'The empty-handed painter from your streets / Is drawing crazy patterns on your sheets.' The painter from the streets, one in a series of familiar Dylan figures of carnivalesque overturning, invades the private space of her bedroom and 'draw[s] crazy patterns on [her] sheets.' As an image this might suggest a bloodying sexual encounter, but more likely he is making art out of her painful personal loss, the rag-tag remnants of a relationship (the sheets are literally what is left since 'the lover who just walked out [her] door / Has taken all his blankets from the floor'). Presumably what is required is for her to do the drawing herself, to take up the mantle of creating the world that will follow the one that is collapsing.

In the final verse, she is asked to see herself anew: 'The vagabond who's rapping at your door / Is standing in the clothes that you once wore.' The vagabond dressed in her cast-offs is her own distorted mirror image who might be seen to mock her with his transvestism, making her a precursor to the soundly trounced debutante Miss Lonely in 'Like a Rolling Stone', who 'once upon a time . . . dressed so fine', but then again he might also offer a way forward; he may be an Orpheus leading her out of the realm of the dead. Another of Dylan's outcasts, the vagabond, like the painter, is a figure for the radical freedom that comes with the admission that it is in fact all over now. But the song doesn't let us know how Baby Blue will respond to these exhortations; what we are left with is the sense that, like Connie in Oates's story, her house is being invaded – by rappings at the door and painters in the bedclothes.

The couplet 'Yonder stands your orphan with his gun / Crying like a fire in the sun' has come in for a fair amount of critical attention. But interestingly it is the second part of the couplet which is usually focused on. 'Crying like a fire in the sun' is a compressed image of loss and impotence – a fire in the sun is unlikely to make any sort of visual impression.[13] However, I find that the real mystery is in the first half of the couplet. 'Yonder stands your orphan with his gun' is at least as paradoxical as that 'fire in the sun'. Addressed to Baby Blue it makes the orphan belong to her, placing her structurally in the position of a dead mother. She appears to be, at the beginning of the song, one of the dead whom she will later need to leave behind. Not only that but she is a dead mother who is threatened with yet another death by the weapon in the hands of her child. 'Baby' Blue then, is also paradoxically a maternal figure; she is in this sense abandoning, as well as abandoned, dying multiple deaths in this apocalyptic landscape. She is also perhaps, in her implied delusions of grandeur, a parodic version of Helen of Troy – the face that launched a thousand ships into stormy seas: 'All your seasick sailors, they are rowing home / Your empty-handed army is all going home.' 'Baby Blue' is one of Dylan's seductive but bitter harangues that piles failure upon failure upon the woman it addresses before pulling the carpet out from under her feet. But it also presents a dizzying range of subject positions (although not necessarily very happy ones), allusions and possibilities that accrue around its central character. The haunting quality of the song that similarly filters through 'Where Are You Going, Where Have You Been?' emerges from an inability to disentangle the personal (the failure of a relationship, the potential breakdown of the woman who's addressed in the song) and the biblical, mythical or political (the destruction of a world, the confrontation between Death and the Maiden, the end of an era).

Dylan himself suggests another more straightforward way of thinking about 'It's All Over Now, Baby Blue' in his remarks about the song in the liner notes to *Biograph*. His explanation chimes almost too well with Oates's story:

> I had carried that song around in my head for a long time . . . and I remember that when I was writing it I remembered a Gene Vincent song. It had always been one of my favorites, *Baby Blue* . . . 'when first I met my baby, she said how do you do, she looked into my eyes and said . . . my name is Baby Blue.' It was one of the songs I used to sing back in High School. Of course, I was singing about a different Baby Blue.[14]

Dylan, by separating his Baby Blue from Gene Vincent's, clearly distinguishes his creative output from his own high school musical fare. Gene Vincent, the sexy rockabilly singer whose 1956 hit 'Be-Bop-A-Lula' (along perhaps with Little Richard's 'Tutti Frutti') proved once and for all the superfluousness of lyrics to rock 'n' roll, could easily have been one of Connie's favourite heartthrobs. Dylan's 'different Baby Blue' may be one way of reflecting back the questions that Oates's story deftly poses – about the relationship between young women's construction of desire through pop music and pop music's construction of young women as objects of desire and desiring objects – into Dylan's own lyrics.

Different baby blues are beginning to emerge in the songs of the mid-Sixties, but of course those differences don't necessarily produce wholly new or positive images of women. But then do we, should we, must we, look to pop music for those kinds of images? The point that I'm head-butting here is that it's difficult for me (a woman academic, a Dylan fan) to write about Dylan and women without sounding either self-righteously accusatory or sheepishly apologetic. At the heart of this article are some questions I can only state without answering analytically: what does it mean to consider oneself simultaneously a feminist and a fan of some wrenchingly misogynist music? Wrenching, because smart, not wrenching because dumb?[15] (The only truly classic 'dumb' misogynist Dylan song is probably 'Just Like A Woman', and it's a classic that, in my experience, few people admit to actually liking any more, except perhaps in the splendidly camp version by Nina Simone.)[16] Structures of identification and desire that produce much of the pleasure associated with activities such as listening to music cannot and should not be patrolled by thought police, and yet I still sometimes feel more than a little queasy when I hear Dylan sing 'Can you cook and sew, make flowers grow / Do you understand my pain?/ Are you willing to risk it all / Or is your love in vain?'[17] I'd like simply to pass that one off as a joke, but if I can't do that with a clear conscience, should I toss that song to the lions, in exchange for the right to defend anything on *Blonde on Blonde* to the death? (And then we're back to the 'Just Like A Woman' problem.) Could it be that Dylan just purveys interesting misogyny – you know, the 'good' misogyny, while other artists don't? My heart sinks as I write that line. In the end I don't have satisfying answers to these questions; I just have faith in the dazzling array of Dylan's characters, male and female. Ellen Willis writes about the multitude of personae who inhabit the world of *Blonde on Blonde*:

> The songs did not preach: Dylan was no longer rebel but seismograph, registering his emotions – fascination, confusion, pity, annoyance, exuberance, anguish – with sardonic lucidity. Only once, in 'Just Like a Woman,' did his culture shock get out of control ... Many of the songs were about child-women, bitchy, unreliable, sometimes vulnerable, usually one step ahead: 'I told you as you clawed out my eyes/ I never really meant to do you any harm.' But there were also goddesses like Johanna and the mercury-mouthed, silken-fleshed Sad-Eyed Lady of the Lowlands, Beatrices of pop who shed not merely light but kaleidoscopic images: 'these visions of Johanna are now all that remain'.[18]

But of course, long before the seismographic impressions of *Blonde on Blonde*, Dylan's rebellions were compelling. In one sense Dylan's attacks have always been more wide-ranging and interesting than a simple charge of misogyny can encompass. Misanthropy – political and personal – is certainly as germane a context for exploring the vicious side of Dylan as misogyny. Dylan has always alternated between adapting the prophetic voice and, quite sensibly, refusing to take on the demands of his disciples. The responsibilities of the prophet towards the community have never interested him even when the oracular mode has made him more compelling. As Ron Rosenbaum writes of him during his late Seventies conversion to Christianity: 'hasn't he always taken the stance of a biblical prophet using the word and fables of both Testaments to convey his outrage? . . . Hasn't he always been arrogant and self-righteous in his jeremiads?'[19] The same accusatory voice that is exhilarating when damning the masters of war continues to exhilarate when damning his exes and soon-to-be exes, although we may occasionally feel a pang of guilt towards Suze Rotolo or Joan Baez. Talking about 'Don't Think Twice It's Alright', Jon Landau claims that Dylan usually:

> casts himself in the same light with reference to his subjects, i.e., above them . . . his lack of sympathy for the girl, the totalness of the putdown, the necessity to come right out and say it, the lack of subtlety, are all characteristics of Dylan's one-dimensional myth-making. It's just that in 'Don't Think Twice' the beauty of Dylan's vocal-guitar-harmonica performance doesn't really say what the words do, and, in fact, really transforms the verbal meaning of the song into something much deeper and much less coarse.[20]

This contrast may explain part of the power of 'Don't Think Twice', but it doesn't explain the power of 'Positively 4th Street'. The sneering contempt Dylan's voice wrenches from the word 'you' in songs such as 'Positively 4th Street' and 'Like a Rolling Stone' is exhilarating, because listening to those songs involves identifying with Dylan's rage, not with the object of it. And of course hatred is by no means solely directed towards women. The object of 'Positively 4th Street' 's rage is very likely male, but even 'Miss Lonely' of 'Like a Rolling Stone' is a moving target, sliding from contempt-drenched object to exemplary subject. After all, in the wake of the historical upheavals of the Sixties or the personal upheavals of dislocated identity, we're all like rolling stones; we all have no direction home, as the title of Robert Shelton's biography of Dylan suggests.[21] But let us also not forget that one dimensional myth-making has its uses. Anger is an energy, as Johnny Lydon said a little later on. 'You've got a lot of nerve . . .' will always thrill me.

Greil Marcus argues that Dylan's leaving behind the folk revival was in part a leaving behind of those angry political myths – the supremely satisfying but ultimately unsustainable righteous wrath of the protest world. Dylan's work from *Another Side of Bob Dylan* in 1964 shifted from politics to relationships, from black and white certainty to shades of grey. He lets in the complexity, the ugliness, the basic ambiguity of desire. Marcus writes of 'Blowin' in the Wind', 'With God on Our Side', 'A Hard Rain's A-Gonna Fall':

> These songs were embraced as great social dramas, but they were not really dramas at all. Whether one hears them ringing true or false, they were pageants of righteousness, and while within these pageants there were armies and generations, heroes and villains, nightmares and dreams, there were almost no individuals. There was no room for them in the kind of history these songs were prophesying – and certainly none for the selfish, confused, desirous individual who might suspect that his or her own story could fit no particular cause or even purpose. These songs distilled the values of the folk revival better than any others,

and what they said was that, in the face of the objective good that was the Grail of the folk revival, there could be no such thing as subjectivity.[22]

The selfish, confused, desirous individual gains the upper hand from *Highway 61 Revisited*, and Dylan's women and men become ever more intricate, even in their fleeting appearances. If it is visions of that Beatrice-like absence, Johanna, that conquer the singer's mind in 'Visions of Johanna', then it is a song that is also chock-full of other iconic and quotidian women: Mona Lisa, Madonna, the primitive wallflower, the jelly-faced women (one with a mustache), the countess, and the anti-Johanna, Louise. At first it seems that Louise might be a mysterious seer herself, as the song's magnificent opening lines indicate:

> Ain't it just like the night to play tricks when you're
>   trying to be so quiet?
> We sit here stranded, though we're all doing our best to
>   deny it
> And Louise holds a handful of rain tempting you
>   to defy it

Achieving quiet is a sometime pursuit of the cranky visionary Dylan persona, who at the end of 'Farewell Angelina' claims 'I must go where it is quiet'. In the late-night end-of- the-party/end-of-the-world atmosphere of 'Visions of Johanna' quiet is the shared attribute of the isolated community – the 'we' who are together but simultaneously 'stranded' and alone. Louise, doing the seemingly impossible, holds a handful of rain, but she is finally too fleshly to fulfil the ultimate muse function. Entwined in the arms of her lover, she is 'all right' but 'just near' – too accessible. 'She's delicate and seems like the mirror / But she just makes it all too concise and too clear / That Johanna's not here.'[23] Louise makes a poor mirror for the singer – the absent Johanna is a better reflector for the singer's narcissism. Yet it is in that poor mirroring that Louise truly comes into her own; in those lines Louise manages to become a more interesting because inaccurate imitation of both the singer and Johanna.[24] She accentuates Johanna's absence concisely and clearly and this listener, at least, likes her all the better for it. Johanna, like the iconic Madonna she resembles, still has not showed, but that is hardly surprising – she's not the type of woman who shows. Like the Sad-Eyed Lady of the Lowlands, she is the type of woman who makes the singer wait. It is Louise who gets the last spoken word in the song, however: 'But like Louise always says/ "Ya can't look at much, can ya man?"' (although the fiddler does get the last written word, scrawling 'ev'rything's been returned which was owed / On the back of a fish truck that loads' and of course the singer gets the final vision. Of Johanna.). Louise is at the heart of the song and her (Brooklyn accent-inflected?) undercutting of men who 'can't look at much' seems to throw the whole practice of vision and visions into question. Romantic visionaries beware; she is certainly no Baby Blue, of either the Gene Vincent or Bob Dylan variety.

There is of course much more to say on the ever-expanding topic of Dylan and women. A comparison of 'Shelter from the Storm' (1974) from *Blood on the Tracks* and the unreleased variant 'Up to Me' (available on *Biograph*) also reveals the range of Dylan's women, which may often begin with a fine line in madonnas and whores but which often go on to undercut each other in spectacular reversals. In 'Shelter from the Storm' the welcoming maternal goddess 'with silver bracelets on her wrists and flowers in her hair' relieves the singer from the burdens of art and martyrdom: 'She walked up to me so gracefully and took my crown of thorns'. Doing that eternal feminine thing, in the first verse she gives shape and coherence to the exhausted, emasculated biblical wanderer: 'I came in from the wilderness, a creature void of form / "Come in," she said, "I'll give you shelter from the storm"'. She's as old as time, and as basic as beauty: 'Beauty walks a razor's edge, someday I'll make it mine / If I could only turn back the clock to when God and her were born.' The heroine of 'Shelter from the Storm' corresponds to the embodied mother/lover rather than the ethereal vision Johanna, but she still embodies a plethora of feminine archetypes. 'Shelter from the Storm' is a song about a man's longing for completion in the feminine ideal even if that ideal is always retrospective, always already lost.

The sister song to 'Shelter from the Storm', 'Up to Me', signals from its title a different account of male–female relations. In this world, rather than finding completion in another, the singer relies on himself. Even when the beloved is missed: 'Well, I just can't rest without you, love, I need your company, / But you ain't a-gonna cross the line, / I guess it must be up to me'. She doesn't in any sense belong to the singer: 'And the girl with me behind the shades, she ain't my property / One of us has got to hit the road, / I guess it must be up to me.' It's a song full of partings, comic and tragic. In the intricacies of the lyrics (much like in the differing versions of 'Tangled Up In Blue') the 'you' may possibly refer to several different characters, but it definitely refers to several different variants of love and friendship. My favourite verse has the singer working for the post office:

Oh, the only decent thing I did when I worked as a
  postal clerk
Was to haul your picture down off the wall near the cage
  where I used to work.

Was I fool or not to try to protect your identity?
You looked a little burned out, my friend,
I thought it might be up to me.

This version of love – removing the beloved's mugshot from the most wanted board – is a perfect antidote to the undoubtedly compelling but comparatively clichéd relation between the sexes established in 'Shelter from the Storm'. The assumption is that the singer is not necessarily the outlaw in the relationship; the girl behind the shades graces the walls, while he does the distinctly un-macho job of postal clerk. It's hard to imagine that in the 'world of steel-eyed death, and men who are fighting to be warm' of 'Shelter from the Storm' one would find many employees of the postal system. The woman in that song is inevitably assigned the role of the angelic presence, the keeper of the hearth; she gives shelter and the man receives it. 'Up to Me', by contrast, ends with the promise of a gift from the male artist which seems not to be bound up in this dynamic of completion and incompletion:

And if we never meet again, baby, remember me,
How my lone guitar played sweet for you that old-time melody.
And the harmonica around my neck, I blew it for you, free,
No one else could play that tune,
You know it was up to me.

Dylan returns to the subject of what women want in the rambling epic 'Highlands' which concludes his 1997 album *Time Out of Mind*. In the song the burnt-out singer who 'don't want nothing from anyone' and 'wouldn't know the difference between a real blonde and a fake' has an encounter with a waitress in a restaurant in Boston:

She got a pretty face and long white shiny legs
I said 'do you know what I want?'
She said 'you probably want hard-boiled eggs'
I say 'that's right – bring me some.'
She says 'we ain't got any, you picked the wrong time to come.'
Then she says, 'I know you're an artist, draw a picture of me!'
I say 'I would if I could, but,
I don't do sketches from memory.'
'Well,' she says, 'I'm right here in front of you, or haven't you
      looked?'

Some more negotiations ensue, eventually resulting in a sketch
of the waitress done on a napkin. The waitress is not impressed:
'I make a few lines, and I show it to her to see / Well she
takes a napkin and throws it back / And says "that don't look
a thing like me!"' Next the waitress flings a disparaging question
at the singer:

'You don't read women authors, do you?'
Least that's what I think I hear her say,
'Well', I say, 'how would you know and what would it
      matter anyway?'
'Well', she says, 'you just don't seem like you do!'
      I said, 'you're way wrong.'
She says, 'which ones have you read then?' I say, 'I read
      Erica Jong!'

In 'Highlands' the singer first asks the waitress if she knows
what he wants ('If you can read my mind, why must I speak?'
says the singer in 'Angelina'); she guesses successfully that he's
hankering for some hard-boiled *eggs* – symbolically at least still
fascinated by the mystery of the feminine after all these years.

But the dynamics of supply and demand soon shift when the waitress recognizes him as an artist. Unlike in 'Up to Me' when the harmonica is blown 'for free', this masterpiece is bullied out of the artist. And it doesn't satisfy. Once again the waitress is no Baby Blue; neither is she like Connie of 'Where Are You Going, Where Have You Been?', who doesn't seem to notice that Arnold Friend describes her as his 'sweet little blue-eyed girl' despite the brownness of her eyes. She recognizes a false portrait when she sees one and she speaks a different language entirely to the aging reluctant artist. When she puts him on the spot about his feminist credentials, and he can only come up with the author of *Fear of Flying* before wandering out of the diner, we feel that we have witnessed Dylan making fun of himself, placing himself as old (the only woman author he can think of wrote her trashy opus in the Seventies) to the waitress's young, as well as male to her female. As Michael Gray puts it, 'The whole gift of Bob Dylan giving us a cameo of feminist debate, and wholly free of any unpleasant reactionary sneering, is a delightful surprise, totally outside the range of subject matter we expect from him.'[25] Of course this may be a little over-indulgent – I suspect that Dylan is also making fun of the waitress who pesters him for a picture and then complains. There's an implied sneer at almost everyone in some of his most successful recent songs such as 'Not Dark Yet' and 'Things Have Changed' as well as 'Highlands'. For me, perhaps the most amusing line is the 'Least that's what I think I hear her say'. Is the artist going deaf? Or is he now being scrupulous about what women actually say, when they no longer seem to offer shelter from the storm, or even, for that matter, hard-boiled eggs? Perhaps in another version of the song the answer to the question might be that he's read Joyce Carol Oates. From my perspective, it seems as if they've effectively read each other.

13

LOOKING FOR NOTHING: DYLAN NOW

Aidan Day

In the earlier part of his career Dylan's vehement moral sense was directed – not exclusively but most famously – outwards. It castigated masters of war and cauterised white judges who handed out six-month sentences to white murderers of black kitchen maids. But the rich vein of interiority which also characterised the first sixteen years of his work had, by the Christian phase of the late 1970s and early 1980s, developed into a tortured moral self-scrutiny. Dylan had always been haunted by a sense of mortality –

> Death kept followin', trackin' us down, at least I heard
> your bluebird sing.
> Now somebody's got to show their hand, time is an
> enemy ...

> ('Up to Me', 1974)

– but in songs from 1979 he started reviewing his life in the context of a 'spiritual warfare' where there is 'no neutral ground' ('Precious Angel'). Reviewing his life in the face of an impending Judgement, a final reckoning, a cataclysmic separation of the evil from the good when 'darkness ... will fall from on high / When men will beg God to kill them and they won't be able to die' ('Precious Angel'). In this Christian phase, disgust at the licence of his own profession – particularly the masculinist licence – is cast in absolute moral terms:

You might be a rock 'n' roll addict prancing on the stage,
You might have drugs at your command, women in a cage ...

But you're gonna have to serve somebody ...
Well, it may be the devil or it may be the lord ...

('Gotta Serve Somebody')

Self-disgust grounds the discontent in another song of the same period, 'Trouble in Mind'. It grounds the song's anxiety about death. It is not just sudden death that is feared in this song, but death that is unprepared for. Because the voice of conscience intimates that both itself and the chance of ultimate salvation are threatened by the egoism of a commanding career:

I got to know, Lord, when to pull back on the reins,
Death can be the result of the most underrated pain ...
Here comes Satan, prince of the power of the air,
He's gonna make you a law unto yourself, gonna build a
   bird's nest in your hair.
He's gonna deaden your conscience 'til you worship the
   work of your own hands,
You'll be serving strangers in a strange, forsaken land.

('Trouble in Mind')

The chance of salvation is threatened also by an inveterate sexual exploitativeness. People notice appropriation and scorn in some of Dylan's images of women ('Ah, you fake just like a woman . . . You make love just like a woman . . . Then you ache just like a woman / But you break just like a little girl'; 'Just Like a Woman', 1966). They notice less his troubled self-consciousness about masculine drive:

> Satan whispers to ya, 'Well, I don't want to bore ya,
> But when ya get tired of the Miss So-and-so I got
>   another woman for ya'.
>
> ('Trouble in Mind')

A variant on the association made in the Christian lyrics between forces of darkness and ungoverned sexual drive appears in a later song, 'Man in the Long Black Coat' (1989). The scene at the opening of this visually very graphic song paints the aftermath of a powerful natural force:

> Crickets are chirpin', the water is high,
> There's a soft cotton dress on the line hangin' dry,
> The window's wide open, African trees bent over
>   backwards from a hurricane breeze.

The delicacy and vulnerability of that dress are germane to the song. Because the impact of the hurricane is a motif for a force that has swept away the woman or girl who might have worn it. A man:

> Not a word of goodbye, not even a note,
> She gone with the man in the long black coat.

The mysterious traveller who comes into town and effects some transformation before disappearing is an archetype of American film. The transformation may be redemptive, life-giving. The traveller may fulfil a Christ-like function. But here the traveller has a distinctly disturbing aspect. Concealing another countenance, he is, in part, a figure of death:

> Somebody seen him hanging around
> At the old dance hall on the outskirts of town,
> He looked into her eyes when she stopped him to ask
> If he wanted to dance, he had a face like a mask.
> Somebody said from the Bible he'd quote
> There was dust on the man in the long black coat.

Death and the erotic court each other here. The man in the long black coat, wearing not just the dust of journey but that of death, figures at the same time a sinister, even Satanically seductive masculinity. His attractiveness, his power of compulsion, sufficient to provoke the girl to approach him, is strong enough to cause her to abandon home, to leave the safe and the known. And she made a mistake.

In the fourth stanza Dylan criticises a certain view that there are no mistakes in life, that everything happens, fundamentally, without our consent. Such a view is cast as the easy attitude of people who neither live life to its fullness nor face death in its extremity. The girl had sought to break out of superficial routine. She took a risk:

> There are no mistakes in life, some people say,
> It is true sometimes you can see it that way,
> But people don't live or die, people just float.
> She went with the man in the long black coat.

She took a risk and she made a mistake. Just how serious a mistake is captured in the way the final stanza defines the scene of the lyric as witness to an energy that is menacing in its frustration, an energy that is the opposite of anything vital:

> There's smoke on the water, it's been there since June,
> Tree trunks uprooted 'neath the high crescent moon.
> Feel the pulse and vibration and the rumbling force,
> Somebody is out there beating on a dead horse.

If Dylan attributes, in 'Man in the Long Black Coat', a negative, destructive dimension to masculinity itself, then, at the same time, he raises doubts about whether there is a human faculty which can take the measure of that dimension. In the third stanza he has lines which question the idea that human beings have any capacity for morally pure judgement:

> Preacher was talkin', there's a sermon he gave,
> He said every man's conscience is vile and depraved,
> You cannot depend on it to be your guide,
> When it's you who must keep it satisfied.

St Paul may have said that the conscience of the 'defiled' is itself defiled, but at least he allowed that for 'the pure all things are pure' (Titus, 1:15). The darker vision in these lines, where the last two isolate their point with the ticking discrimination of 't' sounds, is that there is no such thing as purity. No such thing as a reliable faculty of conscience for anyone. Conscience is, rather, complicit in the evil that it judges. It doesn't stand above the evil that one does. It depends, instead, *on* one doing wrong. It *needs* one to do wrong so that it can itself exist. The conscience shares in the interest of the ego. The disturbing point in the passage is that the conscience may be seen as *causing* one to do wrong, itself generating evil in a self-fulfilling and self-justifying loop. The point may apply to the girl, who made a mistake and followed danger but whose real mistake was to be tricked by a corrupt conscience into making the mistake. It may apply to the figure in the long black coat who would be taking the girl to keep, as it were, his conscience satisfied.

The Christian songs maintain a sense of conscience as something that will speak of things like the negativity of certain forms of masculine drive. There is a conviction – although it sometimes sounds more like an assertion – that renovation is possible. 'Man in the Long Black Coat', again figuring a doubtful potency of masculinity, has lines which deny the integrity of conscience. But the Southern Gothic ambience of the song maintains a sense of the right even as it conjures the prevalence of evil. What is different about Dylan now – in his recent work from *Time Out of Mind* (1997), through 'Things Have Changed' (2000), to '*Love and Theft*' (2001) – is that everything has been demythologised. And not just the Gothic. Good and evil have lost their metaphysical significance. The conscience has lost connotations of the pure and neither is it worth considering for its dark treacheries. Dylan's moral self-scrutiny and the associated unease are still apparent, particularly in matters to do with sexual desire, but it is a kind of secularised scrutiny, a scrutiny without spiritual issue. It is not held within a viable apparatus of self-transformation. 'I was born here and I'll die here, against my will, / I know it looks like I'm moving, but I'm standing still', says Dylan in one of the songs from *Time Out of Mind* ('Not Dark Yet'). Where he once made poetry out of change and mutation ('he not busy being born / Is busy dying'; 'It's Alright, Ma (I'm Only Bleeding)', 1965), Dylan is now making poetry out of stasis.

'Highlands', the one-hundred-line talking blues song which closes *Time Out of Mind*, focuses many of the preoccupations of the entire album, as indeed of much of his work since 1997. In the second stanza of 'Highlands', what is nightmarish is not something that lies outside the ordinary but the exact opposite – the nightmare is that there is nothing more to the ordinary than the ordinary. The preternatural meaning in the Gothic trope of bad dreams is reversed: 'Windows were shaking all night in my dreams / Everything was exactly the way that it seems'. Dylan's feeling is of being trapped in a monochromatic, exhausted normality where nothing is imaginatively or spiritually rich. This lack of any transfiguration of the commonplace undermines his ability to distinguish between the authentic and the false: 'Wouldn't know the difference between a real blonde and a fake', he tells us. Artificial blonde is a tampering, not a transfiguration. Authentic blonde is invested with a richness of the real. Where the whole of reality was once rich, full of hints, mysteries, untract conclusions, it has now lost that fertile dimension. And so Dylan's sense of the authentic, his passionate, imaginative apprehension of the real, is lacking.

The condition leaves him in limbo – a state repeatedly defined in the songs from *Time Out of Mind*. 'I've been walking through the middle of nowhere', he sings in 'Tryin' to Get to Heaven'. In 'Not Dark Yet' we hear that 'There's not even room enough to be anywhere' and that 'Every nerve in my body is so vacant and numb / I can't even remember what it was I came here to get away from'. 'Night or day, it doesn't matter where I go any more; I just go', we are told in 'Can't Wait'. Towards the end of 'Highlands' he is reduced to having to think up things that he might need. Having to make fictions of what might satisfy him, of what might be rewarding. He is so dissociated that he is not even interested in the political process, his lack of interest heightened in the flatly ironic delivery of Dylan's singing:

> I'm crossing the street to get away from a mangy dog,
> Talking to myself in a monologue.
> I think what I need might be a full length leather coat,
> Somebody just asked me
> If I registered to vote.

Comparable kinds of verbal and vocal irony – comparable kinds of self-deflating humour – are used by Dylan in songs from '*Love and Theft*'. The speaker of 'Lonesome Day Blues', for example, confesses that the metaphorical wind of inspiration, of mystery and insight, is unintelligible: 'Last night the wind was whispering something, I was trying to make out what it was / Yeah, I tell myself something's coming, but it never does'.

The sensation of internal and external diminishment on *Time Out of Mind* is conceived as a function of ageing. When he was young Dylan was able to attack the *mores* of his elders with a maturity of vision that outstripped theirs. And he was always good at imagining the depredations of older age. In 'Shelter from the Storm' (1975):

> I've heard newborn babies wailin' like a mournin' dove
> And old men with broken teeth stranded without love.

This is appreciating old age from the outside. In *Time Out of Mind* he is speaking from inside the state of being stranded. Dylan's regret at ageing on this album is very frank: 'All the young men with their young women looking so good / Well, I'd trade places with any of them / In a minute, if I could'

('Highlands'). But it is not crass envy of the young. It is regret at having lost youth's engagement with reality's abundance and variety. No longer fired by the world – 'I ain't looking for nothing in anyone's eyes' ('Not Dark Yet') – there is 'nothing left to burn' ('Standing in the Doorway'). Even the conscience is spiritually void:

> If I had a conscience, well I just might blow my top.
> What would I do with it anyway?
> Maybe take it to the pawn shop.
>
> ('Highlands')

The sense of conscience as no more than a commodity touches the scrutiny of masculinity, the examination of the compulsion of male sexual feeling, that Dylan also undertakes both in 'Things Have Changed' and in 'Highlands'. It is a moral scrutiny where nothing hangs on the morality of the scrutiny.

The opening lines of 'Things Have Changed' tell of a sense of displacement in older age, a sense of not being able to connect with the past and of having no expectations of the future: 'A worried man with a worried mind / No one in front of me and nothing behind'. Then, there is a nameless woman:

> There's a woman on my lap and she's drinking champagne,
> Got white skin, got assassin's eyes.
> I'm looking up into the sapphire tinted skies,
> I'm well dressed, waiting on the last train
> Standing on the gallows with my head in a noose.
> Any minute now I'm expecting all hell to break loose.

The woman's assassin's eyes identify as much his susceptibility to her as any threat offered by her. To this extent, the danger comes from within. 'I've been trying to get as far away from myself as I can', comments Dylan, later in the song. But the extent to which the woman is threatening defines the barrenness of the relationship that is being described. A part of him may be after her white skin, but she is after something too – a kind of kill, seducing this man of authority, position, power. So it's not straightforward, who is hooking whom. They are both extracting something from it. Each, in a sense, exploiting the other. A metaphorical hell might be about to break loose, but in this loveless situation he is already implicated in a kind of purgatory. The 'last train', the 'gallows', and the expectation of 'hell', contradict such positive content as the experience with the woman holds. The man's worry comes in part from ambivalence about his own indulgence in the woman and equal ambivalence about her assault on him, and partly from his knowing that, while he should be getting ready for the last train, preparing for death, he finds himself in this uncertain condition, still addicted to the sexual appeal of women, resigned to that addiction, yet recoiling from the woman's possible motives in being drawn to him. Nor is it just that he should be attending to graver things than the pleasures of the senses. There's a suggestion not merely of death approaching but – in the gallows and in the prospect of hell breaking loose – an anxiety about judgement. As if he's morally compromised in his susceptibility to the appeal of those 'eyes'.

Morally compromised, also, in the power which he exercises in the sexual relation described, whatever power the woman may be exercising. Dylan knowingly provides a patriarchal cliché in the phrase 'woman on my lap'. He summarises all the seigneurial force of his position in this picturing of the woman as little girl: him older, moneyed, famous. But the self-consciousness of the summary dispels any crass celebration of the position, just as the woman's own self-command as assassin undermines it. What is interesting is the way in which the moral unease in the passage as a whole qualifies the masculine power that is defined at its outset. The complex response to his own response to the woman unsettles and re-imagines the stereotypical figure of male sexual authority.

None of this leads anywhere. There is no resolution. The judgement is not Judgement. There is no possibility of spiritual reconstruction. Just self-division and unrelieved distress. A sense either of entrapment or of alienation. There is no middle ground: 'I'm locked in tight, I'm out of range', as Dylan sings in the refrain. But there is an awareness of a problem within masculinity itself. An awareness of intense conflicts of interest within the masculine self. The problem is something Dylan addresses at greater length in 'Highlands'.

Across seven of the twenty stanzas of this song Dylan pictures himself encountering a waitress in a restaurant. The episode is a kind of allegory and, in Dylan's performance on *Time Out of Mind*, a clue to its meaning comes in the first stanza of the sequence as he observes that there is 'Nobody in the place but me and her'. He sings 'her' with an insinuation that stresses not simply her gender but her sexuality. It is, from his perspective, an erotically charged moment; a point stressed three lines later when we hear that 'She got a pretty face and long white shiny legs'. In his performance of the succeeding lines Dylan recounts a drily funny exchange between himself and the waitress about what he wants and whether the restaurant has any hard-boiled eggs. But those long, white, shiny legs have already told us one of the things, at least, that he wants, and it's obviously not actual hard-boiled eggs. It is no mystery. The rest of the episode with the waitress bears the point out. She suddenly – in what is apparently a

mixture of flattery and flirtation – insists that he make a portrait of her:

> Then she says, 'I know you're an artist, draw a picture
>   of me'.
> I said, 'I would if I could, but,
> I don't do sketches from memory'.
>
> 'Well', she says, 'I'm right here in front of you, or
>   haven't you looked?'
> I say, 'all right, I know, but I don't have my drawing
>   book'.
> She gives me a napkin, she says, 'you can do it on that'.
> I say, 'yes I could but,
> I don't know where my pencil is at'.
>
> She pulls one out from behind her ear,
> She says 'all right now, go ahead, draw me, I'm standing
>   right here'.
> I make a few lines, and I show it for her to see.
> Well she takes the napkin and throws it back
> And says 'that don't look a thing like me!'
>
> I said, 'Oh, kind miss, it most certainly does'.
> She says, 'you must be jokin''. I say, 'I wish I was'.
> Then she says, 'you don't read women authors, do you?'
> At least that's what I think I hear her say,
> 'Well', I say, 'how would you know and what would it
>   matter anyway?'
>
> 'Well', she says, 'you just don't seem like you do'.
> I said, 'you're way wrong'.
> She says, 'which ones have you read then?' I say, 'I've
>   read Erica Jong'.

She goes away for a minute and I slide up out of
    my chair.
I step outside back to the busy street, but nobody's going
    anywhere.

There's mild comedy in the man's attempts to resist drawing the picture, his attempts to deflect her confrontations. But what is it that he finally draws which she is so contemptuous of? And why the business about women authors and Erica Jong?

The woman's reminder, 'I'm right here in front of you', puts one in mind of something Dylan said in his foreword to the collection of his own sketches published in 1994 as *Drawn Blank*:

> My drawing instructor in high school lectured and
> demonstrated continuously to 'draw only what you can
> see' so that if you were at a loss for words, something
> could be explained and even more importantly,
> not misunderstood . . . draw it only if it is in front
> of you.

The great majority of the drawings of women in *Drawn Blank* show them in various degrees of undress. They reveal the gaze of an implacably male sexual imagination. It is possible that the man in 'Highlands', having focused on the woman's pretty face and long legs, has indeed drawn only what he sees – her body and her sexuality, or, rather, his sense of her sexuality. He is himself uneasy with the image of her that he has made. When she rejects the drawing – 'that don't look a thing like me!' – his reply, amplified in the tonalities of Dylan's performance of the lines, carries so much darkness, so much awareness that the picture of her in his mind and now in the drawing has in a fundamental way violated her: 'Oh, kind miss, it most certainly does'/ She says, 'you must be jokin', I say, 'I wish I was'. The comedy here is very black. He had tried hard to avoid drawing how he sees her, tried hard to avoid not being misunderstood, tried hard to avoid exposing the masculine gaze.

Having had that gaze and its objectifications exhibited, the woman immediately asks: 'you don't read women authors, do you?' The man's eventual reply that he has read Erica Jong fits the terms of the scene, read like this, precisely. It is another provocation in the repartee that has seen the man and the woman each turn the other's statement on its head. The mention of Jong is an aggressive act rather than a simple listing. Because Jong – as we are reminded in the entry on her in the *Cambridge Guide to Women's Writing in English* (1999) – 'introduced', in her most notorious novel, *Fear of Flying* (1973), 'the concept of "the zipless fuck": an ideal of casual, fulfilling, guilt-free sex which liberated the sexual expectations of a generation of women'. If the waitress rejects a particular kind of sexualised drawing of herself and implies that, not reading women authors, the man doesn't know anything about women, then he responds by pointing out that his familiarity with the work of a female author who has been classified as a feminist might very well lead him to expect the same objectifying compulsions in women as he finds in himself. That it *might* lead him to expect that his drawing would *not* simply be rejected. The scene as a whole is about uncertainty and turmoil in the man's mind (Jong aptly rhymes with 'wrong'). He may be unclear about what women want. But this is part and parcel of his perplexity about what he cannot help himself from wanting. The indignation in his riposte to the woman's presumption that he doesn't read women authors – 'How would you know . . . ?' – is endorsed in his sarcastic, sneering performance of the question. More significant is his observation – 'what would it matter anyway?' – which implies that, whether he read them or not, it would make little difference to his underlying sexual response. Erica Jong may have sought to free women from guilt about sexual compulsion, but Dylan is riven with disorder and guilt about the relentlessness of his own male eye: '... "you must be jokin'". I say, "I wish I was"'.

The depth of Dylan's anxiety about the whole issue is signalled by the line in which we hear: 'At least that's what I think I hear her say'. It is this observation which, more than any other single thing, turns this passage of the song into an exploration – rather than a mere description – of an exchange. The whole thing is so interiorised that it's perhaps even *his* inner voice which has come up with the point about women's writing and self-expression. He is not sure that the waitress has said it but that's what he hears because, ever since he saw those long white shiny legs, he's been going over his reaction to them in his mind. The peculiar honesty of Dylan's verse here lies in the recognition that the problem of conflicting impulses and perspectives within the man – his gaze and his simultaneous recoil from that gaze – may be irresolvable. But it's not irresolvable just for the man in this song. The sequence with the waitress ends with him returning to the 'busy street' where 'nobody's going anywhere'. The ancient business of confusion about, and mutual incomprehension between, the sexes concerning what and how the other sex wants has not been resolved by debates about gender in the last half-century or so and the issue is not advancing anywhere, for anyone, however much we may think we have sorted the matter.

The sense of impasse affects matters of love as well as of plain sex. Throughout *Time Out of Mind* Dylan articulates the feeling of being stranded without love. This is more than the question of the emptiness of casual encounters. Experiences of the loss of real love are part and parcel of the exhaustion registered in the album. In 'Love Sick', for example, there is the felt oppression of, and the frustrated rage at, desertion and betrayal:

> Sometimes the silence can be like thunder,
> Sometimes I wanna take to the road and plunder.
> Could you ever be true?
> I think of you
> And I wonder.

'Standing in the Doorway' confides vulnerability and yearning after abandonment:

> I can hear the church bells ringing in the yard,
> I wonder who they're ringing for.
> I know I can't win
> But my heart just won't give in.
>
> Last night I danced with a stranger,
> But she just reminded me you were the one,
> You left me standing in the doorway crying
> In the dark land of the sun.

'My heart just won't give in'. *Time Out of Mind* is instinct with open-heartedness ('It always means so much / Even the softest touch'; 'Standing in the Doorway'. And what is crucial is that the intimacy, the rawness, lie at the heart of songs which speak of older age in terms of its alienation, its displacement, its distancing. Songs which speak authentically of having lost any sense of authenticity. Songs which speak of an inability to understand new ways of understanding ('Feel further away than ever before / Some things in life, it just gets too late to learn'; 'Highlands'). Songs which speak of not wishing to speak about love ('I see nothing to be gained by any explanation / There are no words that need to be said'; 'Standing in the Doorway'). Songs which speak of having lost any political message ('my sense of humanity has gone down the drain'; 'Not Dark Yet'). Songs which tell of un-heroic, un-Herculean defeat ('Reality has always had too many heads . . . There are some kind of things you can never kill'; 'Cold Irons Bound'). Songs which speak, paradoxically, of having nothing at all left to communicate ('The party's over, and there's less and less to say / I got new eyes / Everything looks far away'; 'Highlands').

But it is the emotional trueness and the acutely discriminating self-consciousness with which the irresolutions of older age are explored that make the album specially valuable. Love doesn't stop. Hurt doesn't stop. The libido won't lie down. Anxiety about it doesn't cease. The sense of new, hungry generations bearing down is overwhelming. 'Peace will come', sang Dylan in 1978, just before entering fully into his period of Christian belief, 'with tranquillity and splendor on the wheels of fire' ('Changing of the Guards'). The refrain of 'Highlands', beginning each time with 'my heart's in the Highlands', alludes to Robert Burns's song of that title. Burns reworked an old piece from the folk tradition, 'The strong walls of Derry', in his song of yearning for some better state of heart and mind, imaged in a nostalgically idealised Scottish Highlands: 'My heart's in the Highlands, my heart is not here; / My heart's in the Highlands a-chasing the deer'. Dylan's 'Highlands' massively redefines the Burns song and is of an altogether different order of achievement. But in his refrain Dylan does maintain, in a generic way, the spirit of yearning for release:

> Well, my heart's in the Highlands, gentle and fair
> Honeysuckle blooming in the wildwood air . . .

> my heart's in the Highlands, wherever I roam
> That's where I'll be when I get called home.
> The wind, it whispers to the buckeyed trees in rhyme
> Well, my heart's in the Highlands,
> I can only get there one step at a time.

In the last refrain of the song Dylan claims peace of mind in being able to imagine, as in a fairy tale, peace in mind:

> Well, my heart's in the Highlands at the break of day
> Over the hills and far away.
> There's a way to get there, and I'll figure it out somehow
> But I'm already there in my mind
> And that's good enough for now.

'Over the hills and far away'. It is an evocative line from the English nursery-rhyme, fairy tale tradition. It suggests an ultimately inexpressible yearning. But it doesn't reassure that solid grounds for peace have been established. In a comparable way, in the song 'Bye and Bye' from '*Love and Theft*', there is an invocation – through the references to 'briars' and 'wild roses' – of stock properties of fairy-tale and romance. But where the torment suggested by the briars is defined also in other terms, the promise of the 'wild roses' remains only a stock property:

> Well, I'm scufflin' and I'm shufflin' and I'm walkin' on briars,
> I'm not even acquainted with my own desires.
> I'm rollin' slow, I'm doin' all I know
> I'm tellin' myself I've found true happiness,
> That I still got a dream that hasn't been repossessed,
> I'm rollin' slow, goin' where the wild roses grow.

Neither in 'Bye and Bye' nor in 'Highlands' does peace arrive with splendour on wheels of fire. The last lines on the last song of *Time Out of Mind* do lift a little the mood of the album as a whole. That said, the abiding impression of *Time Out of Mind* is one of near despair as it shows, uncompromisingly, the ways in which older age brings neither peace, nor joy, nor love, nor certitude, nor help for pain.

Something about Dylan's voice and the sensuousness of the music bring it all vividly home. But it is there, centrally, in the words. The peculiar power of the lyrics on *Time Out of Mind* is their sheer confessionality. Dylan comes from a culture much given to self-revelation. But he does not subscribe to the vulgarity that can make displays of the self seem forms of self-disguise. He pursues the inner reaches of the self with a ruthless honesty and intelligence. His song poems – finely crafted as they are – succeed in speaking as if there were no wall of poetic convention separating the statement from the listener. It is that capacity to conjure a sense of there being no poetic distance, in lyrics which are about other, graver kinds of distance, that constitutes one of Dylan's major contributions to lyric poetry in English.

14

AMERICAN RECORDINGS:
ON '*LOVE AND THEFT*' AND
THE MINSTREL BOY*

Sean Wilentz

It is May 24, 1966, and at the Olympia in Paris, also known as 'la salle la plus importante d'Europe,' time slips.

Exactly two years after this night of music, many of the young people who are in the audience will be rioting in the Paris streets, their heads full of ideas that will drive them to proclaim a revolution of the imagination, fight pitched battles with the police and the National Guard, and try to burn down the Paris Stock Exchange, in what would become known forever in Left Bank lore as 'la nouvelle nuit des barricades,' the most dramatic cataclysm of May '68. Seven hundred and ninety-five rioters are arrested, and 456 are injured.

But now it's exactly two years earlier, to the minute, and the rebels-to-be sit expectantly, waiting for the second half of the show, when the curtain parts, and there they see to their horror, attached to the backdrop, the emblem of everything they are coming to hate, the emblem of napalm and Coca-Cola and

---

* This essay was commissioned by bobdylan.com, where a slightly shorter version originally appeared in 2001.

white racism and colonialism and imagination's death. It is a huge fifty-star American flag.

What's the joke? But it is no joke. They are here to hear the idol, and know full well that the idol now will play electric (after what turned out to be a frustrating-to-all-concerned acoustic set), but this stars-and-stripes stuff turns a musical challenge into an assault, an incitement, as in your face – more so – to the young Left Bank leftists as any Fender Telecaster. In England, the idol had traded insults with the hecklers, but in Paris, on this, his twenty-fifth birthday, he strikes first.

Whether they like it or not, the idol will give them his own version of 'America', a place that they have never learned about in books, and, if they have, that they do not comprehend.

Not quite five months after this concert, the French pop singer Johnny Hallyday plays the Olympia. He has two young women back-up singers, one wearing a miniskirt, the other, vaguely resembling Marianne Faithfull, dressed in trousers and a vest. He also has a back-up band that doubles as his warm-up act, a new group, still in formation and a little rough, that is introduced to the audience as hailing from Seattle, Washington, and that performs, among other numbers, a bent-out-of-shape version of the Troggs' top-40 summer smash 'Wild Thing'. There is no flag, and by now the Paris audience has caught up – musically enough to be amazed, not dismayed, by the Jimi Hendrix Experience, in its fourth public appearance.

Suddenly, it's May '66 again, Hendrix and company have vanished, and the star-spangled banner is back. An organist and a drummer and a bunch of guitarists take the Olympia stage. The organist is the guy from the Sir Douglas Quintet, and the lead guitarist is only ten years old or so, and the headliner, skinny as a fence rail, has swapped his Mod-cut houndstooth suit for a black and silver Nashville number, and he wears a five-gallon hat; and somehow during the intermission he has sprouted a Dapper Dan pencil moustache. Then the kid guitarist turns into a grownup and the band rips into, not 'Tell Me, Momma,' but a faster version of 'From a Buick 6,' curling the ears of the rebels-to-be. The headliner rasps the opening lines:

> Tweedle Dum and Tweedle Dee
> They're throwin' knives into the tree

Love and theft, Bob Dylan has said, fit together like fingers in a glove. But don't quote somebody when you can steal.

The new album's title, people have noticed, is the same as a book by Eric Lott on the origins and character of American blackface minstrelsy. In the 1820s and 1830s, young working-class white men from the North began imitating Southern slaves on stage, blacking up and playing banjoes and tambourines and rat-a-tat bones sets, jumping and singing in a googly-eyed 'Yass suh, Noooooo sah' dialect about sex and love and death and just plain nonsense. The minstrels stole from blacks and caricatured them, and often showed racist contempt – but their theft was also an act of envy and desire and love. Bluenoses condemned the shows as vulgar. Aficionados, from Walt Whitman to Abraham Lincoln to Mark Twain, adored the minstrels for their fun, and for much more than that. '"Nigger" singing with them,' Whitman wrote of one blackface troupe in 1846, 'is a subject from obscure life in the hands of a divine painter.'

Whether Dylan stole his title from Lott is anybody's guess. But there is plenty of theft and love (and divinity) in '*Love and Theft*,' some of it obvious. One needn't know much more about the songs of Robert Johnson and the rest of the Delta blues players than the versions copped by the Rolling Stones in order to recognize the po' boy prodigal son or the line in

'Tweedle Dee and Tweedle Dum' about someone's love being 'all in vain.' Johnson again, but also the upcountry white pickers Clarence Ashley and Dock Boggs get plundered on 'High Water (For Charley Patton),' the best song on the album. Patton, who is something of the presiding shade of '*Love and Theft*,' also wrote and recorded a song about the great 1927 flood in Mississippi, 'High Water Everywhere.' 'Lonesome Day Blues' was the title of a song by Blind Willie McTell of Georgia.

Dylan has been committing this kind of theft all of his working life, right down to swiping his own surname. The tune of 'Song to Woody,' on his very first album, is a direct steal of Guthrie's own '1913 Massacre.' At a press conference in San Francisco late in 1965, one questioner, who turned out to be Allen Ginsberg, asked Dylan if there would 'ever be a time when you'll be hung as a thief?' (After a wave of laughter, Dylan replied, almost chuckling, 'You weren't supposed to say that.') Now, as then, Dylan is a minstrel, filching other people's diction and mannerisms and melodies and lyrics and transforming them and making them his own, a form of larceny that is as American as apple pie, and cherry, pumpkin and plum pie, too. Or as American as Chang and Eng, the original Siamese twins, who, though born in Siam, started touring the United States in proto-carny style in 1829, coming to town right beside the minstrels, before they signed up in 1832 with P.T. Barnum, for whom they worked for seven years and then retired to Wilkesboro, North Carolina, became American citizens, married a pair of sisters, and raised two families before showing up on '*Love and Theft*', for 'Honest with Me.'

But Dylan is a modern minstrel – a whiteface minstrel. The hard-edged racism taken for granted by the nineteenth-century troupes is of another age. The disguises that Dylan has sported on stage – 'I have my Bob Dylan mask on,' he told his New York audience, off the cuff, on Halloween night, 1964 – are more of himself, his time, and his America. While he has tipped his hat to the old-time minstrels, he has inverted their display, as when he actually whitened his face for the Rolling Thunder Revue.

As a modern minstrel, he has continually updated and widened his ambit, never more so than on '*Love and Theft*,' lifting what he pleases from the last century's great American songbook. Folksongs, as ever: the wonderful tag line of 'Mississippi' comes from an old folk tune called 'Rosie.' 'The Darktown Strutters' Ball' is here, plain as day. But there are also melodies and lyrics reminiscent of songs from the 1930s and 1940s and 1950s, and bits and pieces of the rockabilly 'Hopped-Up Mustang' appear on 'Summer Days' and 'High Water.'

(In a disarming little story about three jolly kings that became the liner notes to '*John Wesley Harding*', Dylan pokes fun at the Dylanologists who search for the great true meaning in his songs. 'Faith is the key!' one king says, 'No, froth is the key!' the second says; 'You're both wrong,' says the third, 'the key is Frank!' In the story, the third king is right, sort of – but who would have ever imagined that Frank might turn out to be someone like Sinatra?)

And, of course, among the great old last-century songwriters whom Dylan recycles is himself – and not just from his songs or his adaptations of other people's. In New Orleans, there was a streetcar that had as its destination a street called 'Desire.' Tennessee Williams used it for the title of his play; Dylan appears to have adapted it (or used Williams) for the title of an album. (*Streetcar*, the play, seems to turn up elsewhere in Dylan, as in Blanche Dubois's immortal line about how her family's 'epic fornications' led to the loss of its estate on a called-in mortgage: 'The four-letter word deprived us of our plantation,' Blanche remembers, the word in question being either fuck or love.) Well, 'Desire' is back on '*Love and Theft*'. 'Tweedle Dee and Tweedle Dum' and 'Honest With Me' and 'Cry A While' are all variations of standard 12-bar blues, but listen hard and I think you'll catch the musicality of 'Buick 6' (especially the rare withdrawn version, if you've had the chance to hear it) and of 'Leopard-Skin Pill-Box Hat' (like 'Song to Woody,' a standard number in Dylan's recent live shows) and of 'Pledging My Time.' (Same thing with the 8-bar blues 'Po' Boy' and the 8-bar 'Cocaine,' yet another recent concert standard.) The opening guitar lick of 'High Water' brings my ear back to 'Down in the Flood'; and the rest of the song recalls John Lee Hooker's 'Tupelo,' as rendered on the complete bootleg version of '*The Basement Tapes*'. Dylan's been singing his own version of 'The Coo Coo' at least since his Gaslight days forty years ago.

There's no message to this modern minstrel style. It is a style, a long-evolving style, not a doctrine or an ideology. But that's not to say that Dylan, a craftsman, is unaware of that style, or that we should be either. Several years ago, Johnny Cash released an excellent album of traditional songs which he called '*American Recordings*'. '*Love and Theft*' could have the same title, though Dylan's musical reach is even wider than the great Cash's, and his minstrelsy more complicated. He's unfurled that American flag once again.

In keeping with the seemingly miscellaneous but highly struc- tured randomness of the minstrel shows, '*Love and Theft*' is an album of songs – greatest hits, except they haven't become hits yet, Dylan has said. And like the shows, the album is funny, maybe the funniest Dylan has produced since he was writing songs like 'Outlaw Blues.' Some of the jokes, like the minstrels', read flat on the page – 'Freddy or not here I come' – but Dylan's delivery of them makes me laugh out loud. Here's another one, a rimshot pun that could have come right from an old minstrel show – dull to read, but funny when sung:

> I'm stark naked but I don't care
> I'm goin' off into the woods I'm hunt'n' bare

When asked who his favourite poets were in 1965, Dylan mentioned a flying-trapeze family from the circus, Smokey Robinson, and W. C. Fields (who through vaudeville had his own connections to minstrelsy); now, in 'Lonesome Day Blues,' he pays a little homage to Field's snowbound gag-line in *The Fatal Glass of Beer*: 'T'aint fit night out for man nor beast!'

Many of the other jokes are high – low literary and operatic. Don Pasquale's 2 a.m. booty call in 'Cry A While' comes right out of Donizetti's *Don Pasquale*, a farce about an old man's lust for young women, first performed in Paris in 1843 – high-minstrel time in America. Then there are the Shakespearean jokes about shivering old Othello and the bad-complexioned Juliet. All of these high–low jokes, too, are in the updated minstrel style, last heard from Dylan in this humorous way on '*Highway 61 Revisited*': the blackface companies regularly performed spoofs of grand opera and Shakespeare (*Hamlet* was a particular favourite) – works as familiar to popular American audiences a century and a half ago as *Seinfeld* and Walt Disney are today.

Dylan delivers every joke poker-faced, like someone out of something by the minstrel show patron Twain. And some of the jokes are sinister. To the steel-guitar background in 'Moonlight,' all is songbirds and flowers in the heavy dusk, when, lightly lilting, the crooner sings:

> Well, I'm preachin' peace and harmony,
> The blessings of tranquillity,
> Yet I know when the time is right to strike.

> I'll take you 'cross the river, dear,
> You've no need to linger here;
> I know the kinds of things you like . . .

Ah, the silver-tongued devil. Rudy Vallee turns into Robert Mitchum. It's scary, and yet it's hilarious.

And there is plenty more serious and fearful play on '*Love and Theft*'. More than any old-time minstrel (and more like later bluesmen and 'country' singers) Dylan thinks about the cosmos contained in every grain of sand. All of those floods aren't just floods, they're also The Flood. Why else do Charles Darwin and his ultra-materialist friend George Lewes (lover of the great novelist, George Eliot) turn up in 'High Water,' wanted dead or alive by a snarling Mississippi judge? Lewes tells the believers, the Englishman, the Italian and the Jew (Protestant / Roman Catholic / Hebrew?) that, no, they can't open their minds to just anything, and for that the high sheriff's on his tail. 'Some of these bootleggers,' Dylan sings on 'Sugar Baby,' 'they make pretty good stuff.' Beware of false prophets. (Or is the minstrel just tipping his hat again here, to the clever thieving fans who secretly record his concerts?)

The Lord's messenger is vengeful. Hear what Dylan does with 'Coo Coo' on 'High Water':

> Well, the cuckoo is a pretty bird, she warbles as she flies
> I'm preachin' the Word of God, I'm puttin' out your eyes

And Jesus isn't any pushover either. Listen to 'Bye and Bye,' another crooner's tune, and imagine that, alongside Augie Meyers's wickedly goopy organ, the crooner is Christ Himself, in some of the verses anyway, singing lyrics written by the biblical prophet John of Patmos:

Bye and bye, I'm breathin' a lover's sigh
I'm sittin' on my watch so I can be on time
I'm singin' love's praises with sugar-coated rhyme

I'm gonna baptize you in fire so you can sin no more
I'm gonna establish my rule through civil war
Gonna make you see just how loyal and true a man
   can be.

Christ comes with peace – and a sword.

And there are other seers and magicians here too, the hoo-doo men of the Delta blues – bragging mannish boys with their St John the Conqueroos who say if you can do it, it ain't bragging. From 'High Water':

I can write you poems, make a strong man lose his mind
I'm no pig without a wig, I hope you treat me kind

'Summer Days':

Yes, I'm leaving in the morning, just as soon as the dark
   clouds lift
I'm breakin' the roof, set fire to the place as a partin' gift

'Honest With Me':

When I left my home the sky split open wide

'Cry A While':

I don't carry dead weight, I'm no flash in the pan
All right, I'll set you straight, can't you see I'm a union man

Feel like a fightin' rooster, feel better than I ever felt

And this, from 'Lonesome Day Blues':

I'm going to spare the defeated, I'm going to speak to
the crowd
I'm going to spare the defeated, boys, I'm going to speak
to the crowd
I'm going to teach peace to the conquered, I'm going to
tame the proud

That last one may just also be a paraphrase from Virgil's
Aeneid.

There is a richness to all of these musical and literary references
in '*Love and Theft*' that was only foreshadowed in 'Tombstone
Blues,' with its mere glimpses of Ma Rainey and Beethoven –
just as there is a richness to Dylan's silk-cut voice and to his
diction and timing (he has been listening to Sinatra, and maybe
Caruso and surely Allen Ginsberg) uncaptured on previous studio recordings. He's mastered so much more, including his own
performing style, or at least his recorded performing style. Listen
to the break-neck opening lines of 'Cry A While' – 'didn't havta'
wanna' havta' deal with' – then the sudden bluesy downshift; or
the killer long-line about repeating the past in 'Summer Days';
the pause in Juliet's reply to Romeo; the 'High Water' Judge's
creepy, 'Either one, I don't . . . care,' the last word dropping and
landing with a thud like one of the song's lead-balloon coffins.

And with his expert timing, Dylan shuffles space and time
like a deck of playing cards. One moment, it's 1935, high atop
some Manhattan hotel, then it's 1966 in Paris or 2000 in West
Lafayette, Indiana, or this coming November in Terre Haute,
then it's 1927, and we're in Mississippi and the water's deeper
'n as it come, then we're thrown back into biblical time, entire

epochs melting away, except that we're rolling across the flats in a Cadillac, or maybe it's a Mustang Ford, and that girl tosses off her underwear, high water everywhere. Then it's September 11, 2001, eerily the date this album was released, and we're inside a dive on lower Broadway, and, horribly beyond description, things are blasted and breaking up out there, nothing's standing there. And it's always right now, too, on '*Love and Theft*'.

Dylan, remember, has been out there a very long time. He spent time with the Rev. Gary Davis, and Robert Johnson's rival Son House, and Dock Boggs, and Clarence Ashley, and all those fellows; he played for Woody Guthrie, and played for and with Victoria Spivey; and Buddy Holly looked right at him at the Duluth Armory less than three days before Holly plane-crashed to his death; and there isn't an inch of American song that he cannot call his own.

He steals what he loves and loves what he steals.

15

BOB DYLAN'S LAST WORDS

Patrick Crotty

Rhyme plays a more prominent and yet in certain vital senses a
less important role in song than in poetry. Almost all popular
song is structured around end-rhyme, the recurrence of the
rhyming sound closing one melodic phrase and/or semantic unit
and making possible the opening of the next: think of pop, rock,
Music Hall, the Border Ballads, the songs of Robert Burns and
Thomas Moore, the vocal material collected in the *Anthology
of American Folk Music*. Unrhymed song is much less usual
than unrhymed verse. In this respect Bob Dylan's songs are
representative of popular song in general. Indeed it is somewhat
surprising to find, in view of Dylan's manifest appetite for technical innovation and his occasional outings in unrhymed verse,[1] that
every single lyric reproduced on the official website depends either
upon end-rhyme or upon rhymes which appear internally in the
transcriptions but are registered as end-rhymes on the recordings.
He seems never to have been tempted, as the Beatles were in
'Across the Universe' and the opening section of 'Happiness Is
A Warm Gun', to explore the possibilities of unrhymed song.

For all its omnipresence, however, rhyme contributes less to
song than to poetry, in that its function is principally – and, in the
great majority of cases, simply – structural. The mere occurrence

of a loosely rhyming word is sufficient for the purposes of most songs. The ambient musical congruence makes up any leeway in the listener's acoustic satisfaction deriving from an artist's recourse to less than full rhyme. The nuances of half-rhyme are not available – or at least not richly available – to the songwriter since the impact of the music is to convert what in a purely poetic context would be an approximation of rhyme into the genuine article. Melody and accompaniment rob pararhymes and half-rhymes of the subtly dissonantal powers they display in, for example, Yeats's 'Easter 1916' or the lyrics of Emily Dickinson. Full rhymes, too, have less potential in song than in poetry, as their capacity to complement, contradict or undercut the meanings of their chiming partners – exploited so ingeniously in the Renaissance sonnet, for instance – is almost inevitably dampened by the musical environment.

To acknowledge this, however, is not to argue that there is no scope for cunning and resourcefulness in a songwriter's employment of rhyme, and in fact one of the characteristic excellences of Dylan's art is its sophisticated approach to rhyming. It is extraordinarily difficult to generalise about Dylan's use of rhyme, not least because he works much of the time comfortably within the limits of genres – blues, country, rockabilly – in which the status of rhyme is crudely functional. It is probably true to say that he is at his most interesting as a songwriter when he mixes genres to create modes which are distinctively his own (how are we to categorise 'Visions of Johanna'; 'You Ain't Goin' Nowhere'; 'Mississippi'?) or when he takes familiar modes and with the help of irony or sheer plenitude of figurative invention puts them to the service of subject matter or attitudes at odds with their inherited conventions – as he does respectively with bebop in 'Bye And Bye' and with the Anglo-Scottish 'folk' ballad in 'A Hard Rain's A-Gonna Fall'. My intention in this essay is twofold, firstly to examine examples of Dylan's rhyming in a selection of what seem to me his most successful songs and, secondly, to explore some of the ways in which his interest in the last words of his lines relates to other finalities in his work, both formal (last lines and last stanzas of individual songs) and thematic (last things).

In 2001 I attended a lecture called 'Bob Dylan: The Rhyme Schemer'[2] in which Christopher Ricks brought his celebrated powers of formal analysis to bear upon Dylan's achievement as a practitioner of rhyme. The lecture had much to say about rhyme in general and had at its centre intensive readings of two songs, 'If Not For You' and 'The Lonesome Death of Hattie Carroll'. Ricks demonstrated in detail how the sustained use of feminine rhymes in the Hattie Carroll ballad created the context for an enactment, in the formal being of the song, of the murderous violence of William Zanzinger: the delayed arrival of masculine line-endings in the 'slain', 'cane', 'air', 'room' progression in the stanza describing the flight of the cane puts the actuality of the killing at the centre of the proceedings, exactly where it should have been, but was not, at the trial.

It might be observed that a song concerning real people with the names Zanzinger and Carroll, names which, like the majority of Western surnames, end on an unstressed syllable, was likely to have extensive recourse to feminine rhyme in any event (though one notices that Rubin Carter is never cited at the end of the line, unlike his end-stressed nickname 'Hurricane', in the song of that title). There is evidence, however, that Dylan was alert to the possibilities of feminine rhyme before he wrote 'The Lonesome Death of Hattie Carroll', and in fact he uses feminine rhymes to a significant and unusual degree in other songs on the album on which that seminal protest ballad appeared, *The Times They Are A-Changin'*. Some of these songs will be examined in due course, but first I should like to say a good deal about the previous year's 'A Hard Rain's A-Gonna Fall', in which their use is prevalent.

'A Hard Rain' is often said to have been based upon the Border Ballad 'Lord Randal', a song which, like the overwhelming majority of the traditional ballads, employs masculine rhyme. (Perhaps the best-known exception is 'Barbara Allan', where the recourse to the heroine's surname at end of a line in most of the verses accounts for the departure from customary practice.) In point of fact it is only in the opening couplets of its stanzas that 'A Hard Rain' draws on 'Lord Randal', following the ballad's gambit of repeatedly addressing a distressed young man:

> 'O where ha you been, Lord Randal, my son?
> And where ha you been, my handsome young man?'

> And wha met ye there, Lord Randal, my son?
> And wha met ye there, my handsome young man?' etc

The structure of Dylan's song diverges radically from that of its supposed model. 'Lord Randal' is arranged in quatrains, with the second couplet in every verse rhyming the same two words, 'soon' and 'down', words so close in sound to the 'son' and 'man' rhymes of the first couplet that the stanzas could almost as truly be said to rhyme *aaaa* as *aabb*. After the question in the opening pair of lines in each of his stanzas, Dylan works up through the main body of the verse to the 'hard rain' refrain, occasioned on its first occurrence by the rhyme between the unstressed syllable of 'graveyard' and 'hard'. In the subsequent stanzas the refrain has no such structural link with the lines immediately preceding it, though this is scarcely important given that the listener is by now waiting for it to recur. The opening couplet is divided from the refrain by five lines in the first stanza, by seven, seven and six lines in the second, third and fourth stanzas respectively, and by no fewer than twelve lines in the final stanza. Of these thirty-seven 'dividing' lines, which carry the central weight of the song, only three end with a stressed syllable, and in the case of each of them ('world', 'dog' and 'love') the masculine ending is in any case visual rather than aural – on the *Freewheelin'* performance Dylan brings them more or less into uniformity with their thirty-four companions by (albeit very lightly) breaking them into two notes, with the stress falling on the first. (The contribution of his vocalisation to his rhyming is matter enough for a separate essay – 'mirror', for example, fully partners 'near' and 'clear' in 'Mama, You Been On My Mind', and both of those words and 'here' in 'Visions of Johanna'.) The entirety of the unrepeated portion of 'A Hard Rain', then, is presented in a series of feminine rhymes.

This hardly happened by accident. There would appear to have been two reasons for Dylan's choosing to write the song in this rhyming style, one practical, the other relating to his almost uncanny instinct for fusing form and feeling. The practical one is that it is much easier for a songwriter wishing to sustain a rhymed sound over many lines to find serviceable rhymes among the feminine than among the masculine resources of English. (The opposite is true of the poet, because of the much greater exactitude required of rhymes facilitated by language alone.) For a song driven forward as insistently by its rhythm as this one is, the supply of feminine rhymes is almost inexhaustible. Listeners to Dylan's recordings of 'A Hard Rain' register 'mountains', 'highways', 'forests', 'oceans' and 'graveyard' as rhyming words, though it would scarcely occur to them to do so if they encountered them on the page. (These are from the first stanza – some of the later rhyme clusters are more visually recognisable – 'around it'/ 'on it', for example, 'breathe it'/ 'see it' or 'sinkin''/ 'singin''.) Conventionally regarded as a quality entirely separate from rhyme, rhythm in these instances is an aspect of the rhyming procedure to the extent that it is rhythm that makes it possible for the ear to pick up resonances between words which in other contexts would be audited as widely, not to say utterly disparate. If the stress fell on the last syllable of the lines in the main body of 'A Hard Rain' – if the song were written in iambs and anapests rather than trochees and dactyls – much closer consonance between the end-words would be needed to achieve a comparable effect of cumulative rhyme. Of course it is not poetic rhythm *per se* that facilitates these effects, but a combination of poetic and musical rhythm.

The other, more important aspect of the predominance of feminine rhyme in 'A Hard Rain' is that the so-called 'weak ending' characteristic of metres which close on an unstressed syllable is entirely appropriate to the song's psychology. The 'falling' rhythm underscores the vulnerability of the young man (or boy – the indeterminacy of the speaker's age is part of the song's power), giving a tentative and plaintive quality to his account of what he has experienced. (How many voices are at work in 'A Hard Rain'? Certainly two, those of the young man and his questioner, but it is arguable that the prophetic refrain introduces a third presence encompassing the perspectives of both.) Dylan would employ feminine rhymes for the same reason and with even greater pathos in the Hattie Carroll ballad, sketching his protagonist's character in terms of the associations of 'gentle', 'children' and 'kitchen', and distinguishing her in the verbal fabric of the song from the monosyllabic, heavy-stressed brutality of her killer.

Though Dylan's songs are considerably, even astonishingly, diverse in theme, imagery and emotional colouring, they are somewhat less so in form. Most of them are structured on linear principles. Their recourse to bridges, 'middle eights' and other interludes which can have the effect of splicing the horizontal plane with a vertical axis are relatively infrequent. Dylan characteristically prefers to repeat the broad pattern set down at the beginning, or to alternate verse and chorus in a conservative, or at least not particularly adventurous, manner. While he can exhibit an acute appreciation of the possibilities of form, he is not in a strict sense a formalist. Thus in 'Desolation Row' he adheres to a twelve-line stanza throughout, but chooses not to sustain the alternation of masculine and feminine line endings with which the song begins. It could be argued, of course, that his readiness to sacrifice stanzaic tidiness to narrative momentum reflects his understanding of his medium, a medium in which the stanza's 'narrow room' is not a site of pleasure as it is on the page. (He can nonetheless be guilty, even at his best, of a disfiguring verbal sloppiness. How, for instance, can Ophelia's eyes be 'fixed upon' Noah's rainbow if she 'spends her time peeking into' Desolation Row? The substitution of 'mind is' for 'eyes are' would have removed the incoherence.[3]) The structure of 'A Hard Rain', lying somewhere between the stanzaic and the improvisatory, allows him a latitude which it would be foolish to register as looseness. The pattern introduced at the beginning is a matter not of verse length but of filling the gap between the fixed points of opening couplet and closing refrain with the answers of the young man. The variation in the length of these answers is dramatically appropriate; it is also what makes possible the song's movement towards climax. The piling in of more and more lines in the last verse builds tension by deferring the refrain, endowing the latter on its eventual arrival with an aspect of finality and release. The repetitions within one of the late lines ('tell it and think it and speak it and breathe it') both body forth the passionate commitment of the young man and lend a sense of pre-climactic acceleration to the versification.

'Visions of Johanna' employs a markedly similar structural technique. (The copyrighted lyrics present that song in stanzas of nine, ten, nine, nine and fourteen lines, though the third and fourth stanzas are sung as eight-liners on the studio and live versions.) The 'piled in' material of the last verse in this instance includes seven consecutive lines ending on the same (or almost the same) masculine rhyme. These lines serve a single, complex syntactical moment to facilitate one of Dylan's most notable crescendos. The sequence of rhyme words – 'showed', 'corrode', 'flowed', 'road', 'owed', 'loads', 'explodes' – culminates in a verb which might be said to enact its own content, blowing away the images of social degeneracy marshalled earlier and leaving in its tensionless aftermath only the eponymous visions of Johanna to – as the song's last word puts it – 'remain'. Literally, of course, it is the speaker/singer's 'conscience' which explodes, but Dylan understands that words carry symbolic as well as literal freight and there is a high degree of technical cunning behind his decision to detonate the spiralling pressure of the last stanza on the verb 'explodes'.

The closing stanza of 'A Hard Rain' brings matters to a climax, but it also, in a manner typical of much of Dylan's best work, endorses a position at odds with the implications of the preceding stanzas. Their catalogue of the miseries and injustices of a world overshadowed by the imminent hard rain had projected the speaker as a passive, helpless witness. Now, however, in response to a question in the future tense, he emerges as an active agent, who will embrace experience while he still can, and bear *un*solicited witness ('tell it and think it and speak it and breathe it') to the actuality of things before the hard rain engulfs him. 'But I'll know my song well before I start singin'', the last line before the refrain, elevates the final stanza to the status of an artistic credo, one moreover which is informed by a fundamentally moral impulse.

Something strikingly similar – in both formal and ethical terms – happens at the end of 'Desolation Row'. The first nine stanzas of this immensely long song seem to present a gallery of grotesques. The blind commissioner, the tight-rope walker, Cinderella, the Good Samaritan, Dr Filth, the historical Ezra Pound and T. S. Eliot (the former still living, the latter newly dead when the song was recorded), the calypso singers, the fishermen and the rest of them all appear to inhabit a fallen and corrupt realm which disgusts but does not involve the speaker/singer. After the harmonica solo which – as in so many other songs – marks off the last stanza from the rest, Dylan switches from the third to the second person and addresses an intimate in tones which seem at first to be as cold and sardonic as those used to describe the characters encountered thus far. An apparent confusion in the song is – arguably, at least – resolved by his parting instruction to him/her not to send any letters 'unless you mail them / From Desolation Row'. Desolation Row had been identified in the first stanza as the location from which the speaker and his 'Lady' 'look out' on the unfolding scenario. Cinderella's sweeping takes place on the Row, and the Good Samaritan is getting ready for the carnival that will be held there. Ophelia peeks in there from outside, and Dr Filth plies his trade somewhere a little beyond, but within earshot of the Row. If Casanova is punished for going there, his punishment presumably takes place elsewhere. The superhuman crew check to see that nobody escapes thereto, and the lovely mermaids of the penultimate stanza represent the distractions used to keep people from thinking about the place.

Desolation Row, then, is clearly not the habitation of the majority of the characters. The closing injunction about the letters seems to indicate that it is not a location of any kind in the physical sense, but rather a state of mind, a 'place' where the fatuity of the world can be contemplated. The chastened, disabused, informed perspective on experience it offers punctures the delusions not only of others but of oneself. Hence the ban on letters unless they are addressed from Desolation Row amounts to an invitation to the correspondent to join the speaker in his state of difficult, anguished awareness. The *dramatis personae* of the previous verses turn out in the last one to be less degenerates than victims of an absurdity they unknowingly share with the speaker. The moral quality in this concluding stanza involves an implicit recognition that the speaker and others like him are superior to the song's cast of jongleurs and misfits by virtue only of their greater appreciation of their shared and irremediable dilemma. When the strongly rhymed line about Des – O – lation ROW comes relentlessly round for the tenth and final time it is underpinned by a bitter and pitiless irony. (Other clearly demarcated stanzas which substantially qualify or alter the overall mood of the songs they conclude – or at the very least summarise matters from a different temporal perspective – include those which close 'Ballad in Plain D', 'Tangled Up in Blue', 'Simple Twist of Fate', 'Joey', 'Sara' and 'Highlands'. In the two listed songs from *Blood on the Tracks*, as in 'Desolation Row', the rhymed refrain arrives with a sort of invincible finality on its last appearance.)

There is always a danger of endowing poems and songs with a quality of algebraic abstraction when analysing their technical procedures. The mastery of rhyme displayed at the end of 'A Hard Rain' and 'Visions of Johanna' could not exist without an accompanying mastery of the (theoretically) separate discipline of rhetoric. Rhymes, that is to say, are *verbal* sounds, and the words that embody them carry meanings, which in turn serve the thematic development of the poems and songs in which they occur. The cited instances of sustained rhyming in the *Freewheelin'* and *Blonde on Blonde* songs are instances also of figurative stamina. Indeed for all the sour melancholy of 'Visions of Johanna', there is a palpable self-delight in the scene-painting ingenuity which makes possible the progression from the Madonna who still has not (ungrammatically) 'showed', through the 'corroding' (*sic*) cage where her cape once 'flowed' and the 'road' to which the fiddler takes, writing as he does so about the return of what was 'owed' on the back of the 'loading' (*sic*) fish truck, to the 'exploding' (*sic*) conscience of the speaker/singer.

'Visions' remains one of Dylan's most searing songs, and it is resolutely a song of private experience (by which I do *not* mean that it is an autobiographical song). 'A Hard Rain' by contrast is a public song, arguably more deeply implicated in history and politics than anything else Dylan has written, given the seriousness of the Cuban Missile Crisis and the widespread nature and profundity of the anxiety it evoked. Indeed the ballad is the pre-eminent cultural monument to the dread of nuclear holocaust which characterised the early 1960s. The title finds an image in the natural world for the nuclear fallout which many feared was about to destroy all nature. (A related tension is activated by the deployment of a folk mode, with its inevitably pastoral associations, to engage with the theme of the destructive capacity of high technology.) 'A Hard Rain' is the first, the best-known and perhaps the most comprehensively imagined of Dylan's many apocalyptic songs, and the power of its ending is in part at least a reflection of the power of the sense of the imminent ending of the world which haunted the popular mind at the height of the Cold War. Before proceeding to comment on the development of the apocalyptic motif in Dylan's work from *Freewheelin'* to *'Love and Theft'*, however, I should like to redeem my promise to say something of the way his experiments with feminine rhyme in 'A Hard Rain' were extended in the songs of *The Times They Are A-Changin'* in 1964.

As already acknowledged, and as elucidated so brilliantly in Professor Ricks's lecture, a contrast between feminine and masculine rhymes forms the structural and even in a sense the thematic core of 'The Lonesome Death of Hattie Carroll'. 'North Country Blues' also employs feminine rhymes with considerable pathos. This song, which articulates a sort of early form of anti-globalisation protest, is remarkable for the quality of its sympathy with an embattled community, and for its astute appreciation of the economic forces which brought about the collapse of the iron-mining industry in Dylan's home state of Minnesota. (The left-wing critics of Dylan's subsequent development perhaps had better arguments on their side than the folk purists.) It is written in six-line stanzas, with the third and sixth lines carrying the main weight of rhyme. The other lines rhyme too, but less regularly. The contrast between the prosperous past and the impoverished present is driven home by the oppositional relationship between the meanings of the rhymes at the end of the third and sixth lines, all of them feminine. The rhyming signature is set by the first stanza's 'plenty'/'empty' conflict. The inbuilt 'weakness' of feminine rhyme is accentuated and turned to rhetorical advantage by having the second of the pair (in most instances) carry the burden of emptiness. (Thus 'With the lunch bucket filled every season' is followed three lines later by 'To half a day's shift with no reason', 'digging' by 'nothing', 'drinking' by 'sinking' etc.)

'Boots of Spanish Leather' is a very different kind of song, a desolate love narrative sharing the typical four-line, *abcb* form of the Anglo-Scottish ballad but, atypically, employing rhymes which are in every case feminine. Dylan goes to considerable lengths to keep them so, idiosyncratically writing 'made of silver or of golden' to create a partner rhyme for 'Barcelona'. The effect of these rhymes is to amplify the neediness of the male speaker, who three times refuses offers of gifts from his lover who is sailing to Spain, on the grounds that all he wants is for her to return to him 'unspoiled'. While the exquisite tenderness of the song in the 1964 performance is unreplicated on the page (making 'Boots' an odd choice to represent Dylan in the *Norton Anthology of Poetry*), that tenderness is not entirely a matter of performance. Nor is it, I think, altogether a matter of performance in conjunction with feminine rhyming. The song's plangency derives in significant measure from its tardiness in mentioning the articles cited in the title, and from the symbolic ambiguity of the boots themselves. Would the song have the same power if the title had been altered or withheld? The speaker doesn't refer to boots of Spanish leather until he has learned of his lover's faithlessness, and the boots are the first artefacts mentioned in the song. ('Something fine/ made of silver or of golden' is indeterminate, while such natural objects as the 'stars of the sky' and the 'diamonds of the deepest ocean' are abstract entities alluded to in a rhetorical flourish of denial rather than actual things.) The boots, while admittedly imagined rather than perceived, are doubly specific, in that both their manufacture and their material are qualified by the proper adjective, 'Spanish':

> So take heed, take heed of the western wind,
> Take heed of the stormy weather.
> And yes, there's something you can send back to me,
> Spanish boots of Spanish leather.

There may be a vengeful aspect to the warning here, given that the western wind comes from the same direction as the utterance of the betrayed (presumably American) speaker. But why boots? And why Spanish? Boots could represent the straying of the lover, in which case they might be desired by the speaker so that he, too, could become a traveller. Spanish boots might help him to travel unnoticed in the country into which the lover has disappeared, adding to the possibilities of threat in the first two lines. Alternatively – or simultaneously – the exotic connotations of 'Spanish' could be said to eroticise the boots, making them a fetishistic souvenir of the vanished woman. The repetition of 'Spanish' contributes to the air of finality in the last line – the title had used the word only once, and now that the title's significance has at last been revealed, the reiterated adjective emphasises the sense of closure. On the record Dylan breaks the word in two on its second occurrence – 'Spaan-ish' – as if to emphasise the heartbreak of the speaker whose belated request for an expensive gift marks his realisation that he will never have the only thing he really wants.

Less need be said in relation to feminine rhyme elsewhere on *The Times They Are A-Changin'*. The closing couplets of the verses of the title track provide a series of famous, if from a technical point of view not particularly interesting, examples. 'When the Ship Comes In' employs an almost identical stanza structure to 'North Country Blues', but the much more carefully sustained couplets of ll.1–2 and 4–5 of each stanza, with their sharp masculine rhymes, combine with the tempo, melody and theme of the piece to ensure that the possibilities for pathos in the sixth line of each unit are not activated. Formally, of course, that may be the whole point of the song, which can be seen as an experimental deployment of feminine rhyme in the service of an upbeat mood. The more characteristic tonalities of 'weak' rhyming are restored in the first half of a majority of the verses of the elegiac 'Restless Farewell', at the end of the album. 'Only a Pawn in Their Game' brings to masculine rhyme a somewhat less decorous singlemindedness than Dylan displays in relation to feminine rhyme in other songs of the period. When each of the second stanza's ten lines concludes on more or less the same sound, the ear registers the strain.

At this stage of his career Dylan was flexing his formal muscles, trying things out (and perhaps trying things on). Only occasionally in the subsequent work do his structural designs manifest themselves so explicitly. One thinks of the playful 'Mozambique' on *Desire*, for example, where in the space of a three-minute song he finds six rhymes ('cheek', 'week', 'speak', 'seek', 'peek', 'unique') for the title, which provides the end word of both the opening and closing lines. Or of the cinematic ballad 'Angelina' (1981), in which the entire narrative appears to have been constructed round the search for (necessarily feminine) rhymes with the title character's name. These are duly found ('concertina', 'hyena', 'subpoena', 'Argentina', 'arena') and deployed with consummate skill. Elsewhere, however, Dylan's mastery of rhyme is more tactfully exercised. 'Everything Is Broken' (from *Oh Mercy*) and 'Tryin' to Get to Heaven' (from *Time Out of Mind*) provide two recent showcases of his undiminished skill at playing off masculine and feminine rhymes against each other.

The apocalyptic theme enters Dylan's work in 1963 on *Freewheelin'*, where it has specific reference to fears of a nuclear war. Those fears, though very deeply inscribed, remain implicit throughout the tragic 'A Hard Rain', whereas they are spelled out in comic terms in 'Talkin' World War III Blues'. (That song provides yet another instance of Dylan's success in transforming a genre by bending it to the service of unaccustomed materials.) While he was to turn his back on direct commentary on public affairs almost as soon as his most politically engaged album, *The Times They Are A-Changin'*, reached the shops, the Apocalypse motif which had been introduced under the banner of politics would persist in his songwriting, in a variety of guises, through most of his many changes of style and attitude from 1963 to 2001. A very loose definition of Apocalypse, as what happens when everything else ends, might accommodate a great number of Dylan's songs, so numerous are their scenarios of conclusion, destruction and aftermath. A much more continent definition, however, focusing on the Book of Revelation, appropriately the last book of the New Testament, and on other so-called apocalyptic scriptural writings, particularly as they (in their more popular interpretations, at least) pertain to the end of the world, would be sufficient to supply fruitful approaches to many songs drawn even from what are generally considered to be secular stages of his development.

In fact there may be a number of scriptural citations in 'When the Ship Comes In', the first of the obviously apocalyptic songs to appear on a record after the two nuclear war pieces of 1963. The proverb of the title is colloquially employed as a metaphor for the arrival of worldly bounty, but Dylan's song offers a vision of the end of the world rather than a promise of an end of economic privation. Brewer's *Dictionary of Phrase and Fable* somewhat tautologically traces the proverb's derivation to an understanding that 'argosies return home from foreign parts laden with rich freights'. Its origins may in fact be far older than Brewer suspected, older even than the English language. A key apocalyptic text, the Syrian Apocalypse of Baruch, which is canonical to Catholics, apocryphal to most Protestants and – interestingly, given Dylan's background – of little importance to Jews, includes the following verse about the imminent disappearance of worldly and imperial powers: 'The coming of the times is very near . . . The pitcher is near the well and the ship to the harbour, and the journey to the city, and life to its end' (2 Baruch.

85: 10). The opening phrase of the Baruch quotation raises the intriguing possibility that the title track of *The Times They Are A-Changin'* should be counted among Dylan's apocalyptic songs. (Something more majestic and frightening than a set-to between civil rights marchers and police, that is to suggest, 'will soon shake your windows and rattle your walls'.) 'When the Ship Comes In', at any rate, can be said to configure the relationship between the arrival of the vessel and the destruction of the existing order almost identically to Baruch. The song also appears to allude to what is perhaps the most famous phrase in Revelation, '[A]nd there was no more sea' (21: 1) in its prophecy that 'the chains of the sea /Will have busted in the night/And will be buried at the bottom of the ocean'. The second line's reference to the stopping of the wind echoes Revelation 7: 1.

Dylan's song shares with apocalyptic writings generally a confidence that the wicked – whom he compares to the frankly biblical 'Pharaoh's tribe' and Goliath – will be overthrown and the righteous vindicated. It is as difficult to gauge the extent (if any) to which this breezy millenarian rhapsody is tempered by irony, as it is to determine whether it should be read simply as a rallying song for civil rights activists and other libertarians in early 1960s America. (The piece reportedly had its origins in Dylan's anger at being slighted by the reception staff of an East Coast hotel in 1962.[4]) The rousing 'Paths of Victory' (1964), for all the elemental quality of its language, can more confidently be interpreted as a straightforward song of camaraderie.

The visionary strain in the subsequent work sometimes involves citations of apocalyptic scripture. 'It's Alright, Ma (I'm Only Bleeding)', from the *Bringing It All Back Home* album, echoes Revelation 9: 4 and 16: 10 in the opening phrase, 'Darkness at the break of noon', that sets up the aura of terminal crisis sustained throughout. The 'folding' and 'erupting' skies of 'Farewell

Angelina' (1965), like the 'sky full of fire' in 'Mississippi' (*'Love and Theft'*), are traceable to Revelation 8: 7, 8: 10 and 13: 13, while the 'poison' waters of the latter song probably derive from 8: 11. The most obvious scriptural source for the title and refrain of 'Knockin' on Heaven's Door' (*Pat Garrett and Billy the Kid*), and for the refrain of its slyly intertextual successor, 'Tryin' to Get to Heaven', is provided by 4: 2 ('a door was opened in heaven'). (*The Oxford Companion to the Bible* notes that 'Popular conceptions of heaven have been derived largely from the imagery' of Revelation.[5]) Both Armageddon (16: 6) and 'the tail of the dragon' feature in 'Señor (Tales of Yankee Power)', from *Street-Legal*, the dragon's tail being a precise allusion to the creature in 12: 4 who will be identified as the Devil in 12: 9. The frenzy in Dylan's singing of the line 'There's a lion in the road, there's a demon escaped' – on the same album's 'Where Are You Tonight?' – is presumably to be accounted for by the lion's connection to the first of the four beasts of 4: 7, and the demon's to the dragon/Devil of 12: 3–17.

One might observe that the 'Lincoln County Road or Armageddon' antithesis of 'Señor' formulates a more or less constant dualism in Dylan's work between the immanent and the transcendent, a dualism in the light of which the Christian albums of 1979–81 seem to constitute less of a detour than is customarily said to be the case. (Their subject matter is strikingly continuous with the imagery, if not the themes, of *Street-Legal*.) The suffusion of the material on those albums – *Slow Train Coming, Saved* and *Shot of Love* – with scriptural phraseology, at any rate, is hardly a surprise. Nor is the fact that Revelation features strongly in their songs, by virtue of references such as those to Armageddon and the Last Judgement (20: 11–15) in the closing verse of 'Are You Ready' (on the second of those records). What may be a surprise, however, is that in such a non-devotional, 'stray' song as 'Angelina', from the end of the same period, the biblical imagery is at least as pervasive as in the 'born again' works. When Dylan opposes Jerusalem to Argentina in that song, he is not so much contrasting two geographical locations as a heavenly one with an earthly one. The allusions to Revelation in the closing pair of stanzas are somewhat problematic, as they conflate details in a way that makes interpretation difficult. The 'unknown rider' and 'the pale white horse' glimpsed by the speaker direct us to 6: 2, where the first of the four horses of the Apocalypse is described as 'white', and also to 6: 8, where the fourth horse is characterised as 'pale' and where its rider is identified as Death. (Later on in the text, in 19: 11–13, a lone 'white horse' is encountered, ridden by the Word of God.) Dylan's 'angel with four faces' has no exact prototype in Revelation, though it certainly has a loose one: the angels of destruction are four in number (7: 1; 9: 15). And indeed it is precisely prefigured elsewhere in the Bible, in Ezekial 1: 5, 6, 15 and 10: 14, 20–21. The fact that both songs with 'Angelina' in their titles incorporate allusions to Revelation should alert us to the significance of the first five letters of that forename.

Many of the tropes even in what might at first appear to be blithely secular songs are continuous with concerns raised in the allusively or explicitly Christian work. Dylan approaches paradigmatic situations from so many angles and with such a diversity of attitude that the paradigm can be missed or mistaken by the unwary. Thus it can have occurred to few of those responsible for putting Manfred Mann's version of 'The Mighty Quinn (Quinn, the Eskimo)' to the top of the British charts in January 1968 that they were buying a record about the Second Coming. The syntactical construction of the climactic refrain 'When Quinn the Eskimo gets here' is the key to the song's deep kinship with 'When the Ship Comes In' and 'When He Returns' (*Slow Train Coming*). 'When I Paint My Masterpiece'

(1971) plays a cheerful variation – equally ridiculous and sublime – on the theme of millenarian deliverance. Similarly, many songs across the broad sweep of his career exhibit what might be called Dylan's catastrophic imagination, but by no means all of them do so with overt reference to scripture.

Western culture is so deeply informed by the myths of the Fall, the Deluge and the Last Day that any cultural artefact dealing with the imperfection of things or with large-scale destruction will draw, whether consciously or not, on Genesis and Revelation and indeed on the three 'major' prophets, Isaiah, Jeremiah and Ezekiel. Only in some cases, however, will establishing the extent of the debt to ancient sources aid interpretation. It is hard to believe, for example, that any particular illumination could be gained from determining to what degree the earthquake that destroys everything but a Panama hat and a pair of old Greek shoes in 'Black Diamond Bay' (*Desire*) derives from the earthquakes of Revelation (6: 12; 11: 13; 11: 19). Conversely, Dylan's use of the Deluge motif depends on his audience's awareness of the story of Noah's Flood. Indeed the change of title of the Basement sessions song 'Crash on the Levee' to 'Down in the Flood' (for the re-recorded version on *More Greatest Hits*) is an instance of his anxiety that his listeners get the point. A bid to affect the excitement of imminent catastrophe presumably underlay the title of the Before the Flood tour, as of its Rolling Thunder successor. Dylan returned to the motif in 2001 in 'High Water (For Charlie Patton)', perhaps the most emotionally complex – not to say inscrutable – treatment of the disaster theme in his career to date.

Terminal situations, catastrophic and otherwise, recur in almost every phase of Dylan's work. From 'In My Time of Dyin'', on the first album, through 'This Wheel's On Fire' (*The Basement Tapes*), 'Knockin' On Heaven's Door', 'Romance in Durango'

(*Desire*), 'Señor' and 'Under Your Spell' (*Knocked Out Loaded*) to the relatively recent 'Tryin' to Get to Heaven', his songs present speakers either overshadowed by their own deaths or on the very point of expiry. Third-person protagonists die in the course of such pieces as 'Oxford Town', 'The Ballad of Hollis Brown', 'The Lonesome Death of Hattie Carroll', 'Lily, Rosemary and the Jack of Hearts', 'Joey' and 'Black Diamond Bay'. The work is pervaded by a sense of aftermath, and the narrative perspective frequently – indeed characteristically – involves a retrospective summary of something irretrievably lost: 'Don't Think Twice, It's All Right', 'One Too Many Mornings', 'Ballad in Plain D', 'It's All Over Now, Baby Blue', 'Tomorrow Is A Long Time', 'Mama, You Been On My Mind', 'Just Like Tom Thumb's Blues', 'Nothing Was Delivered', 'As I Went Out One Morning', 'I Threw It All Away', 'Simple Twist of Fate', 'If You See Her, Say Hello', 'Shelter From the Storm', 'Cell Letter Blues', 'Sara', 'Man in the Long Black Coat', 'Standing in the Doorway', 'Mississippi'.

Most of the songs in the list concern broken relationships, and though he protests in 'Sugar Baby' (*'Love and Theft'*) that 'love's not an evil thing', it might be observed that Dylan typically constructs love as a matter of residue rather than substance. (Indeed the powerful 'Love Sick', from *Time Out of Mind*, paints the aftermath of a relationship as a post-apocalyptic wilderness.) Other finalities in the work relate to a termination of social intercourse and a withdrawal into solitude. 'Maggie's Farm', 'Tombstone Blues', 'Stuck Inside of Mobile with the Memphis Blues Again' and 'Highlands' feature prominently on the long list of pieces in which the terminal solitude constitutes a bitter experience, as do 'Mr Tambourine Man', 'You Ain't Goin' Nowhere', 'Time Passes Slowly' and 'Watching the River Flow' on the inevitably shorter one of songs in which it has the character of bliss. One of the most engaging and most frequently performed of Dylan's songs, 'All Along the Watchtower', dramatises the prelude to a mysterious finale. The great charm of 'Watchtower' – as of the title track of the *John Wesley Harding* album on which it appears – is its refusal of disclosure: we are not sure whether the event foreshadowed in the narrative will come to pass or not, or whether it will be cataclysmic or redemptive if it does.

From a very early stage of his career Dylan appears to have appreciated that in his capacity as a recording artist (as the American term puts is) he was involved in the making not just of songs and performances, but of records as well. In the course of this essay I have tried to highlight the meticulous care he devotes to the rhymes at the ends of his lines and to the stanzas at the end of his songs, as well as to other kinds of endings in his thematic mediations of varieties of personal, cultural and political finale. Dylan brings a comparable pressure of attention to bear upon the endings of his individual albums, and I should like to say something about these by way of moving the essay itself towards conclusion. *Bob Dylan* and *The Freewheelin' Bob Dylan*, the first and second albums, sign off with elegiac and obstreperous pieces respectively. 'See That My Grave Is Kept Clean' and 'I Shall Be Free' fulfil an obvious valedictory function in relation to what precedes them, a little portentously in the first case, perhaps a shade too knowingly in the second. From 'Restless Farewell' on *The Times They Are A-Changin'* to 'Sugar Baby' on *'Love and Theft'*, however, Dylan has asked rather more of many of the songs chosen to bear the burden of closure on his records. Their positioning contributes to the network of reverberations within the collections and helps set up a self-reflexive commentary on the *oeuvre* and ways of interpreting it. To go through Dylan's work album by album in an attempt to illustrate this point would be a tedious exercise, given the scale of the output of a career which this year enters its fifth decade, and the interested reader is in any case free to pursue such a course independently. Some examples will suffice.

'Restless Farewell' brings a gathering of largely political songs to a close on a bleakly and even discordantly personal note, and includes a caution against reading the songs as propaganda and constructing the singer as a leader of any kind: 'It's for myself and my friends my stories are sung.' The promise implicit in 'till we meet again' was fulfilled later in 1964 with the appearance of the resolutely private and apolitical *Another Side of Bob Dylan*, an album concluding with 'It Ain't Me Babe', a song which can be construed as, among other things, a considerably more emphatic disavowal of prophetic destiny than the previous album's closing track. The personal coda to more than personal material inaugurated with 'Restless Farewell' was beginning to become something of a Dylan trademark by 1965, when he brought *Bringing It All Back Home* to an end with the bitterly elegiac (and characteristically retrospective) 'It's All Over Now, Baby Blue'. Perhaps the career's most moving instance of the manoeuvre happens on *Desire*, when that strange brew of narrative and dramatic songs, set in a range of surreal, mythical or naturalistic locations, comes to rest on the painful gravity of the confessional 'Sara'.

An opposite procedure – summative and climactic – is employed on *Highway 61 Revisited*, when the variously short and middle-length songs, with their explosively electrified arrangements, give way at the end to the extended, acoustic 'Desolation Row'. 'Buckets of Rain' reformulates in terms of rueful humour the emotional turmoil of the *Blood on the Tracks* songs which precede it, as if in an effort to make it possible to envisage a future after the end of the record. (The song also partners the similarly witty 'You're Gonna Make Me Lonesome When

You Go', at the end of what was Side One of the vinyl album and tape, rather as 'Restless Farewell' mirrors 'North Country Blues' – until the advent of compact disc Dylan took a good deal of care over the choice of the material marking the ends of the first as well as of the second halves of his albums.) 'When He Returns' and 'Are You Ready' bring respectively *Slow Train Coming* and *Shot of Love* to end on anticipations of Apocalypse, the former song focusing on the Second Coming, and the latter on Armageddon and the Last Judgement. It is difficult to know what to make of the apocalyptic language in 'Shooting Star', at the end of *Oh Mercy*, though the song can certainly be said to sum up the 'backward glance oe'r travelled roads' melancholy of a very large part of Dylan's work in the admission to its addressee that 'it's too late to say the things to you / That you needed to hear me say'.

The two most recent albums offer extremely interesting samples of closing songs. Simultaneously evocative and rebarbative, 'Highlands' (*Time Out of Mind*) must count as one of the most challenging extended pieces in the career. Its not-quite-consequential narrative of an ageing narrator's uncertain progress through Boston picks up on the theme of wandering introduced in 'Love Sick' and developed in 'Trying to Get to Heaven' and one or two other songs earlier on the album. The location of the speaker's heart in the Highlands, while his feet stay in Boston, gives secular form to a familiar dualism. If the Highlands are not Jerusalem, however, they are not the Highlands either, at least in any recognisably Scottish sense. (The chorus borrows its opening line from one of the lesser songs of Robert Burns, 'Farewell to the Highlands'.) Dylan's strange geography conflates the Borders – in the extreme south of Scotland – with the Highlands in the north-west and Aberdeen in the north-east, while transforming the latter from city to river. In point of fact, of course, so far are they from belonging to the Scottish Highlands that the Border Country and Aberdeen conventionally mark the southern and northern extremities of the Lowlands. Does Dylan not know this? One must assume that he does. The geographical liberties taken by the song, at any rate, should surely be seen as a matter less of confusion or ignorance than of design, as they underscore the mythic otherness of the singer's Highlands. The full opening line of Burns's chorus is, 'My heart's in the Highlands, my heart is not here'⁶, and the portion unquoted by Dylan might provide the motto alike for the album and for the great song that summarises its themes of absence and aftermath.

The stanza before the final chorus offers perhaps the most vivid formulation of *ennui* in the work thus far. The sun shines on the speaker, but to little avail as 'it's not like the sun that used to be'. The 'new eyes', which would have given the subjects in the Christian albums redemptive ways of viewing the world, now only make 'everything' look 'far away'. The final chorus's parting avowal that the speaker is already in the Highlands in his 'mind', and that 'that's good enough for now', does little to alleviate the intense melancholy of the closing verse, and *Time Out of Mind* comes to rest on a note of weariness and exhaustion unsurpassed anywhere even on *Blonde on Blonde*. Dylan had elected to end that album on a long and figuratively extravagant love song which served to dispel the gloom generated by most of the rest of the material. That song was 'Sad Eyed Lady of the Lowlands'. The contradictory echo of its title thirty-one years later in 'Highlands' asserts his disinclination to similarly ameliorate the pervasive pessimism of *Time Out of Mind*. 'Highlands', appropriately, offers conclusion without resolution at the end of Dylan's most disconsolate album.

'*Love and Theft*', far more various in mood than *Time Out of Mind*, and equally vigorous in invention, ends with 'Sugar Baby', one of its two most melancholy songs. (The other, 'Mississippi', as its tonalities might suggest, is a rewritten version of a piece originally recorded for the previous album.) By opening with a line about the sun ('I got my back to the sun 'cause the light is too intense') 'Sugar Baby' can perhaps be seen to comment on the last verse of 'Highlands'. The sun is too strong in this instance, rather than too weak, but the basic situation whereby what should have been dependable has become problematic is repeated. 'Sugar Baby', however, is much more expressly written in a fictional persona than the earlier song, and has a slightly stagy, even ludic character to its sadness. The speaker/singer is a hard-drinking, loose-living man whose experiences belong to a mythic America of bootleggers and the Darktown Strut – the few details about his life we are granted seem appropriate to the Wild West of the nineteenth century, the Chicago of the twentieth and the New Orleans of either. One of the attractions of the piece is the way it reprises themes and situations from the entire span of Dylan's career. Just before the last chorus comes round Dylan reanimates the rhetoric of the Christian albums he recorded twenty years earlier, offering what in this instance is a less than wholeheartedly apocalyptic scenario:

Look up, look up – seek your Maker – 'fore Gabriel blows his horn.

It is remarkable that after four decades of making records, Dylan can still find new ways of engineering valedictory conclusions for them. Rather than have his speaker say goodbye and leave – as in 'Restless Farewell', for example – he creates a situation in which we overhear the weary and somewhat misogynistic protagonist enjoin his 'Sugar Baby' to arrange her own departure:

Sugar Baby, get on down the line
You ain't got no sense, no how
You went years without me
Might as well keep going now

One can only hope that Bob Dylan will take his own advice and keep going, providing us with many more last songs to discuss before we or others have to discuss his last songs.

NOTES

Preface

1 As a result I've always been struck by what of course seems to me the coincidence that Warner and Dylan appeared together in the BBC TV play *Madhouse on Castle Street* in 1963, Warner in the role apparently originally intended for Dylan.

2 *Dont Look Back* is *sic*: that is, like the first word of *Finnegans Wake*, 'don't' has no apostrophe. Don't ask me why.

3 Barry Miles, 'Patti Smith', in John Bauldie (ed.), *Wanted Man: In Search of Bob Dylan* (Harmondsworth: Penguin Books, 1992) p.103.

4 David Kalstone (ed.), *The Selected Poetry and Prose of Sir Philip Sidney* (New York: Signet Classics, 1970), p.220.

5 John Bauldie, 'You Know Something Is Happening', *The Telegraph* 36 (Summer 1990), p.69.

Introduction: Writing aloud

1 Nat Hentoff, 'The Playboy Interview: Bob Dylan', reprinted in Craig McGregor (ed.), *Bob Dylan: A Retrospective* (New York: William Morrow and Company, 1972), p.139.

2 When I use the word 'career' I am reminded that Dylan says in an interview that 'I don't feel like what I do qualifies to be called a career. It's more of a calling.' See Mikal Gilmore, 'The Rolling Stone Interview', *Rolling Stone* no. 882 (22 November 2001), pp.56–69 (p.68).

3 Hentoff, p.140.

4 I am grateful to Dr Margaret Anne Daniel for information about this medal and the occasion of its award.

5 See Robert Crawford, *The Modern Poet: Poetry, Academia*

and Knowledge since the 1750s (Oxford: Oxford University Press, 2001).

6 Nora Ephron and Susan Edmiston, 'Bob Dylan Interview', McGregor, p.84.

7 Elaine Scarry, *Dreaming by the Book* (Princeton: Princeton University Press, 2001), p.7.

8 Roland Barthes, *The Pleasure of the Text*, trans. Richard Miller (New York: Hill and Wang, 1975), pp.66–7.

9 Quoted in Hubert Saal, 'Dylan is Back', *Newsweek*, February 1968, reprinted McGregor, p.245.

10 Stephen Scobie, *Alias Bob Dylan* (Red Deer: Red Deer College Press, 1991), p.30.

11 Frank Kermode and Stephen Spender, 'The Metaphor at the End of the Funnel', *Esquire*, May 1972, reprinted in Elizabeth Thomson and David Gutman (eds.), *The Dylan Companion* (London: Macmillan, 1990), p.155.

12 Hentoff, p.129.

13 Jan Wenner, 'The Rolling Stone Interview: Dylan', reprinted McGregor, p.356.

14 Ruth Padel, *I'm a Man: Sex, Gods and Rock 'n' Roll* (London: Faber & Faber, 2000), pp.303–4.

15 ibid., p.300.

16 ibid., p.301.

17 See Robert Shelton, *No Direction Home: The Life and Music of Bob Dylan* (London: New English Library, 1986), p.28.

18 Sam Shepard, *Rolling Thunder Logbook* (1977; Harmondsworth: Penguin Books, 1978), p.100.

2 Bob Dylan's names

1 With a couple of exceptions I have based my study on songs which have been released by Dylan on individual albums or compilations. I know some of these bootleggers make pretty good stuff, but there's just too much of it. I have not taken account of anything not sung. In quotations I have followed published versions of lyrics except where these are obviously wrong, and I have occasionally changed the layout.

2 'The Grand Coulee Dam' is the name of a Woody Guthrie song which Dylan has recorded, and which he sang at a Guthrie memorial concert in 1968.

3 'Bob Dylan's 115th Dream' (1965) is a wild comedy on this theme; in other songs it's not so funny.

4 'Sara' (1975) is an exception, but the theme of that song is the blurring of the line between a real person (Sara Dylan) and a mythologised and fantasised figure.

5 The reference is to the (white) boxing champion 'Gentleman Jim' Corbett (James John Corbett, 1866–1933).

6 The assassin will acquire a name (though we are not told it) when 'the shadowy sun' sets on him: 'He'll see by his grave / On the stone that remains / Carved next to his name / His epitaph plain: / Only a pawn in their game'.

7 'The Metaphor at the End of the Funnel', *Esquire*, May 1972; repr. Elizabeth Thomson and David Gutman (eds), *The Dylan Companion* (London: Macmillan, 1990), pp.158–9.

8 Compare the first two lines of 'Joe Hill', Earl Robinson's 1938 tribute to the radical songwriter and labour martyr, framed for murder and executed in Utah in 1915: 'I dreamed I saw Joe Hill last night / Alive as you and me'.

9 Dylan found a beautiful answer to this in 'Jokerman' (1983): 'You look into the fiery furnace, see the rich man without any name'. The parable of the rich man and the beggar (Luke 16: 19–31) is proverbially known as 'Dives and Lazarus' but 'Dives' is simply the Latin word for 'rich man'. He truly has no name of his own.

10 The character of Jimmy Ringo is (very) loosely based on that of John Ringo, a gunfighter associated in legend with the Earp–Clanton feud in Dodge City. See Jack Burrows, *John Ringo: the Gunfighter Who Never Was* (Tucson, AZ: University of Arizona Press, 1987).

11 In 'Sweetheart Like You' (1983) the prospect of making a name for oneself 'in a dump like this' is filled with disgust: 'You know you can make a name for yourself, / You can hear them tires squeal, / You can be known as the most beautiful woman / Who ever crawled across cut glass to make a deal'.

12 In the best biography to date, *Dylan: Behind the Shades* (London: Penguin Books, 1991), Clinton Heylin discusses these theories and suggests that Dylan's name-change was 'more an attempt to disavow his small-town background than his Jewish heritage' (p.4), but also that 'he saw it as a denial of his father' (p.16). It seems plausible to see all these elements as connected, though in what proportion is hard to determine.

13 Cited in Barry Miles, *Bob Dylan in his Own Words* (London: Omnibus, 1978), p.21.

14 The American trickster side is nicely illustrated by 'Talkin' John Birch Paranoid Blues' (1962): 'Well, I quit my job so I could work all alone, / Then I changed my name to Sherlock Holmes. / Followed some clues from my detective bag / And discovered they wus red stripes on the American flag!'

15 Cited in Robert Shelton, *No Direction Home: The Life and Music of Bob Dylan* (London: New English Library, 1986), p.49.

16 *Bob Dylan in his Own Words*, p.19. He is equally uncooperative in a song dating from the same year, 'Bob Dylan's 115th Dream': 'They asked me my name / And I said, "Captain Kidd"'; failure to conceal his name brings an ominous rhyme into play in 'Lo and Behold!' (1967): 'The coachman, he hit me for my hook / And he asked me my name. / I give it to him right away, / Then I hung my head in shame'. Reluctant either to admit or conceal his identity when the waitress in 'Tangled Up In Blue' (1974) says 'Don't I know your name?' the singer says: 'I muttered somethin' underneath my breath'. I have found only one positive instance, from an early unreleased track called 'Farewell' (1963): 'I've heard tell of a town where I might as well be bound, / It's down around the old Mexican plains. / They say that the people are all friendly there / And all they ask of you is your name.' It didn't take Dylan long to conclude that this was a bad bargain.

17 Bob Spitz, *Bob Dylan: a Biography* (London: Michael Joseph, 1989) pp.67–8.

18 Shelton, *No Direction Home*, pp.49–50. In the 1968 interview cited above (n. 13), Dylan said: 'If I thought he [Dylan Thomas]

was that great, I would have sung his poems, and could just as easily have called myself Thomas'.

19 From an exchange with a Canadian TV reporter in 1968: 'We're speaking with Bob Dylan. Do you say Dylan or Dielan? – Oh, I say Dylan. Dielan. I say anything that you say really.' (*Bob Dylan in his Own Words*, p.19).

20 Shelton, *No Direction Home*, pp.49–50, 68.

21 Compare Byron, lowering Robert Southey's dignity in the opening line of the Dedication to *Don Juan*: 'Bob Southey! You're a poet, poet laureate'.

22 I mean in his professional life; plenty of friends refer to him as 'Bobby' in biographies and on film.

23 The name of the director and star, Tim Robbins, has the same stress pattern as 'Bob Dylan' and 'Bob Roberts'; as far as I know it's his real name.

24 David Rensin and Bill Zehme, *The Bob Book* (New York: Dell Publishing 1991), p.15.

25 Versions of this Christian precept appear in several Dylan songs, e.g. 'Do Right to Me Baby (Do Unto Others)' (*Slow Train Coming*, 1979).

26 *The Bob Book*, p.134. Harrison was not the only friend to play the Bob card. Neil Young can be heard in the Madison Square Garden 30th Anniversary Concert (1992) saying to Dylan, 'Thanks, Bob. Thanks for having a Bob Fest'. A reviewer on Amazon.com in 1997 called for an update of *The Bob Book* to take account of developments such as the Bob Fest in Avon, Colorado, 'home of the bridge named Bob'. Dylan fans in the Midwest held a Bob Fest in 2000, and the term is probably more widespread than even I am willing to believe. As for Neil Young, Dylan paid him tribute (or back) in 'My Heart's in the Highlands' (1997): 'I'm listening to Neil Young, I gotta turn up the sound / Someone's always yelling turn it down . . .'

27 Robert Lowell, 'Under the Dentist', in *History* (1973); I owe this observation to Christopher Ricks (*Browning Society Notes* 10, no. 3 [December 1980], p.3).

28 I don't mean to suggest that 'Bob' can never be a sinister name; the doppelgänger fiend in *Twin Peaks* is a memorable American

instance, and *The Bob Book* adds Bad Bob, the 'vicious albino outlaw in the film *The Life and Times of Judge Roy Bean*' (p.121). But the recent popularity of the computer-animated children's figure 'Bob the Builder' on both sides of the Atlantic testifies to a dominant strain of cheery blandness. *The Bob Book* opens by remarking that 'Hurricane Bob' in 1985 was sniggered at by newscasters and downgraded to a tropical depression after only one day (p.10).

29 Press conference, 1986, cited in Chris Williams, *Bob Dylan in his Own Words* (London: Omnibus 1993). This compilation has the same name and publisher as the Barry Miles book (see n. 12) but quite a lot of the material is different and it covers a longer period.

30 Interview, 1978, cited in Williams, *Bob Dylan in his Own Words*, p.15.

3 Dylan and the academics

1 Michael Gray, *Song and Dance Man III: The Art of Bob Dylan* (London: Cassell, 2000), pp.54f.

2 ibid., pp.92f.

3 Robert Shelton, *No Direction Home: the Life and Music of Bob Dylan* (New York: Beech Tree/William Morrow, 1986), p.353.

4 Robert Christgau, in Elizabeth Thompson and David Gutman (eds), *The Dylan Companion* (Da Capo Press 2001), p.142.

5 The awfulness of *Renaldo and Clara* is fairly definitively analysed by Pauline Kael in Thompson and Gutman, op. cit., pp.224ff.

6 Christgau, op. cit., p.142.

7 Aidan Day, *Jokerman: Reading the Lyrics of Bob Dylan* (Oxford: Blackwell, 1998), p.7.

8 Day, *Jokerman*, p.16.

9 For a detailed study of Springsteen, see Daniel Cavicchi, *Tramps like Us: Music and Meaning among Springsteen Fans* (New York: Oxford University Press, 1998).

10 Gray, *Song and Dance Man III*, p.121. A judgement that has

survived from the London 1973 edition of his book, p.161.

11 In a *Playboy* interview, cit. Gray, op. cit., p.53.

12 John Fiske, *Understanding Popular Culture* (London and New York: Routledge, 1989), pp.23, 43 etc.

13 Joan Baez, cit. David Hajdu, *Positively 4th Street* (Farrar Straus Giroux, New York 2001), p.236.

14 Cf. the arguments used by John Shepherd in his *Music as Social Text* (Cambridge: Polity, 1991), ch. 10, including the claim that the sociology of pop music is in itself a challenge to the methods of musicology, which have to be adapted to it in seeing such music itself as a 'social text'. But instrumental music alone cannot make social or any other linguistic statements.

15 I sang along with this as a teenager without any sense at all of its political importance or of its historical context; and it even seemed to me to apply to a schoolboy existence quite well. It's not that pop songs can't often have their sharp little repetitive message – one can care about a heart of glass or hanging on the telephone; it nags away at you the way such music can, but such songs do more to make you dance than to make you think, which is a good thing too.

16 Conversely, where Dylan's myth, e.g. of the outsider, overwhelms fact, the result is a disaster, as Lester Bangs shows for the awful 'Joey'. This evocation of the life of the gangster Joey Gallo may be fine in the light of the American affair with the gangster myth:

> Always on the outside of whatever side there was
> When they asked him why it had to be that way,
> 'Well,' he answered, 'just because'.

but is way astray on the basic facts of Gallo's career and moral character. Hence Bangs's judgement that 'Joey' is 'one of the most mindless amoral pieces of repellently romantic bullshit ever recorded'. He compares the facts of Gallo's career and death with Dylan's myth, in *The Dylan Companion*, pp.214–22. The quotation above is from p.214.

17 Alexander Bloom (ed.) *Long Time Gone: Sixties America Then and Now* (New York: Oxford University Press, 2001), p.76.

18 Shelton, op. cit., p.282.

19 Gray, op. cit., p.787.

20 Wayne C. Booth, *The Company we Keep: an Ethics of Fiction* (Berkeley, Los Angeles, London: University of California Press, 1998).

21 Gray, op. cit., p.859.

22 Gray, op. cit., p.215.

23 Christopher Ricks, 'What Can I Do for You', in Michael Gray and John Bauldie (eds), *All Across the Telegraph* (London: Futura, 1987), p.186.

24 Michael Roos and Don O'Meara in Thompson and Gutman (eds), op. cit., p.47.

25 Simon Frith, 'Towards an aesthetic of popular music', in Richard Leppart and Susan McClary (eds), *Music and Society* (Cambridge: Cambridge University Press, 1987), pp.139, 140.

26 Cf. John Pasmore, *Serious Art* (London: Duckworth, 1991).

27 This is because many commentators would add to my characterisations above descriptions of mass art which are also (often false) descriptions of their audiences, such as 'uncouth', 'unrefined', 'common' and so on.

28 Robert Pattison, *The Triumph of Vulgarity: Rock Music in the Mirror of Romanticism* (New York: Oxford University Press, 1987), p.172.

29 Allan Bloom, *The Closing of the American Mind* (New York: Simon & Schuster, 1987), p.75.

30 ibid., p.79.

31 Paul Williams, *Bob Dylan: Performing Artist 1974–1986: The Middle Years* (London: Omnibus Press, 1994), pp.9, 78, 83, 86.

32 Wilfrid Mellers, *A Darker Shade of Pale* (London: Faber & Faber, 1984), p.121.

33 Gray traces some extraordinarily complex chains of influence between popular records: for example in his riff on rockabilly discs: op. cit., pp.91–4. He argues that Dylan has an encyclopaedic knowledge of past popular music.

34 And, to meet an obvious objection, you can read Heine either as Heine alone, or as Heine-plus-Schubert, but not both at the same time.

35 Betsy Bowden, *Performed Literature: Words and Music by Bob Dylan* (Bloomington, Indiana: Indiana University Press, 1987), p.74

36 ibid., p.82.

37 ibid., p.40.

38 Cit. in *The Dylan Companion*, p.64.

39 In pointing to this stylistic transparency I am not suggesting in the least that rock is 'simple' – quite the opposite, as Edward Macon's study of English progressive rock, *Rocking the Classics* (Oxford 1997), has shown.

4 Big brass bed: Bob Dylan and delay

1 'Window' in the sequence 'Redcliffe Square' in Robert Lowell, *The Dolphin* (London: Faber & Faber, 1973).

5 Playing time

1 Jon Bream in *Star Tribune* (23 May, 1991); Larry Katz in the *Boston Herald* (24 May 2001).

2 See the 'Introduction' to *The Dylan Companion*, ed. Elizabeth Thomson and David Gutman (Da Capo Press, 2001), p.xvii.

3 'Search the Lyrics' at bobdylan.com; database searched at 10.45 a.m. 27 December 2001.

4 Sleeve notes of *Bringing It All Back Home*.

5 'Bob Dylan by Mikal Gilmore', *Rolling Stone* (22 November 2001), pp.56–69, at p.61.

6 'Introduction' to *The Dylan Companion*, p.xvi.

7 See Frank Kermode and Stephen Spender, 'The Metaphor at the End of the Funnel', in *The Dylan Companion*, p.158, and Robert Shelton, *No Direction Home: The Life and Music of Bob Dylan* (London: Penguin Books, 1987), p.282.

8 'Who killed Davey Moore?'; 'Like a Rolling Stone'; 'Ballad of a Thin Man'; 'Queen Jane Approximately'.

9 For a discussion of '[w]hy she is like "some raven with a broken wing"', see Christopher Ricks, 'Bob Dylan', in *Hiding in Plain Sight. Essays in Criticism and Autobiography*, ed. Wendy Lesser (San Francisco: Mercury House, 1993), p.157.

10 'Chimes of Freedom'; 'Love Minus Zero / No Limit'; 'Blowin' in the Wind'; 'A Hard Rain's A-Gonna Fall'; 'Gates of Eden'; 'All Along the Watchtower'.

11 'Bob Dylan's 115th Dream'; 'Just Like Tom Thumb's Blues'; 'Clothes Line'.

12 See Philip Larkin, *All What Jazz* (London: Faber and Faber, 1985), p.151, and 'Absences' in *Philip Larkin. Collected Poems*, ed. Anthony Thwaite (London: Faber and Faber, 1988), p.49.

13 See Tom Constanten, 'Dr Z. Agonistes: an Appreciation', in *The Dylan Companion*, p.3, and 'The Metaphor at the End of the Funnel', in *The Dylan Companion*, pp.158–9.

14 *Poems, Chiefly in the Scottish Dialect, by Robert Burns* (Kilmarnock, 1786), p.v.

15 BBC broadcast 'Dylan among the Poets' (11 February 2001).

16 References are drawn from *The Dylan Companion*; Clinton Heylin, *Bob Dylan Behind the Shades: The Biography – Take Two* (London: Viking Books, 2000); Anthony Scaduto, *Bob Dylan* (London: Sphere Books Ltd, 1972); Shelton, *No Direction Home*; Howard Sounes, *Down the Highway: The Life of Bob Dylan* (London: Transworld Publishers, 2001).

17 Paraphrasing the final stanza of 'Just Like a Woman': 'Please don't let on that you knew me when / I was hungry and it was your world'.

18 See John Keats to Richard Woodhouse, 27 October 1818, *The Letters of John Keats, 1814–1821*, ed. Hyder Rollins (2 vols, Cambridge, Mass: Harvard University Press, 1972), I, pp.386–7.

19 See Jim Miller, 'Bob Dylan', in *The Dylan Companion*, p.19.

20 'My Life in a Stolen Moment'.

21 Remark to Robert Shelton, quoted by Jim Miller, 'Bob Dylan', in *The Dylan Companion*, p.19.

22 See Heylin, *Bob Dylan Behind the Shades*, pp.4–7 and Shelton, *No Direction Home*, pp.27–8; Bevis Hillier, *Young Betjeman* (London: Sphere Books, 1989), pp.2–3; and John Millman, 'A Betjeman

Pedigree', *The Betjemanian: The Journal of the Betjeman Society*, 12 (2000/2001), pp.26–49 and especially pp.42–3.

23 See *Young Betjeman*, pp.3–4, and John Betjeman, *Summoned by Bells* (London: John Murray, 1960),

24 See Heylin, *Behind the Shades*, p.33, and Shelton, *No Direction Home*, pp.27–8, 32.

25 See Gino Castaldo's interview with Bob Dylan, *La Repubblica* (24 June 1993).

26 Mikal Gilmore, 'The Rolling Stone Interview', *Rolling Stone* (22 November 2001), pp.56–69.

27 *Rolling Stone* (29 November, 1969); *Rolling Stone* (22 November 2001), pp.56, 58, 64.

28 *Rolling Stone* (22 November 2001), p.68.

29 ibid., p.68.

30 ibid., p.61.

31 Quoted from *William Shakespeare. The Complete Works*, ed. Peter Alexander (London and Glasgow: Collins, 1951; 1975).

32 On Dylan and the renewal of clichés, see the discussions in Christopher Ricks, *The Force of Poetry* (Oxford and New York: Oxford University Press, 1984; 1987), chapters on 'Clichés' and 'American English and the Inherently Transitory'.

7 Trust yourself: Emerson and Dylan

1 J. T. Trowbridge, 'Reminiscences of Walt Whitman,' first published in *Atlantic Monthly*, vol. 89, 1902, p.166, rpt. in *My Own Story* (Boston: Houghton, Mifflin, 1903), p.367. The conversation took place in 1860.

2 *Wait Whitman: The Complete Poems*, ed. Francis Murphy (Harmondsworth: Penguin Books, 1975), pp.762–3.

3 ibid., p.746.

4 *Song & Dance Man III: The Art of Bob Dylan* by Michael Gray (London and New York: Continuum, 2000), pp.75–9.

5 *Lyrics, 1962–1985* by Bob Dylan (London: HarperCollins, 1994; first published 1987), p.155. Dylan's lyrics are also available at http://www.bobdylan.com, to which songs after 1985 are sourced.

6 Whitman, p.737.

7 ibid., p.702.

8 Dylan, *Lyrics* p.371.

9 Luke 24: 31.

10 Whitman, p.737.

11 *Essays & Lectures* by Ralph Waldo Emerson (New York: The Library of America, 1983), p.448.

12 ibid., p.465.

13 ibid., p.450.

14 ibid., p.466.

15 This concert has been released as *The Bootleg Series Vol. 4: Bob Dylan Live 1966*.

16 For an illuminating discussion of the uses made of Thoreau by the counter-culture, see Lawrence Buell's *The Environmental Imagination: Thoreau, Nature Writing, and the Formation of American Culture* (Cambridge Mass: Harvard University Press, 1995), pp.311–70.

17 John Winthrop, 'A Modell of Christian Charity' (1630), rpt. in *The Heath Anthology of American Literature* (Lexington: D.C. Heath and Company, 2nd edition, 1994), vol. 1, p.233.

18 See in particular 'The Ritual of Consensus', Chapter 2 in his *The Rites of Assent: Transformations in the Symbolic Construction of America* (New York and London: Routledge, 1993), pp.29–67.

19 Emerson, p.260.

20 Dylan, p.147.

21 Though recorded in 1983, this song is not included in *Lyrics, 1962–1985*, but is printed in full in Gray, pp.473–5, and at http://www.bobdylan.com.

22 Emerson, p.274.

23 Quoted by Clinton Heylin in *Dylan: Behind the Shades* (London: Penguin, 1991), p.127.

24 Dylan, p.295.

25 Emerson, p.10.

26 Dylan, p.349.

27 Heylin, p.127.

28 Emerson, p.49.

29 Heylin, p.127.

30 Whitman, p.737.

31 Emerson, p.265.

32 'I'm Not There (1956)' remains unreleased.

33 *Call Me Ishmael* by Charles Olson (London: Jonathan Cape, 1967 (first published 1947)), p.15.

34 Dylan, p.659.

35 *Moby-Dick* by Herman Melville, ed. Harold Beaver (Harmondsworth: Penguin, 1972 (first published 1851)), p.93.

36 Emerson, p.271.

37 Dylan, p.508.

38 Emerson, pp.404, 414.

39 Dylan, p.300.

40 Emerson, p.266.

41 Quoted in Heylin, *Behind the Shades*, p.364.

42 Emerson, pp.266, 489.

43 *The Journals and Miscellaneous Notebooks of Ralph Waldo Emerson*, ed. William H. Gilman *et al.* (Cambridge, Mass: Harvard University Press, 1960–82) vol. 5, p.831.

44 Dylan, p.276.

45 Reprinted in *Seventeenth-century American Poetry*, ed. H.T. Meserole (New York: New York University Press, 1968), p.55. In line 4 'ure' means 'condition'.

46 Dylan, p.42.

47 ibid., p.612.

48 ibid., p.604.

49 Reprinted in Heath, p.588.

50 Emerson, p.471.

51 ibid., p.473.

52 ibid., p.403.

53 ibid., p.473.

54 Emerson, p.471.

55 ibid., pp.473, 476.

56 All Dylan quotations in this paragraph can be found at http://www.bobdylan.com.

57 'Dignity', http://www.bobdylan.com. The song was intended for *Oh Mercy* but then – for reasons hard to fathom – left off the album. Dylan re-recorded a vastly inferior version in 1994

which is included on his *Greatest Hits Volume III* (1995).

58 Emerson, p.482.

59 Whitman, p.679.

60 ibid., pp.731, 736; cf. these lines from the first version of 'Caribbean Wind': 'Would I have married her? I dunno – I suppose: / She had bells in her braids and they hung to her toes / But I heard my name and destiny said to be moving on' (quoted in Gray, p.450).

61 Emerson, p.490.

8 Death's honesty

1 Nat Hentoff, 'The Playboy Interview: Bob Dylan', reprinted in Craig McGregor (ed.), *Bob Dylan: A Retrospective* (New York: William Morrow and Company, 1972), p.130.

2 Robert Shelton, *No Direction Home: The Life and Music of Bob Dylan* (London: New English Library, 1986), p.201.

3 Michael Gray and John Bauldie (eds.), *All Across the Telegraph: A Bob Dylan Handbook* (London: Sidgwick and Jackson, 1987), p.190.

4 My transcript from the movie *Dont Look Back*, dir. D. A. Pennebaker, 1967.

5 Mikal Gilmore, *Night Beat: A Shadow History of Rock & Roll* (1997; London: Picador, 1998), p.45. Gilmore interviews Dylan years later in *Rolling Stone*, 22 November 2001, and gets a fascinating response when he asks him about this episode. Dylan more or less admits, of course, that he doesn't really remember his daddy saying any such thing.

6 Barry Miles, 'Patti Smith', in John Bauldie (ed.), *Wanted Man: In Search of Bob Dylan* (1990; Harmondsworth: Penguin Books, 1992), p.103.

7 Sam Shepard, 'True Dylan', *Esquire*, July 1987 (pp.59–68), p.59.

8 ibid., p.68.

9 Michael Gray, 'Deaths Around Bob Dylan's Life: Last Thoughts on David Blue', in Michael Gray and John Bauldie (eds.), *All Across the Telegraph: A Bob Dylan Handbook* (London: Sidgwick and Jackson, 1987), p.190.

10 A full account of the episode, and of William Zantzinger's (*sic*) subsequent life, is provided in an article from *The Telegraph* entitled 'The true story of William Zantzinger', which can be accessed at http://users.powernet.co.uk/barrett/The Telegraph/extracts/zanzinger42.html. No author's name is given.

11 Christopher Ricks, 'The Lonesome Death of Hattie Carroll', a talk delivered in Berkeley in 1989, first published in *The Threepenny Review*, reprinted in *The Telegraph*, can be accessed at the site given in note 10.

12 But they are not necessarily so; and one of Dylan's finenesses as a political writer at this time is his appreciation of the plight of poor whites in the South too. 'Only a Pawn in Their Game' is uneasy about apportioning blame too readily, about burying the rag in its face too early, and devotes itself to nosing out where the truest blame might lie.

13 'Maid of the kitchen' is what the printed lyrics give. Dylan in fact sings 'maid in the kitchen' on the version on *The Times They Are A-Changin'* (1963) – with, I always think, a tiny hesitation. In 1965 he certainly sang 'maid of the kitchen', and the transcript of the song from *Dont Look Back* has it so. See D. A. Pennebaker, *Bob Dylan: Dont Look Back* (New York: Ballantine Books, 1968), p.56.

14 Greil Marcus, *Invisible Republic: Bob Dylan's Basement Tapes* (Picador, 1997), p.xi.

15 Ezra Pound, 'Date Line' (1934), reprinted in T. S. Eliot (ed.), *Literary Essays of Ezra Pound* (London: Faber & Faber, 1954; 1968), p.86. My historicising of the album in this way need not, I think, be dependent on specific dating. Nevertheless, it helps to know that *Highway 61 Revisited* was recorded between 12 May and 4 August and released 30 August 1965. In March of that year the first American combat troops arrived in Vietnam; in April President Lyndon Johnson authorised their use for offensive operations; and later that month the Students for a Democratic Society sponsored the first major anti-war rally in Washington, DC.

16 Santa Fe: Twin Palms Publishing, 2000.

17 Paul Fussell, *Abroad: British Literary Travelling Between the*

Wars (Oxford: Oxford University Press, 1980), p.26, where he also says that 'the passport picture is an example of something tiny which has powerfully affected the modern sensibility, assisting that anxious self-awareness, that secret but overriding self-contempt, which we recognise as attaching uniquely to the world of Prufrock and Josef K. and Malone.'

18 I always think 'Million Dollar Bash', written subsequently, comments on the technique of 'ransack' in mid-1960s Dylan: 'Ev'rybody from right now / To over there and back / The louder they come / The harder they crack'.

19 I have introduced obliques into the version of the song printed in *Lyrics* to indicate where Dylan's performed version actually heavily insists caesurae: these have, I think, a manifest dramatic and emotional point.

20 William Shakespeare, *King Lear*, III. iv. 63.

21 Kierkegaard's *Fear and Trembling* is an extraordinarily inward and original meditation on the story. Alastair Hannay's introduction to his translation employs some lines of Dylan's song as epigraph, and observes that, compared to certain earlier interpretations, 'faith, obedience and mercy have here given way to disbelief, arbitrariness, and intimidation'. See Søren Kierkegaard, *Fear and Trembling*, translated with an introduction by Alastair Hannay (London: Penguin, 1985), p.7.

22 It is the track on which Dylan plays the final instrument of those credited to him on the album cover: 'guitar, harmonica, piano and police car' – in fact a whooping siren. So 'discrepancy' might be *le mot juste*: OED gives 'to sound discordantly', with an etymology from *crepare*, to make a noise, creak.

23 My historicising of the song like this is not intended to deny the plausibility of a psycho-biographical reading, in which its vehemence would be seen to issue also from a difficult filial relationship, since Bob Dylan's father was called Abram (usually abbreviated to Abe) Zimmerman.

24 Herbert Marcuse, 'The philosophy of art and politics', in Richard Kearney (ed.), *States of Mind: Dialogues with Contemporary Thinkers on the European Mind* (Manchester: Manchester University Press, 1995), pp.207–8.

9 Jokerman

1 *Pat Garrett and Billy the Kid* © 1973 Metro-Goldwyn-Mayer, Inc. Directed by Sam Peckinpah and written by Rudolph Wurlitzer.
2 'Gotta Serve Somebody' (1979).
3 'Maggie's Farm' (1965).
4 'Tombstone Blues' (1965).
5 'Talkin' World War III Blues' (1963).
6 'Po' Boy' (2001).
7 Bob Dylan. *Tarantula: Poems.* (New York: The Macmillan Company, 1966), p.72.
8 Recounted in Howard Sounes, *The Life of Bob Dylan.* (New York: Grove/Atlantic, 2001), p.xi.
9 ibid., p.209.
10 ibid., p.198.
11 'Wiggle Wiggle' (1990).
12 Sounes, *The Life of Bob Dylan*, p.30.
13 ibid., p.190.
14 ibid., p.15.
15 D.A. Pennebaker. *Dont Look Back*. 1967. Distributed by New Video, New York.
16 San Francisco press conference, 3 December 1965. KQED TV San Francisco CA. Available on bootleg videotapes.
17 *Lenny Bruce Without Tears* © 1972 Fred Baker Films Inc.
18 Quoted in newswire copy soon after Bruce's death.
19 'Talkin' John Birch Paranoid Blues' (1970).
20 'Honest with Me' (2001).
21 'I Shall Be Free' (1963).
22 'Subterranean Homesick Blues' (1965).
23 'Bob Dylan's Dream' (1963).
24 'Talking New York' (1962).
25 'All Over You' (1968).
26 As note 24.
27 As note 20.
28 'Shot of Love' (1981).
29 'Highlands' (1997).

30 Constance Rourke. *American Humor: A Study of National Character.* (New York: Harcourt Brace Jovanovich, Inc., 1931, 1959)

31 Recorded 23/11/36 in San Antonio, Texas, for Vocalion Records 03416 © ARC 7-03-56.

32 'Summer Days' (2001).

33 'Boom Boom', written by Lewis for ARC Music Corp. in 1955, © 1965 Chess™ MCA Records.

34 'Ace of Spades' by Deadric Malone © 1970 Back Beat Single 615 © 1972 MCA Records, Inc.

35 Mark Twain. *How to Tell a Story and Other Essays,* 1897. (Oxford: Oxford University Press, 1996)

36 'From a Buick 6' © 1965 Warner Bros. Inc.

37 © 1966 Dwarf Music.

38 'Brownsville Girl' (1986).

39 'I Shall Be Free' (1963).

40 'Bye and Bye' (2001).

41 'Po' Boy' (2001).

42 © 1973 Special Rider Music.

43 'Rita May' written with Jacques Levy © 1975, 1976 Ram's Horn Music.

44 'Tiny Montgomery' (1967).

45 James Fenton from *Out of Danger* (New York: Farrar Straus Giroux, 1994)

46 Charles Bernstein. 'Comedy and the Poetics of Political Form.' *A Poetics.* (Cambridge, Mass. and London: Harvard University Press, 1992), p.220.

47 © 1961, 1963 Ludlow Music, Inc.

48 Christopher Ricks. *The Force of Poetry* (Oxford: Oxford University Press, 1984), pp.417–41.

49 'Bob Dylan's Blues' (1963).

50 'Positively Fourth Street'.

51 'She's Your Lover Now' (1971).

10 Highway 61 and other American states of mind

1 Aidan Day, *Jokerman* (Oxford: Blackwell, 1988), pp. 19–21, 133–43.

2 Mick Gidley and Robert Lawson-Peebles (eds.), *Modern American Landscapes* (Amsterdam: VU University Press, 1995), pp. 1–2.

3 Paul Williams, *Bob Dylan: Performing Artist 1960–1973* (London: Omnibus Press, 1994), p. 159.

4 Henri Lefèbvre, *Everyday Life in the Modern World*, trans. Sacha Rabinowitch (London: Allen Lane, 1971). Henri Lefèbvre, *The Production of Space*, trans. Donald Nicholson-Smith (Oxford: Blackwell, 1991). Michel Foucault, *The Order of Things* (London: Tavistock, 1970). Michel de Certeau, *The Practice of Everyday Life* (Berkeley: University of California Press, 1984).

5 Michael Gray, *Song and Dance Man III* (London: Continuum, 2000), p. 96. For readings of Dylan's songs throughout see also Clinton Heylin, *Dylan: Behind the Shades* (Harmondsworth: Penguin, 1991).

6 Bob Dylan, *The Definitive Dylan Songbook* (New York: Amsco, 2001), p. 48.

7 Bob Dylan, *In His Own Words*, ed. Christian Williams (London: Omnibus Press, 1993), p. 39.

8 Jack Kerouac, *On the Road* [1957] (Harmondsworth: Penguin, 1989), p. 245.

9 'Spatial Stories' in *The Practice of Everyday Life*, pp. 115–30.

10 Bob Dylan, *Lyrics 1962–1985* (London: Jonathan Cape, 1987), pp. 70–2.

11 Robert Shelton, *No Direction Home: The Life and Music of Bob Dylan* (Harmondsworth: Penguin, 1986).

12 *Lyrics 1962–1985*, pp. 3–4.

13 *The Order of Things*, pp. 12–13.

14 Don De Lillo, *Americana* [1971] (Harmondsworth: Penguin, 1990). Don De Lillo, *White Noise* [1984] (London: Picador, 1986), pp. 12–13.

15 Larry Wilde, '"Desolation Row": The Expressionist Dylan'. Unpublished paper to the Annual Conference of the Political Studies Association (2000).

16 Richard Brown, '"I Want You": Engima and Kerygma in the Love Lyrics of Bob Dylan' in Ann Massa (ed.) *American Declarations of Love* (London: Macmillan, 1990), pp. 174–94.

17 *In His Own Words*, p. 40.

18 *In His Own Words*, p. 49.

19 For a discussion of contemporary culture in terms of the idea of redemption see Leo Bersani, *The Culture of Redemption* (Cambridge, Mass.: Harvard University Press, 1990).

20 Michael Gray and John Bauldie (eds), *All Across the Telegraph: A Bob Dylan Handbook* (London: Futura, 1987).

21 *Lyrics*, pp. 32–6.

22 Gary K. Browning, 'Dylan and Lyotard: Is It Happening?' Unpublished paper to the Annual Conference of the Political Studies Association (2000).

11 On the 'D' train: Bob Dylan's conversions

1 Wolfgang Schivelbusch, *The Railway Journey: Trains and Travel in the Nineteenth Century* (Oxford: Blackwell, 1980), p.44.

2 As Dylan put it in the booklet accompanying *Biograph* (1985), p.41. Michael Billig, *Rock 'n' Roll Jews* (Nottingham: Five Leaves Press, 2000), pp.126–7, has a brief discussion on Dylan and the Holocaust. For the doubleness of the train, as death-camp transportation and endless wandering, see Andrew Benjamin, 'Kitaj and the Question of Jewish Identity', in *Art, Mimesis and the Avant-Garde* (London and New York: Routledge, 1991), pp.89–90.

3 Robert Shelton, 'Bob Dylan: A Distinctive Folk-Song Stylist', *New York Times*, Friday, 29 September 1961, reprinted as part of the sleeve notes to *Bob Dylan* (1962), Dylan's debut album.

4 Shelton, 'Bob Dylan', and Interview with Jonathan Cott, *Rolling Stone* (26 January 1978), p.44, cited in Aidan Day, *Jokerman: Reading the Lyrics of Bob Dylan* (Oxford: Blackwell, 1989), p.61.

5 *Biograph*, p.54. Day, *Jokerman*, and Stephen Scobie, *Alias Bob Dylan* (Red Deer: Red Deer College Press, 1991), are two sustained accounts of Dylan's identityless identity.

6 For an account of Dylan's Bar Mitzvah see Anthony Scaduto, *Bob Dylan: An Intimate Biography* (London: Helter Skelter Publishing, 1996), and Paul Williams, *Bob Dylan: Performing Artist 1960–1973* (London: Xanadu, 1991), p.5. See also Billig, *Rock 'n' Roll Jews*, pp.118–31.

7 'Judaism in Music', in Charles Osborne (ed.), *Richard Wagner: Stories and Essays* (London: Peter Owen, 1973), pp.28–32.

8 Zygmunt Bauman, 'Allosemitism: Premodern, Modern, Postmodern', in Bryan Cheyette and Laura Marcus (eds), *Modernity, Culture and 'the Jew'* (Cambridge: Polity Press, 1998), pp.143–56.

9 Joe Klein, *Woody Guthrie: A Life* (London: Faber & Faber, 1999 edn), p.429.

10 Klein, *Woody Guthrie*, p.425, and Scaduto, *Bob Dylan*, p.67.

11 Michael Alexander, *Jazz Age Jews* (Princeton: Princeton University Press, 2000), and see also Sean Wilentz's essay on '*Love and Theft*' (2001) in this collection.

12 Alexander, *Jazz Age Jews*, p.182, and see also Michael Rogin, *Blackface, White Noise: Jewish Immigrants in the Hollywood Melting Pot* (Berkeley: University of California Press, 1996).

13 This mythology and the phrase 'young Woody Guthrie' can be found in the album notes to *Bob Dylan* (1962), written pseudonymously by Shelton. See also Klein, *Woody Guthrie*, p.427.

14 E. Anthony Rotundo, 'Jews and Rock and Roll: A Study in Cultural Contrast', *American Jewish History* (September, 1982), pp.104–5.

15 *Biograph*, p.38.

16 For this see my 'Clive Sinclair and Philip Roth: Representations of Central Europe in British and American-Jewish Literature', in Ann Massa and Alistair Stead (eds), *Forked Tongues: Comparing Twentieth-Century British and American Literature* (London: Longman, 1994), pp.355–73.

17 Mark Shechner, *The Conversion of the Jews and Other Essays* (Macmillan, 1990), pp.3–4, and Leslie Fiedler, 'The Christianness of the Jewish American Writer', in *Fiedler on the Roof: Essays on Literature and Jewish Identity* (New York: Godine 1991), pp.59–71.

18 Greil Marcus, *Invisible Republic: Bob Dylan's Basement Tapes* (London: Picador, 1997), p.21.

19 Scobie, *Alias Bob Dylan*, pp.9–13: details how Hibbing from the 1920s to the 1950s was moved two miles south to make room for one of the world's largest open-pit mines.

20 Michael Gray, *Song and Dance Man III: The Art of Bob Dylan* (London and New York: Continuum, 2000), pp.39–40.

21 'My Life in a Stolen Moment' (1962), in Bob Dylan, *Writings and Drawings* (London: Jonathan Cape, 1972), pp.80–3, and Day, *Jokerman*, p.80.

22 Gray, *Song and Dance Man III*, p.39 and Chapter One for a thorough examination of the 'Railroad Theme' in early Dylan and its relationship to 'the folk tradition'.

23 Leo Marx, *The Machine in the Garden: Technology and the Pastoral Ideal in America* (Oxford: Oxford University Press, 1972), p.238, cited in Schivelbusch, *The Railway Journey*, p.92, to whom I owe this discussion.

24 This important poem is collected in *Writings and Drawings*, pp.118–27.

25 Scobie, *Alias Bob Dylan*, pp.124–6.

26 See my *Between 'Race' and Culture: Representations of 'the Jew' in English and American Literature* (Stanford: Stanford University Press, 1998), pp.1–17 and Chapter Two for this argument.

27 Michel de Certeau, *The Practice of Everyday Life* (Berkeley: University of California Press, 1984), p.114, and Sigmund Freud, *Standard Edition of the Complete Psychological Works of Sigmund Freud*, ed. and trans. J. Strachey *et al.* (London: Hogarth Press, 1955–74), Volume 12, p.135, cited in Sander Gilman, *Freud: Race, and Gender* (Princeton: Princeton University Press, 1993). I am grateful for this reference to John Schad, whose *Queer Fish: Christian Unreason from Darwin to Derrida* is forthcoming. He kindly let me have sight of Chapter Three of his MS entitled 'Stations: Freud's Christian Trains of Thought'.

28 *The Complete Letters of Sigmund Freud to Wilhelm Fleiss 1887–1904*, trans. Jeffrey Moussaieff Mason (Cambridge, Mass.: Harvard University Press, 1985), p.274, cited in Schad, *Queer Fish*; Sidra Dekoven Ezrahi, *Booking Passage: Exile and Homecoming in the Modern Jewish Imagination* (Berkeley: University of California Press, 2000), pp.110 and 112.

29 'Honey, Just Allow Me One More Chance' (1963) in Dylan, *Writings and Drawings*, p.76. For trains and desire in general see

Laura Marcus, 'Oedipus Express: Trains, Trauma and Detective Fiction', *New Formations*, Volume 41 (2000), pp.173–88.

30 'If Dogs Run Free' (1970) in Dylan, *Writings and Drawings*, p.448, which includes a self-portrait of Dylan as a dog. It is not a coincidence that 'Walk Out in the Rain' (1978), unusually about a woman making her escape on a train, is co-written with Helena Springs.

31 Day, *Jokerman*, p.115. I am grateful to Day for this discussion.

32 'Notes by Bob Dylan', *Writings and Drawings*, pp.297–9, and Gray, *Song and Dance Man III*, Chapter Seven, for the gospel tradition underpinning Dylan's image of the 'slow train'.

33 Klein, *Woody Guthrie*, p.243.

34 Paul Williams, *Watching the River Flow* (London: Omnibus Press, 1996), p.79 and Chapter Eleven.

35 Williams, *Watching the River Flow*, p.66, and Søren Kierkegaard, *Papers and Journals: A Selection*, trans. Alastair Hannay (Harmondsworth: Penguin, 1996), p.21, cited in Schad, *Queer Fish*. Schad also has references to Dostoyevsky's *The Idiot* (1868), which begins with a Christ-like Prince in a third-class carriage, and to Flaubert's *Sentimental Education* (1869), which describes a picture by the artist Pellerin which 'showed the Republic, or Progress, or Civilisation, in the form of Christ driving a locomotive'.

36 Gray, *Song and Dance Man III*, pp.43–4 and 211–12, and Klein, *Woody Guthrie*, p.157. Williams, *Bob Dylan*, p.14, notes that Dylan performed Guthrie's 'Jesus Christ' in late 1960.

37 Woody Guthrie, *Bound for Glory* (London: J. M. Dent & Sons Ltd, 1969 edition), pp.18–19.

38 Scobie, *Alias Bob Dylan*, p.120 and Chapter Seven, and Gray, *Song and Dance Man III*, pp.206–8 and Chapter Seven. The phrase 'Before the Flood' was used of Dylan's 1974 comeback tour with The Band and is repeated in the song, 'In the Summertime', in his *Shot of Love* (1981) album.

39 Day, *Jokerman*, p.96 and Chapter Six. See also Bert Cartwright, *The Bible in the Lyrics of Bob Dylan* (Bury: Wanted Man, revised edn, 1992), and Gray, *Song and Dance Man III*, Chapters One, Seven, Eleven and Twelve.

40 Williams, *Watching the River Flow*, Chapter Eleven, and Clinton Heylin, 'Saved! Bob Dylan's Conversion to Christianity', in John Bauldie (ed.), *Wanted Man: In Search of Bob Dylan* (Harmondsworth: Penguin Books, 1992), pp.141–7, for detailed accounts of these concerts.

41 Day, *Jokerman*, p.84.

42 Heylin, 'Saved!', is a verbatim account of these harangues.

43 Day, *Jokerman*, Chapters Six and Seven, and Scobie, *Alias Bob Dylan*, Chapter Seven. Another key song in this regard is 'Trouble in Mind' (1979), which was inexplicably left off the *Slow Train Coming* album.

44 Cited in Clinton Heylin, *Bob Dylan: Behind the Shades: The Biography – Take Two* (Harmondsworth: Penguin Books, 2001), p.665.

45 Dylan's reference to being 'exiled' and unconverted is taken from 'We Better Talk This Over' from his *Street-Legal* (1978) album.

46 Scobie, *Alias Bob Dylan*, p.133, rightly makes this connection, which can also be found in Muriel Spark's *The Mandelbaum Gate* (1965), p.28, which is set in Jerusalem. Dylan is pictured at the Western Wall in Jerusalem on the cover of his album *Infidels* (1983), which contains the song, 'I and I'.

47 *Biograph*, p.41, and Scobie, *Alias Bob Dylan*, Chapter Eight, for Dylan and outlaws in general.

48 See Billig, *Rock 'n' Roll Jews*, pp.118–31, for these two versions of Dylan's Jewishness.

12 'A different Baby Blue'

1 Thanks to Danny Karlin, for pointing me towards 'Highlands', and to Jim Endersby, for readings and encouragement.

2 Joyce Carol Oates, 'Where Are You Going, Where Have You Been?', *Fictions*, ed. Joseph F. Trimmer and C. Wade Jennings (2nd ed., Orlando, Florida: Harcourt Brace Jovanovich, 1989) pp. 902-15.

3 Interview with Joyce Carol Oates in *Mirrors: An Introduction to Literature*, ed. Christopher R. Reaske and John R. Knott Jr. (New York: Harper & Row, 1988), p.148.

4 Mike Tierce and John Michael Crafton, 'Connie's Tambourine Man: A New Reading of Arnold Friend', *Studies in Short Fiction* 22:2 (Spring 1985), pp.219–24, p.220.

5 Tierce and Crafton, p.224.

6 This recalls one of the few really sweet moments in *Dont Look Back* where Dylan signs autographs for the adolescent Northern English girl fans who have been waiting on the street outside his hotel window. (One of them says 'pinch me' when he appears briefly at the window.) They, like everyone else, want him to keep writing 'Blowin' in the Wind'; he responds that his friends need work, hence the band. What's interesting is the way in which Dylan is perfectly adaptable as a pop idol along the earlier lines of Elvis (although onstage the audience may greet him with rapt silence and restrained applause, the girls' reaction indicates he still fits the earlier mould of a pop idol).

7 James Healey, 'Pop Music and Joyce Carol Oates: "Where Are You Going, Where Have You Been?"' *Notes on Modern American Literature* 7:1 (Spring – Summer, 1983), item 5 (no page numbers available).

8 Of course, we are never obliged to read a work through the lens of what the author might say about her intentions or influences, but in this case I'm interested both in what happens when a story which invites a strong feminist reading is dedicated to Bob Dylan and in the interaction between Dylan's music and the context of the story, including Oates's suggestive statements about her repeated listening to 'Baby Blue'.

9 Although Healey and others have also seen connections between the story and 'A Hard Rain's A-Gonna Fall', presuming that the 'Where have you been my blue-eyed son?' is a source for the story's title, and perhaps for Arnold's final reference to Connie's 'blue eyes' (Healey, 'Pop Music and Joyce Carol Oates: "Where Are You Going, Where Have You Been?"').

10 Michael Gray, *Song and Dance Man III: The Art of Bob Dylan* (London: Continuum, 2000), p.23.

11 'Farewell Angelina' (1965) also uses the sky in a similar Chicken Little-esque way to parallel the ending of a relationship and the breaking up of a world: 'The sky is on fire … The sky

is trembling ... The sky is folding ... The sky's changing color ... The sky is embarrassed ... The sky is erupting/And I must go where it is quiet.'

12 Aidan Day, *Jokerman: Reading the Lyrics of Bob Dylan* (Oxford: Basil Blackwell Ltd., 1988), p.81.

13 Day, *Jokerman* p.80.

14 *Biograph*, Notes, Cameron Crowe with Bob Dylan (Sony Music Entertainment Inc., 1985), p.52 (ellipses included in original).

15 Ruth Padel considers Dylan's misogyny in her book about the aggressive phallicism of rock 'n' roll, *I'm a Man: Sex, Gods and Rock 'n' Roll* (London: Faber and Faber, 2000): ' "It's all over Now Baby Blue" is a giant of a song, wonderful, mesmeric; but also the last word in patronizingness, sung to a woman who can't keep up with him, babe' (p.301). Padel's analysis is both helped and hindered by the fact that she's not a real fan. She misses some of the subtlety and some of the humour involved in the artists she discusses, but she may also make fewer excuses of the kind which take the form, well I like it so it can't be misogynist.

16 According to Marianne Faithfull Dylan wrote 'Just Like a Woman' for Allen Ginsberg, so potentially the parodic excess of the song is fully intentional, and it is in fact a song about how making love just like a woman or breaking just like a little girl is really a drag. (Marianne Faithfull, *Faithfull*, quoted in Padel, p.330.)

17 'Is Your Love in Vain?' *Street Legal*, 1978.

18 Ellen Willis, 'Dylan', *Bob Dylan: A Retrospective*, ed. Craig McGregor (New York: William Morrow & Company Inc., 1972), pp.218–42, p.235.

19 Ron Rosenbaum, 'Born Again Bob: Four Theories', *The Dylan Companion*, ed. Elizabeth Thompson and David Gutman (Da Capo Press, 2001), pp.233–6, p.236.

20 Jon Landau, 'John Wesley Harding', *Bob Dylan: A Retrospective*, ed. Craig McGregor (New York: William Morrow & Company, 1972), pp.248–64 (originally in *Crawdaddy!* 1968), p.251.

21 Robert Shelton, *No Direction Home* (London: Penguin, 1987).

22 Greil Marcus, *Invisible Republic: Bob Dylan's Basement Tapes* (London: Picador, 1997), p.27.

23 I have to admit I've always heard the line about the mirror in two completely different ways: either 'She's delicate and seems like veneer' or my personal favourite, 'She's delicate and seems like Vermeer'. Readings to follow.

24 See Aidan Day's related and comprehensive reading of this scene and the song as a whole (*Jokerman*, p.119). Where Day stresses the inability of Louise to measure up to Johanna – 'The sheer measurability of Louise as human lover emphasizes the extent to which the relationship of lovers does not tap resources comparable to the human mind' (p.119) – I prefer to see Louise as the much-needed anti-muse, that helps to make the song one of Dylan's most anchored in time and place. The late-night remains of the party may simply be a setting for the visions, but we still know that setting precisely – down to the heat pipes coughing, and the lights flickering from the opposite loft. My sense is that Louise is more necessary to this setting than the visions of Johanna that are finally all that remain.

25 Gray, *Song and Dance Man III*, p.819.

15 Bob Dylan's last words

1 For instance the '11 Outlined Epitaphs' on the sleeve of *The Times They Are A-Changin'* and the 'poems' of 'Some other kinds of songs' on the sleeve of *Another Side of Bob Dylan*.

2 Keynote address at the Poetry Now Festival, County Hall, Dun Laoghhaire, 22 March 2001.

3 I do not mean to suggest that Dylan is characteristically careless about verbal precision. On the contrary. The evolution of 'You Ain't Goin' Nowhere' illustrates something of his concern for accuracy and for balancing the demands of sense and form. The website reproduces the official *Basement Tapes* version. This can be said to abjure reason in favour of rhyme in its chorus and thereby – paradoxically – to achieve a radiance some of the other humorous songs from the Basement sessions lack:

> Whoo-ee! Ride me high
> Tomorrow's the day
> My bride's gonna come
> Oh, oh, are we gonna fly
> Down in the easy chair!

Bootleg versions suggest that the penultimate line of each verse originally ran, 'Are we gonna sit', the unrhymed end word giving an effect of plumping bathos to the entire chorus. The airiness of the canonical version is a direct consequence of the substitution of 'fly'. Yet sitting is more easily achieved in an easy chair than flying, at least if we are to speak literally. There may of course be an appropriate metaphorical sense to 'fly', as in 'flying high' (doing very well, feeling good etc), but Dylan was evidently unconvinced that this was sufficient to vindicate the *Basement Tapes* wording. When he re-recorded the song with Happy Traum in 1971 for *More Greatest Hits* he substantially revised the words, changing the last line of the chorus to 'Down *into* the easy chair'.

4 See booklet accompanying the *bootleg series: volumes 1–3 (rare & unreleased) 1961–1991*, pp.9, 21.

5 Bruce M. Metzger and Michael D. Coogan, eds, *The Oxford Companion to the Bible* (New York and Oxford: Oxford University Press, 1993), p.271.

6 'Farewell to the Highlands', in Carol McGuirk, ed., *Robert Burns: Selected Poems* (London: Penguin, 1993), p.156.

CONTRIBUTORS

SIMON ARMITAGE's nine volumes of poetry include *Killing Time* (1999) and *Selected Poems* (2001). His first novel, *Little Green Man*, was published in 2001. He has taught at the University of Iowa's Writers' Workshop and currently teaches at Manchester Metropolitan University. Two further collections of poetry, *The Universal Home Doctor* and *Travelling Songs*, were published in 2002.

RICHARD BROWN is Senior Lecturer in the School of English at the University of Leeds. He is author of *James Joyce and Sexuality* (1985), founding co-editor of the *James Joyce Broadsheet*, and has published a number of articles on modern and contemporary literature. His essay ' "I Want You": Enigma and Kerygma in the Love Lyrics of Bob Dylan' appeared in *American Declarations of Love*, ed. Ann Massa (1990).

CHRISTOPHER BUTLER is Professor of English Language and Literature and Tutor in English at Christ Church Oxford. His publications include *Early Modernism: Literature, Music and Painting in Europe 1990–1916* (1994). *A Very Short Introduction to Postmodernism* is forthcoming. He is currently working on a book on *The Arts and Pleasure*.

BRYAN CHEYETTE holds the Chair of Twentieth-Century

Literature at the University of Southampton. He is the author of *Constructions of 'the Jew' in English Literature and Society* (1993) and *Muriel Spark* (2000). He has also edited *Between 'Race' and Culture* (1996), *Contemporary Jewish Writing in Britain and Ireland* (1998), and, with Laura Marcus, *Modernity, Culture and 'the Jew'* (1998).

NEIL CORCORAN is Professor and Head of the School of English at the University of St Andrews. His books include *English Poetry since 1940* (1993), *After Yeats and Joyce: Reading Modern Irish Literature* (1997), *The Poetry of Seamus Heaney: A Critical Study* (1998) and *Poets of Modern Ireland: Text, Context, Intertext* (1999).

PATRICK CROTTY is Professor of Irish and Scottish Literary History at the Academy for Irish Cultural Heritages, University of Ulster. He has published many essays in books and journals, mainly on twentieth-century poetry. He edited *Modern Irish Poetry: An Anthology* (1995), and is a frequent reviewer in the *Times Literary Supplement*. He is currently co-editing, with Alan Riach, the *Complete Collected Poems* of Hugh MacDiarmid.

AIDAN DAY is Professor of British Literature and Culture at the University of Aarhus, Denmark, and was formerly Professor at the University of Edinburgh. He is the author of *Angela Carter: The Rational Glass* (1998) and *Romanticism* (1996). In 1988 he published *Jokerman: Reading the Lyrics of Bob Dylan*. He has co-edited a 31-volume facsimile edition of Tennyson's poetical manuscripts, *The Tennyson Archive* (1987–1993).

MARK FORD has published two collections of poetry, *Landlocked* (1992) and *Soft Sift* (2001). His critical biography, *Raymond*

Roussel and the Republic of Dreams, was published in 2000. He teaches in the English Department at University College London.

LAVINIA GREENLAW has written two books of poems, *Night Photograph* (1993) and *A World Where News Travelled Slowly* (1997). Her novel *Mary George of Allnorthover* was published in 2001. She lives in London and works as a freelance writer, critic and broadcaster.

DANIEL KARLIN is Professor of English at University College London. His most recent publications are the *Penguin Book of Victorian Verse* (1997) and the *Oxford Authors* edition of Rudyard Kipling's stories and poems (1999). He is working on a study of the figure of the singer in English poetry, one of whose chapters will be devoted to Bob Dylan, whose art he has loved and admired for thirty years.

PAUL MULDOON is Howard G. B. Clark Professor at Princeton University and Professor of Poetry at Oxford. His most recent book is *Poems 1968–1998* (2001). His ninth collection, *Moy Sand and Gravel*, was published in 2002.

NICHOLAS ROE teaches English Literature at the University of St Andrews. His books include *Wordsworth and Coleridge: The Radical Years* (1988), *John Keats and the Culture of Dissent* (1997), *Samuel Taylor Coleridge and the Sciences of Life* (2001), and *The Politics of Nature* (1992; 2002).

WILL SELF is the author of many novels and books of non-fiction, including *Great Apes*, *The Book of Dave*, *How the Dead Live*, which was shortlisted for the Whitbread Novel of the Year

2002, *The Butt*, winner of the Bollinger Everyman Wodehouse Prize for Comic Fiction 2008, *Umbrella*, which was shortlisted for the Booker Prize 2012, and *Shark*. He lives in south London.

PAMELA THURSCHWELL is a lecturer in English at University College London. She is the author of *Literature, Technology and Magical Thinking, 1880–1920* (2001) and *Sigmund Freud* (2000). She has also published an article on Elvis Costello in *Reading Rock'n'Roll* (1999).

SUSAN WHEELER has published three volumes of poetry, *Bag of Diamonds* (1993), *Smokes* (1998) and *Source Codes* (2001). Her work has appeared in *The Paris Review, New American Writing* and *The New Yorker*. She is a member of the Creative Writing faculties at Princeton University and the New School in New York City.

SEAN WILENTZ is Dayton-Stockton Professor of History and Director of the Program in American Studies at Princeton University. For many years his family ran The Eighth Street Bookshop in Greenwich Village. There, in December 1963, in Wilentz's uncle's apartment above the shop, Al Aronowitz introduced to each other Bob Dylan and Allen Ginsberg. Ginsberg, just returned from India, was staying at the apartment temporarily.

ACKNOWLEDGMENTS

The editor, contributors and publishers are grateful for permission to quote from the following works:

'Talking Bear Mountain Picnic Massacre Blues', 'Song to Woody' © 1962 by Duchess Music Corporation. Copyright renewed 1990 MCA

'Ain't A-Gonna Grieve', 'Bob Dylan's Blues', 'Boots of Spanish Leather', 'The Death of Emmett Till', 'Don't Think Twice, It's All Right', 'Down the Highway', 'I Shall Be Free', 'Let Me Die in My Footsteps', 'Long Time Gone', 'Masters of War', 'Talkin' World War III Blues', 'The Times They Are A-Changin'' © 1963 by Warner Bros. Inc. Copyright renewed 1991 Special Rider Music

'Ballad in Plain D', 'I Don't Believe You', 'It Ain't Me, Babe', 'The Lonesome Death of Hattie Carroll', 'Percy's Song' © 1964 by Warner Bros. Inc. Copyright renewed 1992 Special Rider Music

'Ballad of a Thin Man', 'Desolation Row', 'From a Buick 6', 'Highway 61 Revisited', 'It's Alright, Ma (I'm Only Bleeding)', 'Positively Fourth Street', 'Tombstone Blues' © 1965 by Warner Bros. Inc. Copyright renewed 1993 Special Rider Music

'Just Like a Woman', 'Leopard-Skin Pill-Box Hat', 'Stuck Inside

'Brownsville Girl' © 1986 Special Rider Music

'Man in the Long Black Coat' © 1989 Special Rider Music

'Dignity' © 1991 Special Rider Music

'Highlands', 'Love Sick', 'Not Dark Yet', 'Standing in the Doorway' © 1997 Special Rider Music

'Things Have Changed' © 1999 Special Rider Music

'Bye and Bye', 'Cry A While', 'High Water (for Charley Patton)', 'Honest With Me', 'Lonesome Day Blues', 'Moonlight', 'Po' Boy', 'Sugar Baby', 'Summer Days', 'Tweedle Dee and Tweedle Dum' © 2001 Special Rider Music

INDEX

Abraham and Isaac 166–68
'Absolutely Sweet Marie' 132, 238
academics 7–23, 51–70
advertising 202
'Advice to Geraldine on Her
    Miscellaneous Birthday' 41
ageing 282–83
'Ain't A-Gonna Grieve No More' 241
'Ain't Gonna Go to Hell for
    Anybody' 139
'Ain't No Man Righteous' 137
Alcott, Bronson 129
Aleichem, Scholem 236
Alexander, Michael 226–27, 228
'All Along the Watchtower' 94–95,
    210, 328
'All I Really Want to Do' 19
Allen, James 161–62
Allen, Steve 179
'Angelina' 321, 325
Another Side of Bob Dylan 11, 19, 89,
    114–15, 203, 260, 267, 329
apocalyptic motif 317, 321–22, 330
'Are You Ready' 324, 330
Armageddon 244, 251, 324, 330
'As I Went Out One Morning' 145
Ashbery, John 193
Ashley, Clarence 298, 305
Au Pairs 112
Auden, W. H. 215

'Baby, Let Me Follow You Down' 9
Baez, Joan 59, 266
Baker, Chet 73
'Ballad of Donald White' 184
'Ballad of Emmett Till, The' 32
'Ballad of Hollis Brown' 152, 327
'Ballad in Plain D' 88, 219, 316
'Ballad of a Thin Man' 7–8, 21, 55–56
Band, The 130, 134
'Barbara Allen' 310
Bardot, Brigitte 202
Bare, Bobby 69

Barnum, P. T. 298
Barthes, Roland 11
Baruch, Apocalypse of 322–23
Basement Tapes 11, 174
Basement Tapes, The 300
Baudelaire, Charles 22
Baudrillard, Jean 208, 214
Bauldie, John 5, 145
Bauman, Zygmunt 225
Beatles, The 190, 307
Beats, The 128, 200, 206
Beckett, Samuel 5, 148, 197, 218
Before the Flood 66
Before the Flood tour 326
Bercovitch, Sacvan 131
Bernstein, Charles 186
Betjeman, John 87
Biblical allusions 54, 137, 205, 219,
    322, 325 *see also* Abraham and
    Isaac; Apocalypse; Armageddon;
    Last Judgement; Revelation of St
    John; Second Coming
Big Pink 134
Biograph 228, 263, 269
Biograph interview 250–51
'Black Diamond Bay' 213–14, 326
Black Panthers 259
blackface minstrels 226, 297, 298
Blake, William 52, 256
'Blind Willie McTell' 31, 214–16
Blonde on Blonde 18, 86, 92, 93, 116,
    160, 169, 203, 237, 265, 331: place
    in 208–9
Blood on the Tracks 105, 116, 117,
    211–12, 269, 316, 329: place in 212
Bloom, Allan 65, 66
'Blowin' in the Wind' 68, 199, 267–68
blues 150–51, 180, 182, 199, 229, 297;
    talking 186, 187–88
Bob Dylan 1–2, 151, 199, 201,
    207, 328
'Bob Dylan's 115th Dream' 75,
    189, 197

penguin.co.uk/vintage